Our Priorities

Safety

Located in a sheltered harbour protected by the lush green mountains of the Northern range, CrewsInn marina offers more peace-of-mind than just being outside of the Hurricane Belt.

Our qualified dockmen are always on hand to assist berthing your boat and offer advice in rough weather. Our 214-foot floating dock acts as a breakwater stopping surges and unwanted swells.

CrewsInn also has round-the-clock security, so whether you're on board or not, you can rest assure your boat is looked after.

Service

From the consistent cleanliness of our bathroom facilities to complimentary daily newspapers, we take nothing for granted. Front desk staff is available 24 hours to help you get oriented and no request is too small. Our aim is that you'll never want to leave.

Satisfaction

The most important thing to us is that your stay is perfect (or at least as near to perfect as we can get by striving for it all day long). We hope the hotel, freshwater swimming pool, gym, laundry room, free cable TV, direct phone, golf cart service, free water and onsite shopping and marine services will make you look forward to your return.

CrewsInn
HOTEL & YACHTING CENTRE

Call or make your booking online early!

Point Gourde, Chaguaramas, PO Bag 518, c/o Carenage Post Office, Trinidad, West Indies
Tel: 868 634 4384/5 Fax: 868 634 4175 Email: dockmaster@crewsinnltd.com Website: www.crewsinn.com

I

Chris Doyle	Text, charts, layout
Jeff Fisher	
Sally Erdle	Illustrations
Chris Doyle	Photos
Jeff Fisher	
Norman Faria	Barbados consultant and contributor
Cathy Winn	Carnival

PUBLISHED BY
CHRIS DOYLE PUBLISHING
in association with
CRUISING GUIDE
PUBLICATIONS

ISBN 0-944428-59-2

First edition published in
Cruising guide to Trinidad & Tobago,
Venezuela and Bonaire 1994

Published as Cruising Guide to
Triniadad and Tobago 1996

This edition Published 2001

AUTHOR'S NOTES

In the text we give a very rough price
guide to the restaurants. This is an
estimate of what you might spend to
eat out and have a drink:

$A is $50 U.S. or over
$B is $25 to $50 U.S.
$C is $12 to $25 U.S.
$D is under $12 U.S.

We are happy to include advertising. I
gives extra information and keeps the
price of the book reasonable. If you wish
to help us keep it that way, tell all the
restaurateurs and shopkeepers, "I read
about it in the Sailors Guide." It helps
us no end.

KEEP THIS GUIDE UP-TO-DATE!
(at least till the next edition)
Visit: www.Doyleguides.com
go to guide updates.

If you like, tell us about your experiences, good or bad. We will consider you
comments when writing the next edition
Please e-mail your comments to:
sailorsguide@hotmail.com
or fisher@caribsurf.com
If your information is by way of an
update we may post it on our web site.

Printed in Trinidad

ACKNOWLEDGEMENTS

To everyone who helped: from those
who tell us what they are trying to
achieve, to those who have e-mailed
suggestions - the book would not be
the same without your input. Special
thanks to Jack Dausend at Boaters'
Enterprises for proofing the book.

Thank you all, Chris & Jeff

DISTRIBUTION

USA AND WORLDWIDE
Cruising Guide Publications
P.O. Box 1017
Dunedin, Florida 34697-1017
Tel: 727-733-5322
Fax: 727-734-8179
E-Mail: info@cruisingguides.com
www.cruisingguides.com

ST. VINCENT AND THE GRENADINES
Frances Punnett, Box 17
St. Vincent, W. I.
Tel: 784-458-4246
Fax: 784-456-2620

ST. LUCIA
Ted Bull, Box 8177
Castries, St. Lucia
Tel/Fax: 758-452-8177
E-mail: amazona@candw.lc

GRENADA
Jeff Fisher,
Tikal, Box 51, Young St.
St. George's, Grenada
Tel: 473-440-2556
E-Mail: Fisher@caribsurf.com

TRIINIDAD & TOBAGO
Jack Dausend
Boaters' Enterprises
Village Square, suite B8
Chaguaramas, Trinidad
Tel: 868-634-2055
Fax: 868-634-2056
E-Mail:
nfo@BoatersEnterprise.com

SKETCH CHART INFORMATION

Our sketch charts are interpretive and designed for yachts drawing about 6.5 feet. Deeper yachts should refer to the depths on their charts.

LAND   HILLS   ROADS PATHS

LAND HEIGHTS ARE IN FEET AND APPROXIMATE

WATER TOO SHALLOW FOR NAVIGATION OR DANGEROUS IN SOME CONDITIONS

 SURFACE REEF   ROCKS AND/OR DEEPER REEF

NAVIGABLE WATER   60   9 DEPTHS ARE IN FEET AND APPROXIMATE

1.5 KNOTS CURRENT   ✝ CHURCH

MANGROVES   ⚓ ANCHORAGE

    Ⓟ PICK UP MOORING ONLY

WRECK   DAY STOP ANCHORAGE

GREEN BEACON
GREEN BUOY (PORT)

RED BEACON
RED BUOY (STARBOARD)

ISOLATED BEACONS AND BUOYS   IALA B MARKS SHOWING DIRECTION OF DANGER (BUOYS & BEACONS)

YELLOW BUOY

RED & BLACK BUOY   MOORING OR OTHER BUOY

 SECTOR   LIGHTS
 WHITE (W)   FL = FLASHING, F = FIXED, L = LONG,
GREEN (G)   Q = QUICK, M= MILES
YELLOW (Y)   LIGHT EXPLANATION
 RED (R)   FL (2) 4S, 6M
    LIGHT GROUP FLASHING 2 EVERY FOUR SECONDS, VISIBLE 6 MILES

NOTICE

No warranty, expressed or implied, is made by the publisher and authors with respect to accuracy. This guide and these charts are the work of two individuals. There may be errors and omissions, so undue credence should not be placed in this guide. This guide should be used with navigational charts and other navigational aids. This guide should not be used for navigation.

CRUISING GUIDE

TO

TRINIDAD & TOBAGO

Store Bay during Angostura/Yachting World Regatta

PLUS **BARBADOS**

by Chris Doyle
& Jeff Fisher

TABLE OF CONTENTS

PLANNING
& CRUISING

With special thanks to Jody Feavearyear of the Strasenburgh Planetarium, Rochester, NY.

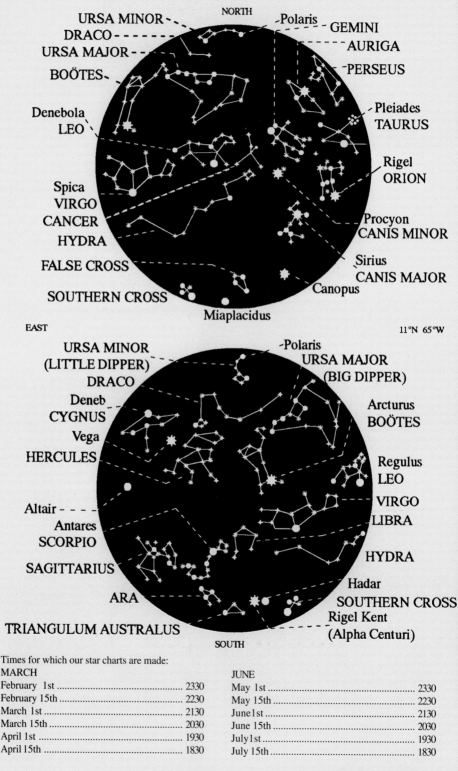

NORTH

URSA MINOR
DRACO
URSA MAJOR
BOÖTES

Polaris
GEMINI
AURIGA
PERSEUS

Denebola
LEO

Pleiades
TAURUS

Rigel
ORION

Spica
VIRGO
CANCER
HYDRA
FALSE CROSS
SOUTHERN CROSS

Procyon
CANIS MINOR

Sirius
CANIS MAJOR

Canopus

Miaplacidus

EAST

11°N 65°W

Polaris
URSA MAJOR
(BIG DIPPER)

URSA MINOR
(LITTLE DIPPER)
DRACO

Deneb
CYGNUS

Arcturus
BOÖTES

Vega
HERCULES

Regulus
LEO

VIRGO
LIBRA

Altair
Antares
SCORPIO
SAGITTARIUS
ARA
TRIANGULUM AUSTRALUS

HYDRA

Hadar
SOUTHERN CROSS
Rigel Kent
(Alpha Centuri)

SOUTH

Times for which our star charts are made:

MARCH		JUNE	
February 1st	2330	May 1st	2330
February 15th	2230	May 15th	2230
March 1st	2130	June 1st	2130
March 15th	2030	June 15th	2030
April 1st	1930	July 1st	1930
April 15th	1830	July 15th	1830

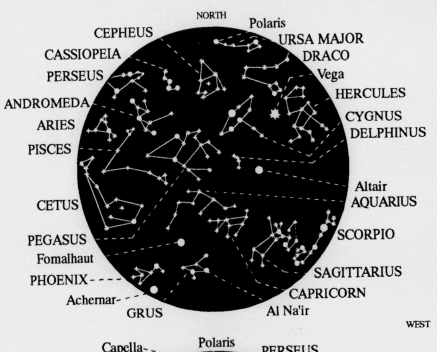

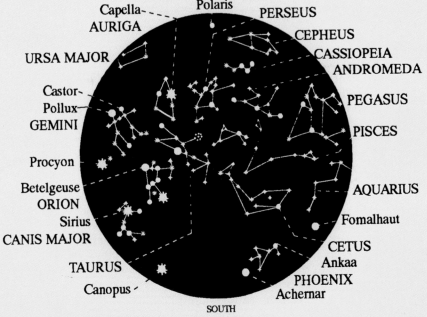

ANI AT ASA WRIGHT

Introduction

*T*rinidad was part of South America as recently as 10,000 years ago and geographically more closely resembles Venezuela than the rest of the Caribbean. While it lacks those perfectly peaceful anchorages backed by powdery palm-fringed beaches that typify the other islands, it offers a rich cultural heritage and an amazing wealth of natural wildlife unseen in the islands to the north. Tobago by contrast is a typically idyllic Caribbean island that runs at a gentle pace under swaying palms, with the added bonus of a much larger diversity of birds than can be found in the islands to the north.

Trinidad and Tobago is now a favorite destination for cruising sailors. Strangely enough, a few years ago, yachts rarely visited these islands. It was felt that Tobago was too far to the east and hard to get to and most yachtspeople thought there was nothing for them in Trinidad.

Attitudes began to change when Don Stollmeyer, the manager of a yard called Power Boats, decided to invest in a used 50-ton travel lift. The only way to justify it was to expand into hauling visiting yachts. Within just a few years this had grown into a thriving industry of hauling and repairing yachts involving many yards and hundreds of people.

It also put Trinidad and Tobago on the map for cruising folk who came to haul out but stayed to discover another side of Trinidad; an island whose exotic and flamboyant nature includes rain forests and swamps with monkeys, parrots, macaws, manatees and giant leatherback turtles. They discovered too, one of the most fun-loving and hospitable people in the Caribbean whose Carnival is considered by many to be the best in the world. When the fun got too much, they found, as Trinidadians have long known, that a week or two in Tobago is the perfect way to relax.

Few nations offer such diverse attractions in such a small area.

Welcome to Trinidad and Tobago!

WATERFALL AT GRAND RIVIERE

Local Lore

CRUISING COMFORT

The wind often dies at night in Trinidad. This can make it warm for sleeping below, especially in marinas. Windscoops or efficient 12-volt fans are useful luxuries. Those planning to spend long periods in marinas might find a small air conditioning unit worthwhile. These can be rented locally.

FISHING

Fishing is excellent throughout this region. The westerly setting equatorial current hits the continental shelf, causing colder nutrient rich water to rise from the seabed. That old lure and line that has been hanging unsuccessfully over the stern of your yacht for hundreds of miles is likely to jump into action and surprise you.

From our questioning of locals it appears that ciguatera poisoning is extremely rare in Trinidad and Tobago. However, to ensure your own safety, avoid really big barracudas, Spanish mackerel and jacks.

SWIMMING

While the water in Trinidad is often colored by run-off from the Orinoco it is perfectly good for swimming and there is also good snorkeling in some anchorages, although the visibility is restricted. The small caimans found mainly in inland lakes and reservoirs and brackish estuaries are not considered dangerous, unless molested.

CURRENCY

Currency is the TT dollar which varies in value to the US. You currently get around 6 TT dollars for one US. US dollars are widely accepted and easily changed into local currencies. EC dollars can also be changed in the banks though the rate of exchange is not very favorable.

Travelers checks and credit cards are very widely accepted.

LANGUAGE

English is the language of Trinidad and Tobago, which makes it easy for many of us.

PHOTOGRAPHY

Photographic supplies are easily available in the large towns in Trinidad. Film is usually reasonably priced. There are first rate facilities for developing and printing your print film. Slide film can also be developed fast and well but it has to be the E6 process type (Fujichrome, Ektachrome). For aquatic shots a polarizing filter brings out the water colors.

MEDICAL CARE

You can get good medical and dental care in Trinidad and Tobago with many doctors and modern facilities. For a current list of doctors check the latest Trinidad and Tobago Boater's Directory. The St. Clair medical Center (628-1451/2/8615) is a private establishment, which will take care of most of your needs. You could also visit the Mount Hope Medical Sciences Complex (645-4673/2640) or the Community Hospital of Seventh Day Adventists (622-1191/2). You can also try the Port of Spain General hospital (623-2951). If you need an ambulance in an emergency you could try calling the coast guard for help on the VHF. 16

DANGERS

Trinidad has a very rich wildlife that includes poisonous snakes like the fer-de-lance, bushmaster and coral snake. There are also scorpions and centipedes. Most of these exist in the wilder regions. They don't present much danger as long as you keep your eyes open and tread carefully. Small ticks and biting insects can be more annoying. The liberal use of repellent or long pants and shoes and socks is advisable when you go exploring in the forest. Insect repellent can also be handy ashore in the evenings.

If you have not yet learnt to identify the poisonous manchineel tree, get someone to show you one. These pretty trees grow close to the water and the sap is highly toxic, as are their little green apples. It can be dangerous to shelter under one in the rain, and a fire made from manchineel sticks produces toxic smoke.

DRUGS

Law enforcement officers throughout this area take illegal drugs very seriously. Anyone getting caught even with one joint can expect confiscation of the yacht, a monster fine and a long jail term.

SECURITY

Trinidad is a bustling and exotic country, bursting with activity, and among other life forms there is a light-fingered brigade and there are also those who rob with guns. Illegal drugs exist in Trinidad and have certainly been linked to some of the crimes. As to theft from yachts, we have been surprisingly lucky so far. There have only been a few break-ins, and occasional items stolen from yachts in the yards.

However, it is sensible to take a few precautions. Do not keep large quantities of cash either on board or on your person. Use credit cards and travelers checks as much as possible, as they are insured. Keep your dinghy locked up, especially at night. If you have anything of special value on your boat hide it really well.

Be streetwise ashore. Stay aware of what is going on around you. Don't set your handbag or brief case down somewhere and move away. If you are renting a car, do not leave anything valuable, even in the trunk. It is also advisable to use a wheel locking device if it is supplied.

Before walking or jogging on your own ask local advice on the safety of the area concerned.

PROTECTING THE ENVIRONMENT

Probably the worst damage yachts do to the environment is to coral when anchoring. Always anchor in sand or mud. If you have to anchor in an area with a lot of coral, dive on your anchor to make sure it is not doing any harm. If necessary, use two anchors to stop your rode from chewing up the bottom as the boat swings around.

Yachtspeople are usually fairly good about garbage here. Take your garbage to a proper facility, recycle glass and batter-

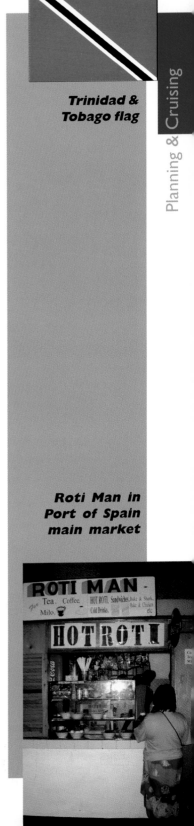

Planning & Cruising

Trinidad & Tobago flag

Roti Man in Port of Spain main market

TRINIDAD-BUILT C-MOS COMPETING IN TOBAGO

ies where possible and put old oil in the right containers. Never throw anything over the side, and never discharge oil or oily bilge water while in Trinidad and Tobago waters.

SAILING EVENTS AND REGATTAS

Trinidad's keen boating community puts on some great races and competitions. Visiting yachts are encouraged to join in.

The premier event is the Angostura/ Yachting World Regatta in Tobago that lasts a week and begins around the middle of May. This is one time of year you do not have to sail to Scarborough to clear in. For a week preceding the race yachts coming from abroad can clear in at Store Bay. There are races for racing, cruising, charter and live-aboard classes. The regatta is big enough to be bustling and fun, yet small enough to be friendly and personal. The regatta kicks off with two days of racing followed by the best Caribbean lay day, then finishes with two more race days. There is plenty of partying and fun after the races, including volleyball competitions, treasure hunts and spontaneous jump-ups.

Trinidad and Tobago Match Racing Regatta is another good racing event. Teams of three compete in 20 ft SR Max sports sloops that are provided by the Sailing Association. It is held late May or early June - apply in plenty of time. A dinner party with live music is held on the night of the skipper's briefing.

The TTSA hold races year round, and you can pick up a complete racing schedule from them (634-4376).

The Bum Boat Regatta in Tobago will be a spectator event for visitors as small open sailing workboats from Tobago and islands as far north as St. Vincent compete in a series of races, usually at Whitsun.

The big event for power boats is the Great Race to Tobago. You will need quite a tender to compete in this, Trinidad's premier power boat race. It is held in August, and the entrants are impressive. The record for the 86 mile open-water course is just 1 hour 4 minutes.

For fishermen the Annual Sports Fishing Competition takes place at Crown Point in Tobago usually in April.

WEATHER

The weather is generally pleasant, with temperatures of 78-85° Fahrenheit year round. There are two seasons, the rainy season (June to December) and the dry season (January to May). These vary from year to year and the starting and finishing times are not exact. During the rainy season Trinidad is considerably wetter than Tobago or the islands to the north, though there are still many pleasant days and lots of sunshine.

Tobago lies in the regular trade wind belt and you usually have a good breeze. The weather along the coast of Trinidad is more variable. Winds often intensify during daylight hours and calm down at night. Many yachts heading from Trinidad to Tobago power overnight in the calm. This rule is not cast in stone and it is less likely to be calm at night when the trades are blowing hard.

A westerly to northwesterly setting current flows past Tobago and along the north coast of Trinidad. It rushes between Trinidad and Tobago. When close to Trinidad, you can sometimes keep out of the current by staying within a mile of the mainland coast.

Trinidad is considered to be below the hurricane belt, which is why many people leave their yachts here during the summer. However, Tobago has had a few hurricanes. It is sensible to listen to the weather, not only because of hurricanes, but because easterly waves and other disturbances can come through with a lot of rain and wind.

Should a storm threaten, you should go to a secure harbor. In Tobago the Bon Accord lagoon is the only safe harbor, so if you draw 6 feet or more be prepared to sail to Trinidad or Grenada. In Trinidad the fishing harbor south of Port of Spain is probably as good a place as any.

The anchorage in Chaguaramas can be rolly during periods of southerly winds. Very rarely, such a wind will reach proportions that make it dangerous to be tied to the outer docks in Power Boats or in the Peake dock, and dinghies can get smashed,

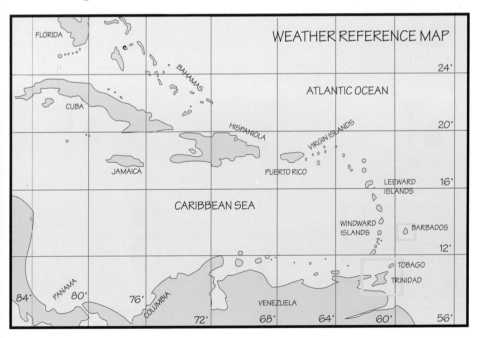

particularly in Power Boats. CrewsInn, Coral Cove and Tropical Marine right up in the eastern corner are generally protected, as are the Power Boats docks in the creek.

While Trinidad is too far south to be subject to cold fronts, swells from these systems do affect the northern coasts of Trinidad and Tobago.

Marine forecasts

Trinidad and Tobago have several radio stations both on the AM and FM bands. Gem Radio on 93.5 MHz FM gives forecasts from the Miami weather bureau following the news every hour on the hour from 0600-1800.

Trinidad radio gives a forecast after the 0600 news on 720 AM.

An informal VHF net comes on the air each morning at 0800 on channel 68. One of its good features is the detailed weather forecast.

North Post radio also gives weather on the VHF at 0940 and 1640 or by special request. They stand by on VHF: 16 and broadcast their weather on 27. They also use 25, 26, 28 and 78.

If you have a ham or SSB radio, the Caribbean Weather net is on 8104 kHz at 0830. The Caribbean safety net is before the weather net on the same channel.

The Boaters' Directory carries tide predictions for the coming year.

NAVIGATION

Tides

The tidal range in Trinidad and Tobago is around 3 feet, which is significantly greater than in the Windwards and Leewards. Currents vary with the tides, and along the north coast you can expect some kind of an east going current from one hour before low water till about two hours before high water. In Chaguaramas the tide seems to turn to the east about two hours before low water, it can create a little chop.

Lights

Major lights in Trinidad and Tobago are generally reliable. In particular the light on Chacachacare Island is a big help to those sailing to Trinidad. The light at Fort George in Scarborough is also reliable, though I would not advise approaching Tobago at night because of the shoals and strong currents. Don't rely on smaller lights marked on navigation charts, some of these have been taken out.

Buoys

The whole area comes under the IALA B system (red right returning). However, buoys are not always in place so treat them with caution.

Fishing Boats

Night sailing along the north coast of

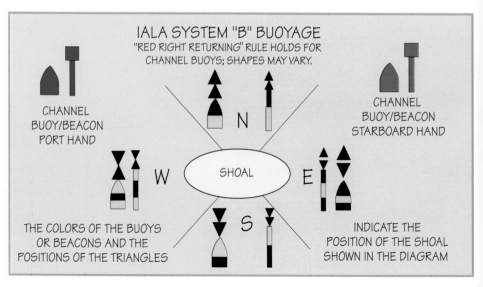

IALA SYSTEM "B" BUOYAGE
"RED RIGHT RETURNING" RULE HOLDS FOR
CHANNEL BUOYS; SHAPES MAY VARY.

CHANNEL
BUOY/BEACON
PORT HAND

CHANNEL
BUOY/BEACON
STARBOARD HAND

N

W   SHOAL   E

S

THE COLORS OF THE BUOYS
OR BEACONS AND THE
POSITIONS OF THE TRIANGLES

INDICATE THE
POSITION OF THE SHOAL
SHOWN IN THE DIAGRAM

GPS POSITIONS
as taken with a Garmin-50 on WGS-84 - for planning

PLACE	LAT (NORTH)	LONG (WEST)
Trinidad	**deg mins**	**deg mins**
Approach to Boca de Monos	10 43.7	61 40.1
Chacachacare I.	10 40.5	61 43.9
Chaguaramas	10 40.7	61 38.4
La Vache Bay	10 46.1	61 29.0
Maracas Bay	10 46.8	61 25.6
Las Cuevas	10 48.0	61 24.0
Grand Riviere	10 50.6	61 03.0
Monos I., Grand Fond Bay	10 41.0	61 40.8
Monos I., Morris Bay	10 41.5	61 40.6
Pointe-A-Pierre	10 19.9	61 28.4
Scotland Bay	10 41.9	61 40.1
Trinidad and & Tobago Yacht Club	10 40.5	61 34.0
Winns Bay, Gaspar Grande I.	10 39.4	61 39.7
Tobago	**deg mins**	**deg mins**
Bon Accord Lagoon, channel entrance	11 11.3	60 50.6
Bulldog Shoal	11 08.8	60 44.5
Castara Bay	11 16.5	60 42.2
Charlotteville	11 19.8	60 33.4
Englishman's Bay	11 17.7	60 40.6
King's Bay	11 15.5	60 32.9
Little Tobago, off the northwest point	11 18.4	60 30.6
Mt. Irvine Bay	11 11.5	60 48.3
Parlatuvier Bay	11 18.2	60 39.3
Pigeon Point	11 10.0	60 50.9
Plymouth	11 12.7	60 46.8
Scarborough	11 10.6	60 44.2

MILEAGE CHART

	Punta Pargo	Boca de Monos	Chaguaramas	Port of Spain	Pointe a Pierre	Store Bay	Scarbourough	Plymouth	Castara	Englishman's Bay	Charlotteville	Anse Bateau
Grenada	80	78	82	90	103	74	84	75	77	78	82	87
Punta Pargo		23	28	34	47	77	83	84	89	92	101	107
Boca de Monos			4	10	26	56	63	63	66	69	79	85
Chaguaramas				8	24	60	67	67	70	73	82	88
Port of Spain					20	66	73	73	76	79	88	94
Pointe a Pierre						82	89	89	92	95	104	110
Store Bay							10	7	10	13	22	28
Scarborough								17	20	23	25	17
Plymouth									5	7	15	21
Castara										3	12	16
Englishman's Bay											9	14
Charlotteville												6

This table is approximate and is offered as a guide to planning. Distances sailed vary greatly due to wind and current.

Planning & Cruising

Trinidad requires great caution. Small fishing boats have no fixed lights, but they will briefly flash a light when they see your yacht coming. Stay well clear of fishing boats whenever you can. Large nets of tough plastic are sometimes set, which could ensnare your yacht.

Oil Rigs

In the Gulf of Paria there are several new and derelict oil rigs and single oil pipes that stick up out of the water. Most of these have lights, but it is far better to sail here during the day when you can keep a good lookout.

A new natural gas rig is being positioned between Trinidad and Grenada about 20 miles north of Trinidad. This one will be well lit.

CUSTOMS AND IMMIGRATION

(See also regulations under harbor headings)

Customs and immigration are simple for entering Trinidad or Tobago. If you are a national of Cuba, the USSR and countries that used to be part of the Socialist block or the Dominican Republic, Haiti, India, Iran, Iraq, Jordan, Kuwait, Lebanon, Libya, Nigeria, Papau New Guinea, Saudi Arabia, Sri Lanka, Syria, Tanzania and Uganda you need a visa. Otherwise you do not.

On arrival in Trinidad, clear in at Chaguaramas. (Port of Spain is also a port of clearance, but reserved for commercial ships). You must proceed straight to the customs dock and are required to check in as soon as you arrive. There is normally someone on duty 24-hours a day.

Tobago has two ports of clearance, the capital, Scarborough and Charlotteville. No entry officials are yet based in Charlotteville so you will probably find yourself having to bus down to Scarborough to do the paper work. (See details under Charlotteville.)

You may want to time your arrival for normal office hours (0800-1600, Monday through Friday, excluding holidays) as you will be charged about $45US overtime outside these hours. There are also reasonable charges that include $50TT for every 30 days spent in the country. Once you have cleared in you are free to move between anchorages in either Trinidad or Tobago. Should you wish to go from Trinidad to Tobago (or vice versa) check with customs and immigration with your papers before you leave. They will endorse them for you and on arrival in the other country you should take them to customs and immigration for a further stamp. (You can go by bus there is no reason to take your boat to a port of clearance for this.) Should you clear into Trinidad and plan to leave from Tobago (or vice versa) you must visit both customs and immigration at the entry port so they can give you your papers to take to the officials in the other island.

Immigration Extensions

Trinidad can be very addictive; the people are wonderfully friendly and cruisers occasionally get stuck here. While immigration officers welcome visiting yachtspeople, they do not expect them to become permanent residents. Arriving yachtspeople are normally given up to three months. If you wish to stay longer than this you must apply for an extension with the immigration about a week before you need it. There is a fee of around $150TT for this. You will be asked why you want to stay longer. Staying for the hurricane season and getting bone fide boat work done are usually considered valid reasons.

Signing crew on or off.

If a crew is leaving or arriving while you are in Trinidad and Tobago you must check with immigration. An arriving crew needs to arrive with a letter signed by the captain stating he or she is part of the crew. If you are in Trinidad, one of the marina offices can help produce an approved letter.

Storing a Yacht

If you are leaving your yacht in storage, you need to check with the yard that is looking after it, and get them to supply you with the necessary paperwork, which is simple. You then take this to be stamped and approved by a customs officer in Chaguara-

Planning & Cruising

mas. You keep one copy with you for your return.

Returning to your yacht

When returning to Trinidad have these papers handy along with a list of any boat parts you are bringing in. Instead of going through the usual customs lines, go to the office to the left off the main customs hall as you face the customs desks. They will allow the captain (and only the captain) a permit to take his parts direct to customs in Chaguaramas. You have to proceed straight there and sort out the delivery of these parts with the customs officer in charge. You may not visit your boat first. The time you leave the airport is phoned through.

When you arrive back into Trinidad you must report to the Chaguaramas immigration within 24 hours.

After you have returned and before you clear out, get a statement from the yard that stored your yacht stating how long your yacht was in storage. Take this along when you clear out, or you will be charged the monthly cruising fee for those months.

Shipping in parts

Parts arriving from overseas via courier will go to the Chaguaramas customs office. You will need your boat papers and passport to get them released.

While yacht parts are duty free, other items including

Pelican rests on Chaguaramas anchorage marker buoy

power tools, food and household items will be charged duty.

Pets

While Trinidad does have rabies in their bat population it has not reached their small land animal population. To keep it this way they have strict regulations with regard to pets. Pets must be kept on board at all times, even when a boat is on dry land. If a pet gets sick, you can get a vet to visit the boat. It is illegal to walk the pet ashore under any circumstances. If you have a pet on board and wish to leave with it by plane (or vice versa) this must be arranged in advance. First you need an in transit permit from the Veterinary services division (phone 622-1221) then you need to arrange a quarantine guard (phone 622-5986). Members Only or Ian Taxi can arrange this for you.

There may be some changes in these laws to make it easier for pet owning visitors in the next year or two.

VHF RADIO

Trinidad is part of the International Telecommunications Union. The VHF is designated specifically for safety and essen-tial communications between vessels. Yacht users are requested to keep their transmissions brief and to use low power where possible. The VHF is not the right medium for exchanging recipes, opinions and post mortems of last nights bridge game. However, if messages are brief no one minds people using the radio to arrange a rendezvous.

General calling channels for yachts are 68 and 16. (68 is also used as a talking channel by commercial craft, so it is sometimes busy). General use channels are (USA): 4, 5, 7, 18, 19, 21, 22, 23, 63, 65, 66, 71, 73, 78, 79, 80, 81, 82, 83. Channels 71 and 73 are USA/international compatible. Yachtspeople should not use other channels.

Several shore places stand by on specific channels, these include:

Peake, 69

Power Boats, 72

CrewsInn, 77

TTSA, TTYC, and IMS stand by on 68.

There is an unofficial radio net on VHF channel 68 at 0800. This shares information among yachts about weather, safety and cultural events.

SON AND MOSE BUILDING MY SAMSON 42

Work In Trinidad

TRINIDAD FOR BOAT BUILDING

Trinidadians have been building boats for years, especially power boats and fishing boats both for export and their own use. Bowen Marine, Formula III and Peake all have a good reputation in the power boat market, including fine cruising boats and some very fancy racing craft that, in the wrong hands, would raise the eyebrows of any customs officer from here to Miami. The sailing yacht market is newer.

Soca Sailboats have a factory on the Eastern Main Road in Trinidad where they build Henderson 30 racing boats, as well as occasional custom boats. One of their craft "Crash Test Dummies", a Henderson 35, cleaned up in the Caribbean racing circuit for a year or two. Last news was they were trying to sell it and build something even faster. They have an impressive factory with their own heating oven for building carbon fiber masts and they mold their own

lead for the keels. The glasswork is first class and their prices reasonable by international standards.

Samson Boats in San Fernando build a variety of custom boats from fishing pirogues to giant cats. If you are interested in building new, drive down and see their work for yourself.

Aikane Yachts, in Chaguaramas, built a very fancy, fast cruising cat 52 feet long. They are geared up for the production of these; the yard is in Chaguaramas.

Yards such as these can get VAT exemptions for material and parts arriving for a yacht that is to be exported.

Trinidad is also excellent for custom projects. I am nearly completing a 42-foot Samson Class Catamaran as I write this. This boat has an island tradition, with no plans, but several examples to work from. I had the hulls molded by Samson Boats in San Fernando, who own the mold, and the rest is being completed in a space I rented in

Skinner's Yard. I hired Steve (Son) Ramsahai as the builder and he in turn hired extra help when he needed it. I also hired other contractors for specific jobs. I have been very impressed by the high quality and care of the workmanship, and so far the whole project is going smoothly, on time and within budget. It has been a very pleasurable experience.

I mention this because I think Trinidad is an excellent place for those who have a boat building project in mind, especially if they have some technical knowledge and are willing to spend quite a lot of time being present during construction. There is no question that first class work in all fields is available. The only discouragement at this time is that there is no VAT exemption for a project of this kind so, unlike visiting yachts, you will have to pay tax on your materials. But even so, the price can be very reasonable.

TRINIDAD AS A SERVICE CENTER

In just a few short years, Trinidad has gone from an island that saw few yachts to being the major service and haul out center for the Eastern Caribbean. TTSA had long had a travel lift and occasionally hauled visiting yachts, but Power Boats was the first yard to make it a serious commercial venture and they became so successful this work soon overtook their traditional business of storing small local power boats. Peake quickly followed as did IMS, then CrewsInn, Hummingbird, Tardieu, Tropical Marine and Coral Cove.

In the meantime contractors and businesses were started up to service the industry. As a result Trinidad today has more yacht services in a small area than anywhere else I know of. There are about a hundred yacht services in Chaguaramas alone.

The industry, which expanded very rapidly has today slowed down. This is not because of a lack of demand, but because the Chaguaramas Development Authority, the landlords for all these businesses are not encouraging further rapid expansion.

Planning & Cruising

YSATT

The meteoric growth of the industry owes much to the determination and dedication of the yards that started it. They realized from the outset that yachts were fickle customers, and that a careless attitude, sloppy work or overpricing would quickly drive the yachts away. In order to prevent this and to get feedback from their customers, they formed the Yacht Service Association of Trinidad and Tobago otherwise known as YSATT.

YSATT, a nonprofit organization, is the watchdog, the helping hand and the voice of the industry. At first it had just a few members – mainly the big marinas, now it has about a hundred members including many of the small businesses. YSATT has done a tremendous amount, for both individual yacht owners and for the industry. I know of no other place in the Caribbean where such an effort is made to try and keep people happy.

Behind the scenes YSATT works hard to make things work well with customs and immigration. They supply the air-conditioners and much of the office equipment in the customs and immigration building. They work with the officials to try and smooth out problems whenever they occur. If some new "rule" pops up and annoys visitors, they are the ones to go and get it rescinded. They are also the spokesperson of the industry in government dealings, and negotiate on laws concerning yachting. They have done much to ensure those on yachts can bring in duty free stores in an easy and hassle free manner.

YSATT makes their members keep to a certain standard and arranges training sessions for their workers.

They also have environmental rules that all members must comply with and these are often reviewed and updated. For example, all YSATT marinas must have recycling facilities for glass, oil and batteries. They also have an annual cleanup day to which yachties are invited.

As the watchdog, they want to know how you found things both good and bad, whether you worked with YSATT members or outside. They feed this information back to the services and, in the case of YSATT members, if there are problems, improvement is demanded.

Up front, YSATT offers the visiting yachtsman several important benefits. If you have a serious problem involving a financial dispute with a member, they will work very hard to solve it, firstly by negotiation, and if that fails, by agreed arbitration. They cannot do this if you work with a non-member (which is a good reason for choosing a member). They are

Diane and Angelie at YSATT

28

also working on a computerized log of complaints and praise they have received about everyone in the industry. By viewing this you can quickly work out where the problem areas are and make rational decisions about which contractors will work for you.

YSATT also work as a general information office both about their members and about tourist information on Trinidad and Tobago.

Their offices are downstairs in the CrewsInn Village, in the big two-story building. Two charming women, Diane and Angelie will greet you. They would like to hear from you and add your experiences to their database. They are well worth consulting before you choose a contractor. They will also be happy to supply a list of their members. The system works, because they now find they are getting fewer and fewer complaints about YSATT members. Pop by, even if it is to say hello. The address is:

P.O. Bag 518, Carenage, Trinidad, e-mail: ysatt@trinidad.net, Phone: 868-634-4938, Fax: 868-634-2160.

TIDCO

Tidco is a company that works for the government to encourage and monitor the growth of industry including yachting and tourism. They run the main tourist offices and YSATT works as a distributor of information for them. They do a lot behind the scenes in the yachting industry and you can check their website: visittnt.com.

HOW TO HAUL AND KEEP SMILING

This is an industry that started with very little and had to hoist itself up on the skill and adaptability of many workers who had little experience with yachts. They have done a tremendous job, but naturally there have been a few problems and mistakes. In talking to people who have hauled here (as I do myself) it was apparent that those of us who had a lot of experience in the Caribbean were highly satisfied with the kind of service we got. Most complaints came from people who had little

local experience. If you are going to haul and keep smiling, it is as well to understand the process and the people a little.

Trinidadians love to please and they generally have an optimistic outlook. This makes them pleasant to deal with, but it can also lead to promises of delivery dates which can only be met under the most ideal conditions and these rarely prevail. This is particularly so if you pressure a contractor and plead with him to be able to do a job sooner than he feels he can. He wants to oblige so he will end up offering to try.

The weather plays a big role in any outside work. Rain is frequent and often unpredictable. Sometimes a small shower will fall on what seems like a clear blue day - it may be light, but it takes very little to destroy a paint job. Those who have serious deadlines for painting should opt to have the boat covered in plastic before they start. They can also have it done under cover at CrewsInn.

Problems also arise with people who want a gold-plate job at rock bottom prices. Trinidad offers a large variety of skill levels and prices. There are many who can produce a reasonable workmanlike job at a fair price. There are a few who can do a superb job and their price is higher.

Your experience will very much depend on whom you get to do the job. On average, satisfaction is higher when you work with a YSATT member than with a non-member. Also YSATT can tell you what kind of comments they have had from other people about most of the local businesses. You should also ask around and get good recommendations. If you do this intelligently, you will find you can get what you need at the level you need it. In general price bargaining is not part of the local culture, and problems can occur when people try to bargain the price down to an unreasonable level. The contractor, with his sunny disposition, may want the job and agree to a lower price. But having done this, it is not going to be his top priority job nor is he going to put his best men on it.

HOW THE YARDS WORK

Yards vary according to how much work they do themselves and how much is passed onto outside contractors. Power Boats is at one end of this continuum. They just haul and chock your boat. After that you discuss what you want done with them and they will put you in touch with a variety of contractors. These contractors are very carefully vetted. Power Boats takes a commission from the contractors which increases the price a little, but is money well spent, for the contract is signed in the Power Boats office and they stand by the work. This means that if you have a problem, you don't have to chase after some elusive contractor, you can go right into Power Boats office to get it sorted out. It also means they do their best to make sure you get your job done on time, which is a big help if you leave your boat and fly home.

Southern Caribbean Yacht Works, the working arm of CrewsInn is just the opposite. They contract to do the job and do it right. They look to the larger, more luxurious end of the market where penny pinching is not an issue. They only want to take on a few boats at a time and concentrate on those boats, giving each one personal attention. Some work they do themselves, and some they subcontract, but they take full responsibility for the final job, and you do not have to deal with any individual contractor. Crew cannot work on a yacht in their yard, and they do not charge for storage while work is being done.

Peake, IMS and Coral Cove lie some-where between these two. You are welcome to work on the boat yourself, but outside contractors have to be approved.

PREPARATIONS FOR YACHT STORAGE

While you are gone your yacht is going to be subject to the ravages of sun and rain. Careful preparation can do much to make your return more pleasant.

The biggest danger from rain is that your boat will fill up with water from mast and other leaks leading to flood damage. It is best to remove a hose from one of your lower seacocks and leave it open, so water entering the hull can flow out again. In addition pay someone reliable to pump your bilge from time to time, and to check your cockpit drains do not get filled with leaves.

On the inside of your boat the damp of the rainy season can play havoc with mold and condensation. This depends on how well your yacht is insulated. If it is prone to condensation then it is probably worth renting a de-humidifier to keep it dry. These are generally in short supply, so it is worth booking one well in advance.

Sun shining through windows can fade fabrics and a combination of heat and direct sunlight will destroy the display on electronic instruments. If possible remove your electronic displays and store them below. If this is not possible, then cover them well from all direct sun. If you have large windows, then curtain them with some cheap fabric to protect the interior of the boat against the sun. If you have windows or hatches made of Lexan or other acrylic sheet, these too will last longer if protected, as the sun can cause them to craze

You can also have a temporary plastic cover made for your yacht. This keeps it in much better shape and helps ongoing jobs. Contact Dynamite Marine or Power Boats.

Electrics

You need to decide how you want to leave your electrics (connected or disconnected). If connected, it is well worth cleaning and putting some protective coating on all major terminals before you leave. You can arrange with the yard to put a charger on your batteries from time to time.

Engines

Many people do just walk away from

their engines and find they work fine when they get back. However, it is worth the work of doing at least a minimum lay-up. Your fuel tank wants to be full to cut down on condensation. The salt water should be drained from the cooling system and flushed out with fresh. The engine oil should be changed. Any airways into the engine should be sealed off. This means the exhaust and the air intake. These can usually be stopped up with plastic bags.

Before stowing your outboard, run the fuel tank dry, remove the spark plug and spray a little light oil in the cylinder. Replace the spark plug lightly.

Before you leave there are some simple customs formalities that need to be dealt with. See our Customs section for details.

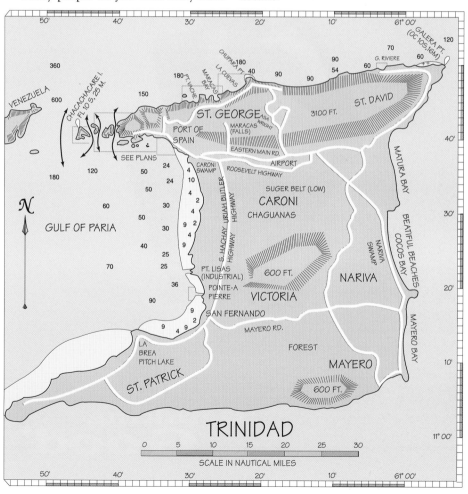

Exploring
Trinidad

Nature Trips

Trinidad has an exceptional variety of birds and animals, whose ranges are restricted to relatively small areas, making it an exceptionally rewarding country for birders and nature lovers. The northern mountain range contains spectacular scenery and some dramatic waterfalls.

Below we mention a few areas visiting yachtspeople might find interesting.

CHAGUARAMAS NATIONAL PARK

Many people spend weeks in Chaguaramas amid the boatyards without realizing that this whole area is part of a national park. Chaguaramas National Park includes the whole of the Chaguaramas Peninsula, from the Tucker Valley west and includes the outer islands to Chacachacare. You can explore some areas on your own; for others you will need a guide. Pass by the Chaguaramas Development Authority (CDA) marketing division, ask for Antoinette, or give her a call at 868-634-4364/4349. She will make sure you have all the information you need. CDA offers many excellent guided tours, but usually for parties of ten or more.

One area of interest is the Macqueripe Mail Road. In days of sail it was hard to get through the Boca against the north going current. Ships could get held up for hours or even days trying to get in and people got fed up waiting for their mail. To get round this, mail was unloaded at Macqueripe Bay and the Macqueripe Mail Road was built to take it overland to Port of Spain. The Chaguaramas golf club (currently 9 holes) is towards the end of this road and many hikes start somewhere in this area.

Edith Falls only exist at the height of the wet season and are easy to find on your own. You can see them from the golf course. Go to the caddy hut and ask to be put on the right track. There is a fee of $7TT per person. This is an easy hike, just over a mile through mixed vegetation on a clearly marked trail. The falls are an impressive 600 feet high and you can find a pool to swim in during the wet season.

You can also take an interesting hike to Macqueripe Bay from here. Pay your $7TT at the caddy hut and ask where the trail begins. This hike is called "moderate," so you want to be reasonably fit. You can swim in the bay when you get there. (If you just want to visit Macqueripe Bay, it is easily accessible by road.)

Another hike you can do on your own (and there is no fee) is the trail up to the tracking station. This offers fairly good views of the north coast and Tucker Valley. The Americans used this station to track ballistic missiles in the 1950's and later it was used for experimental satellite communications. Now it is a monument. The early part of the hike is the most pleasant, when you pass through a tunnel of bamboo with lots of heliconias. The hike is all on road (barred to traffic) and takes about 45 minutes.

The Coving Park River Trail is one you need a guide for, as there is unexploded ordinance about, as well as numerous beehives. The trail begins in a nutmeg grove, follows a river up through a narrow twisting gorge, reaches a waterfall, and ends at an emerald pool where you can get a delightful swim.

You can cycle or hike the road up to Morne Catherine, five and half miles uphill to the top. Take a lot of care on this road because the coastguard uses it and they fly up and down with great abandon in their vehicles.

On the beach opposite the Macqueripe Mail Road you can rent bikes as well as kayaks. Serious bikers should get in touch with Geronimo's in Woodbrook, at the junction of Pole Carew and Roberts Streets. He rents good bikes reasonably, especially on weekends, and knows all about biking in Trinidad.

One of the longest hikes is from Scotland Bay to Macqueripe Bay. This looks like it would be long and arduous. Best get details from the CDA.

With a dinghy, you can easily visit the park on Gaspar Grande Island. To get there, dinghy down toward the far end of Gaspar Grande. Just before you get to the western tip you will see the public landing which has a small rest shelter and a notice board. Take a dinghy anchor and an extra line so you can anchor your dinghy clear of the access dock and tie it to the shore. Follow the clearly marked path.

This is a pleasant park with some big trees and picnic tables. In the park grounds are two large guns in different places left by the Americans after World War II. Both sites have good views. The Gasparee Caves are also in this park, but they are only open on request from Thursday to Sunday and they usually want a sizeable group. (They charge a small entrance fee.) You can call the CDA during the week to try to arrange this, and they may know when they have other groups going that you could join. You will be taken on a guided tour that takes about 20 minutes — down a

Page 35:
Yellow headed
blackbird
Xanthocephalus
Xanthocephalus
at Point-a-Pierre
Wildlife Trust

Opposite:
Matelot Falls

Below:
On the road to
the tracking
station

long staircase into the cave, which is about 100 feet deep and 200 feet across at the bottom. The walls and ceiling are hung with stalactites that form strange patterns. A pool at the bottom reflects the trees overhanging the entrance high above. Fruit bats live in the ceilings and they venture out at night to eat wild balata fruits. The remains of their midnight snacks can be seen on the floor of the cave.

CARONI SWAMP

One of the most famous nature destinations is the Caroni Swamp, where you can see Trinidad and Tobago's national bird, the scarlet ibis. These sociable birds congregate at night on small mangrove islands that can only be approached by boat. The only practical way to see them is to join an organized tour. It is best to call in advance, but you can just turn up at the Caroni Swamp car park after 1500 and make arrangements on the spot. Take the road south from Port of Spain toward San Fernando and look for the turn off to the Caroni Swamp, which is clearly signposted. Bring binoculars, bug spray, and a sun hat or visor and sunglasses, as the sun can be glaring for the first half hour.

You will be taken by boat through a maze of mangrove channels that are home to herons, mangrove crabs, and oddities like the four-eyed fish. The climax of the trip, however, is seeing the scarlet ibis. The beauty of this gorgeous red bird, luminous in the late afternoon sun, is beyond description. The lowest level of the mangrove islands fills with snowy egrets, and little blue herons occupy the mid-level. Then the ibises arrive in small groups from their feeding grounds, gliding gracefully to roost until hundreds of them stand out like brilliant flowers against a dark green background.

The ibis show is at twilight and an earlier stop at Chaguanas, just a few miles farther south, provides an appealing contrast. This town, dominated by East Indians, is a thriving commercial center and an inexpensive place to shop. Vendors used to line the main street, but authorities have been trying to discourage this and move them instead to a separate location. They should not be hard to find.

ASA WRIGHT
NATURE CENTER

This 200-acre nature preserve is set in gorgeous mountain scenery at an elevation of about 1200 feet. To get there, take the eastern main road to Arima and then head north.

The nature center was formerly part of a cocoa, coffee, and citrus plantation. In 1950 William Beebe established a tropical research station nearby and visiting scientists often stayed at the Wright's. One of these, Don Eckelberry, a renowned bird painter, persuaded Asa Wright to turn her property into a reserve after the death of her husband.

Next page (P40): Leatherback turtle digs a nest. The size can be judged by the small human legs just visible in the upper right of the picture

Opposite: Scarlet ibis photo by Roger Neckles

Below: Hummingbird at AsaWright

Roger Neckles photo

It is easy to sit for hours on the verandah of the beautiful old estate house, built in 1907, and watch the birds come to you. Well-stocked feeders bring hummingbirds, honeycreepers, woodpeckers, and many other birds right up close.

The estate has daily tours with local naturalists who will point out many birds you would otherwise miss. You can also hike on any of the marked trails. A day here may not seem enough and they do have overnight accommodation, usually used by birding enthusiasts from the USA. You should book in advance for lunch, as it is miles from anywhere. There is a reasonable admission charge.

Allow time to return by the northern route, which follows miles of breathtaking mountain and cliff-top scenery.

TIMBERLINE

Timberline Resort and Nature Center at Pointe Vache makes an excellent lunch stop when touring the north coast. Do not be intimidated by the road that does a fair imitation of a ski slope. It is not quite as terrifying as it looks, and all but the wimpiest car will make the return trip up the hill. Timberline is set in an old estate and mill that are built on a ridge with views in both directions. On a clear day you can see both Tobago and Venezuela. Beneath is La Vache Bay, one of the best north coast anchorages. Timberline was closed for renovation in 2001, and there was talk of reopening, but plans are uncertain.

THE PITCH LAKE

Noel Coward described this pond of asphalt as: "Twenty two tennis courts badly in need of repair." Perhaps he had some oversize courts in mind, for this million-year-old pit covers 89 acres. Sir Walter Raleigh was the first European to describe it and he used the pitch as caulking compound for his fleet. The quality of the asphalt is high and approximately 300 tons a day are removed. The Pitch Lake is about 10 miles southeast of San Fernando, near the small town of Brighton. The down side to the pitch lakes is the local youth guides who are present in abundance and fairly expensive. They can also be abusive if not made happy.

MARACAS WATERFALL

Maracas Waterfall is 300 feet high, the highest year round fall in the country. Compared with some other waterfalls in the Caribbean, it is not particularly dramatic, but the drive into the mountains and the 1.5-mile hike up to the falls is pleasant through lovely country. There is a good picnicking area at the falls.

FORT GEORGE

When the crowds, bustle, or daily routine start to annoy, drive the five minutes from the yacht club up to Fort George (open 0600 to 1800). It is a different world up here, a peaceful spot with spectacular views over Port of Spain and all the way over to North Post. Fort George was built to defend Trinidad in 1805. It was converted to a signal station in 1902 and was used as late as 1964. The views and the well-tended gardens make it a peaceful place to relax. You often see parrots.

TURTLE WATCH TOURS

Everyone I met who had gone turtle watching was delighted. Seeing these giant reptiles emerge from the sea, their shells glistening in the moon, to struggle up the sand and lay their eggs — a behavior evolved millions of years ago — is enthralling. Trinidad is the best place in the Eastern Caribbean to experience this. Leatherback turtles, six to seven feet long and weighing up to a ton, are most commonly seen. The eggs take 60 days to hatch. From March to June, 30 to 60 turtles may arrive on some beaches in one night. Some nesting continues until September. While the volume of nesting turtles decreases after June, the chances of seeing young hatching out increases. Turtles nest on the northeast and east coast. Matura Bay is a popular and accessible site that is closely controlled and well run. There is a small government fee.

One of the nicest places for a turtle watch is at Grande Riviere on Trinidad's north coast. This is because there is a charming small hotel on the beach called Mt. Plasir Estate. It is run by Piero Guerrini from Italy and makes a perfect dinner spot

and base for a watch. They have several communal rooms with up to six beds for groups. The only disadvantage is the drive from Chaguaramas, which takes three to four hours.

Avoid public holidays, if possible, as this often increases the crowd considerably. The beach and the turtles appear much more beautiful when the moon is close to full. On the other hand, the full moon may also bring more people. If there is a crowd, consider eating dinner and sleeping till 0130, by which time most people will have left. Take plenty of bug spray. I enjoyed having a small beach seat for relaxed viewing. Heavy rain may also affect landings. The easiest way to turtle watch is join a tour or rent a car.

There are many excellent hikes in the Grande Riviere area, so any extra time you can arrange to spend, even half a day, will be well rewarded. Hiking can be arranged through the hotel. There is one small waterfall just a short walk from the hotel, though you will need a guide to find it. If you carry on westward to the end of the road at Matelot and hike up the Matelot River, you will come to some beautiful falls with a big pool for swimming. A guide is recommended and can be arranged through the hotel.

LAKES

Trinidad has three large water storage dams: Hollis Reservoir, Nevit Dam, and Arena Dam. These are all excellent areas for hiking and picnicking, a wonderful way to get away from the boat for a day. They are off the main roads, so it is probably best to rent a car. You can expect to see a good collection of water birds, including cormorants and ducks. You might even get to see caimans.

I have only been to Arena, the largest of these. Here they have built shelters and tables. It covers a large area, so should there be a crowd, you will be able to get well away. Unfortunately, trees do not come all the way down to the water, which is sided by a large area of grass, but it is still an attractive place. You may be able to canoe at the Arena dam, and I would think that includes a rubber dinghy if that is what you have. Take oars or paddles be-

cause outboards are not allowed, and get permission from WASA (Trinidad's Water Authority) before you go. You do need a pass from WASA to visit these dams, and there is a small fee to pay. You can call WASA for details at 662-2301/5, 622-1965.

POINT-A-PIERRE WILDLIFE TRUST

This is a magnificent park area among the reservoirs for the oil refineries. It is written up under Point-a-Pierre.

NARIVA SWAMP

The Nariva Swamp is Trinidad's richest wildlife area. Visiting with Roger Neckles is always an adventure, and there is no one I would prefer to go with. He kindly let me reprint an account he wrote for BWIA magazine:

Of Capuchins and Anacondas
By Roger Neckles

You've got to love the antics of monkeys in their natural settings. The last three outings to a unique part of our emerald isles, Nariva Swamp, were undoubtedly the most thrilling adventures of my professional career as a wildlife photographer and nature guide, apart from hugging and kissing grey whales in Baja Mexico — but that's another story.

It was Friday, the 7th of July 2000, when I was hired by a very charming and admiring fan named Nancy from the USA (temporarily living in Trinidad) to escort her and her family to see our two species of indigenous monkeys, the red-howler and the Trinidad weeping capuchin (endemic to Trinidad). On this day we were fortunate to experience what was certainly my best encounter of capuchin monkeys in 20 years. For my clients it was their first experience of seeing monkeys in the wild. They left there with dilated pupils, their smiles almost touching their ear lobes.

I got too excited and quickly ran out of film that day. I was totally unprepared for such close encounters, I'd seldom shot off more than six rolls of film on monkeys before and my encounters in the past had been brief by comparison. The capuchins were all around us, at waist and eye level, and as close as 15 feet.

As Murphy's Law would have it, they performed some of their best antics when I ran out of film, so I was determined to come back by myself two days later in hope of an action replay, this time armed to the teeth with film, "as a professional should be!"

Well, the 9th of July seemed to be an identical day to my previous visit: the weather was the same, my timing was the same, and my assistant, Bobby, and I searched the same areas that we had searched before to find the capuchins. After a couple hours we got our first encounter as a lone individual came to inspect us, followed moments later by several other members of the troop.

Naturally I got all the shots I needed with lots of film to spare, before the monkeys climbed and bounded through the area en route to their favorite feeding grounds.

I got such good shots and they came so close that I thought this was by far the best experience — not so!

Thursday the 13th, I was hired by a family of three from Massachusetts USA; a chap named Peter and his two well-behaved and enthusiastic daughters. I followed my previous day's plan in terms of timing, as I did not want to break my lucky streak, especially as I had to go and brag to my new clients about the brilliant encounters I had on my last two visits.

Well, Bobby pulled the choke, yanked the cord, the engine smoked and coughed to a start, and we were off, his engine becoming less smoky than on our previous sorties. This must have been a sign of good things to come, as we immediately saw red-bellied macaws and orange-winged parrots flying directly over our heads as they warmed up over the moriche and royal palm trees, before flying off to their favorite feeding grounds. The native lotus lily was in abundant bloom, adding its own share of sublime beauty to this once abused and still threatened jewel of a place.

Once we had completed our first leg of the boat trip, we were ready to walk through the swamp forest. We enthusiastically geared up and proceeded at a slow and deliberate pace in pursuit of our entertainers. About 45 minutes into our sortie, I decided to utter my special capuchin call in the hope that the leader of the troop would respond, enabling me to get a fix on their whereabouts. About 5 seconds later the troop leader called back to me. They were close! Moments later, an individual emerged from the depths of the trees, soon followed by the rest of the troop.

They emerge mysteriously, like little secret forest-tribesmen; you don't really see exactly where they come from; they just seem to appear. I decided to let them pass over us, risking them breaking off dry branches and throwing them down on our heads (a normal behavior), so that they would settle at the cocorite palm tree that I knew they were heading for, several hundred yards on. This would enable us to sneak up on them while they became preoccupied with gorging themselves on the fleshy nuts, which they clearly find irresistible.

When we finally got to them, we noticed that they were all around us, some at eye level and others just a few feet above our heads. Everyone was so excited, my clients were all eyes; they had never seen monkeys in the wild before.

While they were catching their breaths and dodging cocorite palm nuts occasionally thrown by these territorial monkeys, I decided to collect some nuts, which had gathered around the base of the palm, to let my clients experience the sweet taste. As I was gathering the nuts, Bobby yelled out to me, "Roger, move your hand — anaconda", " Where?" I said. He came close to me and pointed to the head and about three inches of the snake's body just peeping out from under the leaf litter. The rest of the body was completely concealed.

My hand was three inches from its head at the time, anacondas are not a poisonous species but they can inflicted a nasty bite with their rows of fine, sharp, inward pointing teeth. I got a twig a few inches long and

Capuchin monkey
Roger Neckles photo

flicked the leaf litter off its head and pinned it down, grabbing the head.

Now, the anaconda's head does not give you a true indication of the size of snake you are dealing with. Its head is disproportionately small compared to its body. So when I thought that this specimen was around six feet in length it turned out to be over ten with a body twice as thick as I had anticipated. It was so strong I could barely control it.

The capuchins scattered in all directions, hundreds of feet away and then slowly came closer, but still nowhere near as close as they were before I caught the anaconda.

They had good reason to be afraid, because this individual was prepared to hide in wait for days until they had exhausted their supply of nuts in the palm tree and descended to collect the fallen nuts on the ground.

They were all extremely alarmed and became quite vociferous, uttering noises that meant "snake" to unwary members of the troop. I'd never heard them utter this call before in all my years of tracking them. They seemed shocked that they were feeding in a tree with an archenemy so close to them, and were clearly surprised.

They began breaking off branches and throwing them down at the snake — I knew I was not really the intended victim. I just happened to be attached to it; tough luck for me! Luckily, their aim was not true.

All this time my clients, who were all armed with cameras, were clicking away at me like I was some sort of movie star. They were ordering me in various poses, then curiosity overpowered their Paparazzi fever and they inched up to the snake and me as I began telling them about the species.

The time came to release the snake, which was beginning to tire me. (This species is so powerful it is said that an individual needs to be only one foot longer than its victim to be able to consume it. Once encircled, the victim feels shortness of breath as its coils tighten around him. His ribs pop under pressure from the powerful constriction and then cardiac arrest follows, as the circulation becomes backed up and the heart has no room to pump). I ordered everybody well back and put it down gingerly, the anaconda wasted not one moment in beating a hasty retreat. It was then that we realized, uncoiled, what a huge snake it was.

When the snake slipped back into a

Avifauna Tours
Trinidad and Tobago
"The Nature Lovers Most Sensible Choice"

Explore Trinidad's nature with Roger Neckles, a world renown wildlife photographer whose pictures have been published in *National Geographic, Natural History, Audubon, and Bird Watchers Digest.*

Roger has been awarded the *Green Leaf Award* in recognition of his contribution to environmental conservation and protection. His realistic bird and animal calls help bring the wildlife to you, and his bird-watching trips are unsurpassed. Roger's wildlife pictures are also on sale, and ten of them are featured on Trinidad and Tobago postal stamps.

Tel: (868)-633-5614, (868)-759-4084
E-mail avifauna@trinidad.net

Howler monkey

**Previous page:
Anaconda**

**Both Roger
Neckles photos**

nearby river, the monkeys descended on overhanging branches and started thrashing around throwing nuts and branches into the water behind the snake, which was long gone. They did not spend much time with us after that, as if it was our fault that the snake was lying in wait for them, and they slowly and deliberately moved off in a single direction to feed elsewhere.

As for my clients, well, talk about dilated pupils and drunken smiles. They were fatigued by the overdose of adrenaline and clearly had to unwind. This was the right opportunity to have breakfast. I could not eat, not because I was not hungry, but because I could not steady my hand enough to get the food in my mouth, I was still shaking from nervous energy.

It was impossible to eclipse that experience, but we did see more: beautiful huge metallic-blue morpho butterflies and a myriad variety of others. We saw what I call the jigsaw puzzle termites. These termites gnaw through the underside of the bark of certain trees, a fallen dead tree in this case, cutting out a perfect shape averaging four inches long and three inches wide.

They then somehow lift this cutout up and toss it to the ground. How? And why? I really do not know. But it was fascinating. We were picking up the puzzle-like pieces of tree bark and trying to fit them back on the tree.

We got a very effortless look at a small troop of red howler monkeys, which were resting just under the canopy some 60 feet up, nowhere near as close as the capuchins. But still, we got very clear and long looks at them before we set off on our return leg of our boat ride of what was, according to my clients, (and certainly for me too) one of the most exciting days of their lives.

WHERE TO GO FOR TOURS:

Those serious about exploring Trinidad might want to approach it in more than one way. Some areas, like the Nariva Swamp, or the Caroni are impossible to see without local knowledge, and a good local guide is the only sensible approach. Exploring the northern mountain range, visiting the Asa Wright Center and turtle watching are all things you can do on your own with a rental car, though excellent trips to these places are also available through tour agencies. The advantage of the tour is that it is very easy and all arrangements are done for you, plus you get a knowledgeable guide. If you go on your own, you will work a little harder, but you get added flexibility. The first turtle watch I did at Grand Riviere was with a tour and it was excellent. However, once there, it seemed a shame to come all that way and not spend more time exploring the beautiful countryside. So the next time I rented a car and spent an extra day hiking to the waterfalls in Matelot. Those with plenty of time could

also do some exploring by bus, but this is will not be as convenient as being on a tour or renting a car.

Avifauna Tours: 868-633-5614, 868-759-4084. Roger Neckles is Trinidad's leading wildlife photographer, and an excellent birder and naturalist. Roger is recommended for small groups serious about either photography or nature. The more exotic wildlife is often best observed early in the morning, so he may suggest starting as early as 0530. Tours are by arrangement only.

Hike Seekers: 632-9746, to join hiking groups.

Members Only: 633-3486, Jesse James organizes lots of tours and is always coming up with new ideas to keep his customers coming. He does nature, cultural, shopping, artisan, and sightseeing tours, and he offers some free shopping trips to supermarkets.

Power Boats: 634-4303, Power Boats arranges a number of tours to make it easy for their customers to see Trinidad. They keep a list of tours posted in the office. The prices look very reasonable.

Sacketteers: 675-1742, enthusiastic hiking club.

Trump Tours: 634-2189, an up-market tour group that provides excellent service and guides. All kinds of tours are arranged, but particularly nature tours and carnival. Free shopping trips to local supermarkets are also on offer.

Winston Nanan Tours: 645-1305. Nanan is one of the operators that has boats doing daily Caroni Swamp trips.

Trinidad's Carnival
by Cathy Winn

Every year, thousands of normally sober, hard-working people come down with a virulent case of Carnival fever that kicks in very soon after Christmas. The poor victims don't get back to normal until Ash Wednesday. Carnival is an integral part of the lives of most Trinidad citizens and it involves people of all age groups, all religions and races. Children start jumping up and wearing costumes when still in diapers and some are still enjoying Carnival today at the age of eighty.

Many of the traditions of Trinidad Carnival originated in medieval Europe and West Africa and were imported by early immigrants from the former, and by their slaves from the latter. The many different peoples and classes created quite different carnivals. French Creole Carnival was exclusive, a culmination of a long Christmas season. It was a time of fancy dress balls, a diversion giving some excitement to their lives. Oddly enough, these whites had a favorite "masque" of imitating their Negro slaves and they reenacted activities on the cane plantations, using torches to portray cane fires. This "canboulay" was a traditional part of the festivities on the plantations.

Slaves were allowed a certain freedom during Carnival times and began to have their own costuming, often mimicking their masters' ways and dress. When emancipation occurred in 1833, it resulted in a withdrawal of Creoles from many of the public festivities and a renewed exuberance from the freed slaves. Gradually, the activities became very rowdy, with glorification of the "jammette" or underworld class. There were stick fighters, devil characters, midnight robbers, and flagrant sexual parody, mimicking the way of life of a deviant working class. Attempts to limit and even outlaw Carnival, were always bitterly fought by mobs and even middle class black nationalists. Overregulation is still sternly resisted by Trinidadians today who insist on having Carnival their way. As Carnival became more law-abiding, the middle class and French Creoles began to come out in the streets again. Competitions sponsored by early merchants were started for the best costumes and Carnival became more respectable, while retaining the working class rear guard that is still active in J'Ouvert. There is growing interest in reviving and keeping alive some of the old ways, and for years now yachties have been thrilled by the Ole Time Carnival parade and show, with many of the characters being portrayed without the lawlessness of previous years.

Carnival season starts right after Christmas, and builds in excitement and anticipation to culminate in the two days before Lent. Then, just like Cinderella's ball, it comes to a crashing halt midnight Tuesday.

Opposite:
Denise Plummer,
Carnival Photos
by Norton
Studios

Opposite:
Carnival Queen

Page 52: Mas

*Page 53: Snake
Charmer*

*Carnival Photos by
Norton Studios*

Trinidad's Carnival is not a show put on for the benefit of tourists or TV coverage; it's every individual masquerader's chance to play a folk or historic character, an animal, or to wear the most popular costume of the day. For two days everyone leaves their cares and worries at home and totally gives themselves up to the music, the color, and the collective excitement of being with thousands of other revellers out on the street.

For those of us not brought up in the tradition of Carnival, it's still possible to appreciate the beauty, creativity, and enthusiasm of everyone involved: from the masqueraders on the street, to the volunteers making costumes late into the night, the Calypso singers trying to come up with a catchy or thought-provoking song, or the many behind-the-scenes organizers. For many, Carnival has become a year-round business, with money and prestige to be had, but all do it for the love of Carnival.

Among the many visitors to Trinidad's Carnival in the last ten years have been increasing numbers of boaters, who have discovered the fun of Carnival in a big way. In the months of January and February, when most anchorages up the islands are crowded with charter boats and cruise ships, Trinidad's marinas and anchorages are also full of sailors eager to discover or experience again this fantastic spectacle. Some sailors are coming back for their tenth Carnival and plan their season's sailing around this event, an event that is by no means is confined to the last two days. There's something for everyone, from little children and teens to retired couples in their seventies. Yachties can participate in — as well as witness up close — the beauty of Carnival.

There's much to do in Carnival season and every activity helps you learn more about the history and culture of Trinidad. This is the birthplace of the steelpan and Calypso music and Carnival is their showcase. There is a huge national steelband competition called Panorama, where bands, most totalling 100 musicians, play original tunes while the whole nation cheers them on. Even their practice sessions are well attended by their fans. The energy that every masquerader needs to jump up on the streets for two days comes from the music which pervades every aspect of Trinidad life. New Calypsos are written each season and each artiste's composition is eagerly awaited, debated, and played over the airwaves and performed in concerts all season. There is also Soca music; its lively, jump-up beat fuelled by brass bands with huge speaker systems and screaming half-naked singers is a big part of every fete (or party) and will be played over and over on the two Carnival days.

By January, most people planning on "playing mas" have already made a down payment on the costume of their choice and all that's left to do is to enjoy and party. Late arrivals can visit the camps where each band has its headquarters to see the drawings showing the costumes and the color schemes. Even close to Carnival you may still be able to buy a costume. All season there are parties called fetes. Most of these have adopted the "all-inclusive" mode. You buy a ticket; then all the drinks, food, and live entertainment are prepaid. Like the costumes, these have escalated considerably in price over the years, but many are held for charities.

Fetes can be great fun; for Trinis they make the whole season - you go to be seen, party with your friends, drink, and hear the most popular music.

Yachties have participated in almost every part of Carnival. They have joined a steel band, learned to play and practiced every night with the band. Yachties have learned to be "moko jumbies" or stilt walkers and performed while six feet up in the air. J'Ouvert is still the most popular parade for yachties to join . This is the opening of

Carnival, beginning at 2 am Monday morning. This wildest of all Carnival celebrations is known for its outrageous "costumes" of mud, oil, blue or red body paint, onion bag outfits, and the like. Most years over 200 yachties take to the streets along with the rest of Trinidad.

It's best to come early to take advantage of the best events, and figure out what you want to do. Taste of Carnival seminars have been given every year for six years by the publisher of the Boaters' Directory. Here you can find out all you wanted to know about Carnival but didn't know to ask. You can get a schedule of events and at the same time be entertained by people involved in every aspect of Carnival. The seminars start three weeks before Carnival.

Transportation is never a problem from the marinas to any event happening at Carnival time, even if it's at 2 am. All you need to do is keep up on what's happening and sign up for what you want to do. There are fetes, concerts, and competitions almost every day of the week, so you only have to pick and choose.

You should definitely consider scheduling Trinidad's Carnival into your Caribbean cruising plans. It's a fantastic experience, impossible to replicate. You can swim, snorkel, or fix the boat anywhere anytime, but Trinidad's Carnival is an experience you'll treasure for years to come.

Trinidad Carnival
"The greatest carnival on earth"

Carnival Dates (Monday and Tuesday)		Taste of Carnival *Three consecutive Wednesdays starting*
Carnival 2002	Febrary 11-12	January 16
Carnival 2003.	March 3-4	February 5
Carnival 2004	February 23-24	January 28
Carnival 2005	February 7-8	January 12
Carnival 2006	February 27-28	February 1

Anchorages in TRINIDAD

& TOBAGO

Passages between Trinidad, Tobago and Grenada

TRINIDAD FROM GRENADA

It is 78 miles from Prickly Bay to the north coast of Trinidad. Some people leave Prickly Bay around dusk and sail overnight; others sail by day, arriving after dark. I usually try to make it in daylight hours, starting at dawn. While I occasionally succeeded both ways in my old 6-7 knot boat, more often I arrived after dark.

The light on Chacachacare is excellent and helps confirm your position. The tidal stream between Grenada and Trinidad is patchy, so if you use a GPS to stay on course, you will be upwind one minute and falling off the next. Better to make an average estimate for current. The northerly component of the current will help you heading north and work against you sailing south. It is highly variable – sometimes you only get the current for a few hours, at other times it will affect you for most of the trip. On the return trip to Grenada, remember that the current can be strongest close to Grenada.

In July 2001 a pipeline was laid from the south of Trinidad through Boca de Monos to a natural gas oil rig, called Hibiscus, which will be permanently stationed about 25 miles north of Boca de Monos, roughly due east of Tobago. This puts it close to the route from Grenada to Trinidad, where it will make a fine landmark. There is no chance of hitting it if you are keeping a good watch; it will be conspicuous by day and well lit at night. Keep at least one mile clear.

The most usual and direct entrance to the Gulf of Paria is through the Boca de Monos. There is a small island about a third of the way between Monos Island and the mainland. Pass between this island and the mainland as there are shoals and rocks between the island and Monos Island.

TRINIDAD FROM VENEZUELA

If wind and sea are against you from the eastern tip of Venezuela, you will probably find it easier to pass on the south side of Chacachacare and the other islands, where you will be out of the ocean swells.

TOBAGO FROM TRINIDAD

Sailing from Trinidad to Tobago can be lovely or rough, depending on the conditions. It is only about 60 miles from Scotland Bay. If the wind is from the south and you leave at about 0430, you should get a lovely calm motor sail up the coast and then a good sail over to arrive in Tobago well before dark. If you go in May, the turtle season, you have a good chance of seeing huge leatherback turtles close to shore. In 2001 we saw more than 40 on this route

If the wind is from the northeast and blowing hard, it is tough because you are bucking both wind and current. The conventional approach is to power up the Trinidad coast at night when the wind is generally lighter, and cross over to Tobago early in the morning. It makes the crossing shorter and more pleasant to set off early in the morning and stop at a north coast anchorage. (See our North Coast Anchorage Section.) If you leave Las Cuevas or Maracas about midnight and power up the coast, you should arrive at Galera Point early the next morning. Don't forget to string out the fishing line during daylight hours to pick up your next meal.

Within about a quarter of a mile of shore, the north coast of Trinidad is very rocky in places. Outside the rocks there is plenty of water. It is difficult to gauge distances at night, so I suggest staying about a mile offshore. Close to shore you sometimes get a counter current which normally goes east at the beginning of the rising tide for about four hours. This can be a mixed blessing when the wind is blowing hard as it creates nasty short seas.

Some Trinidad yachtsmen manage to find a counter current a little way off Trinidad's north coast. They motor sail, staying in the current until it dies out, and then strike out for Tobago.

You can also day-hop up Trinidad's coast, stopping at some of the north coast anchorages. These offer reasonable protection in easterly or southeasterly winds, but will be very rolly in a northeasterly and untenable in a large northerly swell.

When you reach Galera Point at the eastern end of Trinidad, you will find a current of at least two-knots sweeping westward between Trinidad and Tobago. Even if you sail hard on the wind heading to the eastern end of Tobago, you will be lucky to make it close to Crown Point (watch out for the shoals). From Crown Point it is a tough three-hour motor sail to Scarborough. If you want to go to Scarborough, it is easiest to motor sail from Galera Point to make it in one tack.

TOBAGO FROM GRENADA

Yachtspeople with plenty of time who want to visit both Trinidad and Tobago might consider visiting Tobago first, setting off from Grenada's sister island, Carriacou. If you leave in the afternoon and sail round to the northeast side of Carriacou, passing between Carriacou and PSV (there are shoals so you should not do it too late in the afternoon), you get an excellent shot at making Tobago in one tack. When you arrive in Tobago you will still have to make the struggle up wind to Scarborough to clear in, or you can sail further east to Charlotteville, which is now a port of entry.

People also sail from Grenada to Tobago. The speed of this passage varies with the wind direction and current. Most people leave at dusk and go overnight. If you need to tack, don't do it close to Grenada where the current is strongest. If you have a GPS, you can gauge when you are out of the current.

Chaguaramas, the center of Trinidad's yachting industry

A new name to prove our commitment to excellence

Who we are

Southern Caribbean Yacht Works is new name with experience. We've been around for more than five years and worked on well known yachts like Velsheda, Atlantic Goose, Savannah, Cariloy, Charlatan and Naos in just the past year.

What we do

An assigned project manager supervises the quality workmanship on your job, ensuring meticulous attention to detail. SCYW primary focus is on yacht painting, mechanical repairs, interior and exterior refinishing, teak decking, antifouling, osmosis treatment and blister repairs, propeller repairs and balancing and steelwork. That's not to say we cannot accommodate other requests.

What we have

A full-service yacht refit and repair yard, SCYW boasts the largest Travelift® (200 metric tonne) in the Caribbean, as well as a 2.3 acre covered yard.

Where we are

Situated N10°40' Latitude and W61°39' Longitude - outside of the hurricane belt - SCYW is tucked away on Trinidad's northwestern coast, at the southern end of the Caribbean island chain, only seven miles off the South American coastline. Ideally located, the yard is adjacent to a yachting centre, complete with hotel and retail services.

Finally, a professional boatyard with history, focus and dedication you can trust.

SOUTHERN CARIBBEAN YACHT WORKS

**Visit our website: southernyachtworks.com or email us: southernyachtworks@tstt.net.tt
Point Gourde, Chaguaramas, Trinidad • Tel: 868 634 4384 • Fax: 868 634 4828**

Trinidad

Trinidad at a glance

Regulations

Chaguaramas is the main port of clearance for yachts in Trinidad. On arrival, proceed straight to the customs dock in Chaguaramas. For customs details see *Regulations* under *Chaguaramas*. Yachts should not try to clear in Port of Spain as it is reserved for commercial vessels. You can also get clearance in Point-a-Pierre. Customs stand by on VHF: 16.

Holidays

January 1 - New Year's Day

Carnival - the Monday and Tuesday 40 days before Easter are not official holidays - but just try to do anything but fete! (Carnival Monday is Feb 11, 2002; March 3, 2003 and Feb 23, 2004.)

Easter Friday through Monday (Easter is March 31, 2002; April 20, 2003 and April 11, 2004.)

March 30 - Baptist's Day

May 30 - Indian Arrival Day

June 19 - Labor Day

August 1 - Emancipation Day

August 31 - Independence Day

December 25 - Christmas Day

December 26 - Boxing Day

Moveable holidays include Eid (Muslim - April) and Divali (Hindu - October, November).

If you need dates later than those given here, go to doyleguides.com. We give links to a holiday site that gives all the holiday dates for several years ahead. It is on the general information page. The Boaters' Directory also gives carnival dates many years ahead.

Shopping hours

Shopping hours are normally 0800-1630. Most shops close Saturday afternoons and not much happens on a Sunday. Shopping malls often do not open till 1000 but they usually stay open until at least 1900 and some open Sunday mornings. Most banks are open 0800 to 1400 Monday to Thursday, and on Fridays from 0800 to 1300 and 1500 to 1800.

Telephones

Trinidad has public card phones dotted all over the country. You can buy cards at all marinas and clubs. In Port of Spain you can get them at the main Telecommunications Services Trinidad and Tobago (TSTT) in the Maritime Life building on the south side of Independence square on Edward Street. There are two kinds of cards: the ones you put in the phones are good for local calls only. The other kind has special numbers – you have to call a number then punch in interminable codes. This one works for overseas calls. You can also make calls at most internet stations.

For USA, Canada, and other Caribbean islands with a 10-digit code, dial 1 the 10-digit number. For other overseas calls dial 01 + the country code + the number.

The area code for Trinidad is 868

Currency

The currency is the Trinidad and Tobago (TT) dollar which floats with other currencies. At last count it was close to $6TT to $1US.

Transport

Trinidad is well served by major airlines and has a large international airport. It also has its own airline, BWIA, whose schedule is sometimes more convenient than the other carriers. There is a $100 TT departure tax.

Locals who do not have cars usually travel by maxi taxis, which are the cheapest way to get around. These are minibuses that work certain routes and cover most of Trinidad. Like regular taxis they have "H" number plates. Find a bus stop on the road in the direction you want to go and stick your hand out. (This last action is absolutely necessary or they will not stop.) Ask the driver if he or she is going in your direction. They will sometimes go out of the way for a small fee. If the taxi you flag down has no other passengers on board, confirm with the driver that it is a maxi taxi and not a private taxi. If you are leaving from Port of Spain, join the maxi taxi at the starting point, as they always leave full. In 2001 maxi taxi fares from Port of Spain were $2TT up to Carenage, and $4TT beyond.

Occasionally small cars or communal taxis act as maxi taxis. They charge $1TT over the maxi rates.

Rental cars are available (check our directory at the back of the book). US, Canadian, UK ,and most European residents can drive for up to three months on their own licenses. International licenses are also accepted. Drive on the left.

Private Taxis are plentiful. Sample rates (which may well rise) are:

	$TT
All day tours	600
Chaguaramas local drops	23
Chaguaramas to town	45
Yacht Club to town	35
Chaguaramas to airport	150
Power Boats to St. James	45
Power Boats to Caroni Swamp*	120
By the hour	40

*(Round trip, per person, does not include the boat)

Local Radio:
610 or 730 AM,
91, 95, 97, 100, 105 or 106 FM.

Trinidad

Trinidad

They say that when Columbus discovered Trinidad he stumbled into a big party. Today, Trinidadians are a fun loving, hospitable people who do indeed love partying. Steel pan music was invented here, a by-product of the oil industry, and its discarded oil drums. Calypso, too, had its birth in Trinidad. These musical forms combine to help make Trinidad's carnival the world's finest celebration.

Trinidad seems to reach out and almost touch Venezuela. The two were linked together only 11,000 years ago when the last ice age lowered the sea by 300 feet. It shares a rich diversity of plants, birds, and insects with the South American continent. There are also some species that are unique to Trinidad, including the cowboy spider, a clever beast that throws its web at its prey.

South American Indians inhabited Trinidad when Columbus arrived in 1498. The early Spanish colonization in 1776 was not successful as the Spanish were doing too well plundering South America to get too interested in Trinidad. Governor Chacon then offered free land to all comers, and the colonization of Trinidad got under way with help from many French settlers. Port of Spain became the main town.

The British captured Trinidad and Tobago in 1797 and held the two islands until independence. In the early days Trinidad had a flourishing plantation economy based on sugar. The plantocracy found itself short of labor after the abolition of slavery, when former slaves quite naturally wanted no part of working on the plantations. The landowners' solution to the problem was to import some 150,000 indentured servants from India. Today Trinidad's population is a blend of

Indians, Africans, and Europeans; a mix that has generated some exceptionally good looking people. Trinidad has a population of 1.2 million, about 350,000 of whom live in Port of Spain. Trinidad and Tobago became an independent twin-island state in 1962, a democracy in the British tradition. It was led by Dr. Eric Williams for 20 years until his death.

During the last world war the United States established major naval and air bases in Trinidad. They served to protect oil shipments to England, which were prime targets for German U-boats. Trinidad has the good fortune to have large oil deposits and a pitch lake. As a result it is more industrialized than the rest of the Caribbean and produces, among other things, steel and ammonia which are exported, along with oil and natural gas. Shipbuilding and major construction are undertaken.

Trinidad is modern. It has large shopping malls, similar to those in the USA, good roads and excellent repair facilities. Many yachtspeople enjoy spending part or all of the hurricane season here. The sightseeing is good, the hospitality great, and Port of Spain is a thriving, bustling town where something is always happening. It is a great place to overhaul your yacht and enjoy yourself at the same time, and a very secure place to leave your boat in dry storage.

There are a good number of Trinidadian yachtspeople and they have two active yacht clubs, the Trinidad and Tobago Yacht Club (TTYC) and the Trinidad and Tobago Sailing Association (TTSA). They are welcoming and friendly to visiting yachtspeople and love to see everyone have a good time.

Trinidad also has several out-of-the-way anchorages. These make perfect getaways for a few days of peace and quiet. Many of these offer great hiking for the adventurous.

CHAGUARAMAS BAY

Chaguaramas was a major base for the Americans during the last world war, and over 30,000 Americans used to live here. There were major shipyards among other facilities. It is now a national park, which aims at combining park areas with eco-friendly economic activities. Yachting has taken a firm hold in this area, and tourism is encouraged.

Chaguaramas Bay is in hilly country and from the anchorage you get a pleasing view of several islands. The area supports large numbers of pelicans, corbeaus (vultures), and frigatebirds, which ride the thermals like dark kites. Laughing gulls quarrel noisily over scraps of food from fishing boats and parrots fly overhead. On the dock, kiskadees wake you in the morning with their cheerful cries and sound a lot better than an alarm clock.

Most yachting facilities are at Chaguaramas. It is close to

Opposite:
The main market
in Port of Spain

CrewsInn thrives
on an interesting
blend of tourism,
commercial ships
and yachting

Trinidad

CHAGURAMAS BAY

Monos Island, Gaspar Grande, and Scotland Bay. It is within walking distance of the TTSA, access to town is easy, and many yachts use this as their base in Trinidad.

NAVIGATION

The approach to Chaguaramas from the Boca is straightforward. Pass outside the shoal off Delgada Point. It is marked by a buoy which flashes green at night. Most yachts pass north of Gasparillo Island. There is about 35 feet of water in the passage.

If you are anchoring, keep within the marked anchoring area shown on our chart on page 73. Outside this area you will be in the way of commercial vessels, and should one hit you, you will be in the wrong. You can also anchor in Escondida Cove round the headland south of CrewsInn (See our chart, page 99). Watch out for the shoals, marked by a beacon just south of CrewsInn. The cove shoals towards the shore in the northeast corner and there are isolated rocks close to shore, so approach cautiously. This bay is well protected in all conditions except westerlies, and does not get the regular rock and roll at the change of the tide. It is, however, quite far from the dinghy docks.

Though the main Chaguaramas anchorage is generally well protected, it can rock a bit about two hours before low water when the current turns against the wind. It also gets uncomfortable when the wind comes south of east and a surge comes around the corner. This lessens as you get farther in. Very rarely, in a large squall, this surge can become dangerous, especially close to Power Boats, where the water is relatively shallow, increasing the wave height. Westerly winds, luckily very rare, are also bad news here. The holding is in soft mud and not the greatest.

YSATT have put down a number of moorings which you can use for a very reasonable fee. They are orange and marked. If you see an empty one, you can pick it up. If no one comes to collect the rent, drop by YSATT and pay. You can also go into any of the marinas.

REGULATIONS

Chaguaramas is the port of entry for visiting yachts. The officers here are friendly and clearance is simple and straightforward.

On arrival in Trinidad you must go directly to the customs dock and tie up. The customs dock is the closest T-dock to the

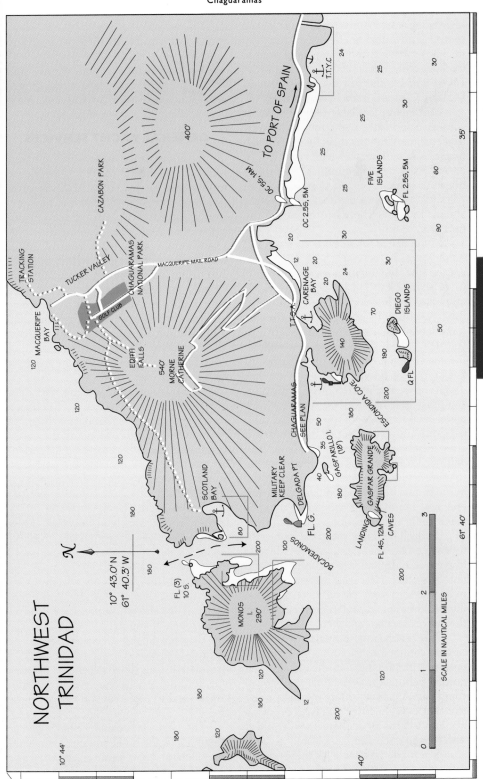

NORTHWEST TRINIDAD

10° 43.0' N
61° 40.3' W

10° 44'

TRACKING STATION

MACQUERIPE BAY

120

120

120

120

180

180

180

120

180

SCOTLAND BAY

MILITARY KEEP CLEAR

DELGADA PT

EDITH FALLS

MORNE CATHERINE
540'

GOLF CLUB

TUCKER VALLEY

CAZABON PARK

400'

CHAGUARAMAS NATIONAL PARK

MACQUERIPE MAIL ROAD

OC 5S, 14M

TO PORT OF SPAIN

T.T.Y.C.

24

25

30

30

35'

25

25

OC 2.5S, 5M

FIVE ISLANDS
FL 2.5S, 5M

20

60

90

20

12

CARENAGE BAY

TT2A

20

24

70

50

DIEGO ISLANDS

140

190

200

Q FL

180

CHAGUARAMAS SEE PLAN

ESCONDIDA COVE

50

35

40

GASPARILLO I.
(18')

FL. G.

180

200

GASPAR GRANDE

LANDING
FL 4S, 12M

CAVES

200

MONOS I.
290'

FL (3)
10 S.

BOCA DE MONOS

100

200

80

120

12

120

40'

61° 40'

0   1   2   3

SCALE IN NAUTICAL MILES

Trinidad

65

Lighthouse at CrewsInn. You are not allowed to stop at any other anchorage on your way in. Those arriving or leaving out of normal weekday office hours (0800-1200 and 1300-1600) will be charged overtime (around $45US). Customs stand by on VHF: 16.

Customs are available 24 hours a day. If you arrive during the night, they will also try to get an immigration officer for you, though he probably will not arrive till around 0700 or 0800 the next morning. The customs house is marked on our sketch chart. If you walk right down the dock, it is straight ahead. Enter at the eastern end of the building.

If you arrive when both customs and immigration are present, check with immigration first. Immigration sometimes wants to see all the crew. The immigration office is upstairs in the big block on the south side of the CrewsInn village square. From the customs door, if you look ahead and slightly to your left, that is the building. Just walk up the outside stairs. Immigration is the first office on the top floor.

If you are signing crew on or off the boat, you must visit immigration with the crew members to arrange it. You will need their passports and tickets out of the country. If crew members are arriving by plane, they will need a letter from the captain stating they are bone fide crew members. Any of the marinas can help you compose these letters, and immigration will stamp them to make their arrival easier.

If you have crew members who wish to leave on another boat, you will all have to go over and sign them off one yacht and onto the other. However, they are unlikely to let you sign someone off if you are leaving and they are staying in Trinidad, unless they have an ongoing ticket.

The regulations covering what you can and cannot do once you arrive are a little open to interpretation. In the old days you needed permission every time you moved your boat. A cabinet minute was put in effect that cancelled this and gave everyone freedom to visit all anchorages in Trinidad and Tobago once you had cleared in. This is still partially in effect. As things stand, you can freely visit all the usual anchorages

in Trinidad and the nearby islands. However, you do need to do some paperwork to visit Tobago.

For information on this, storing your yacht, bringing in spare parts, or returning to your yacht, see *Customs and Immigration* under our Planning section of the book.

GENERAL YACHT SERVICES

Chaguaramas boasts so many yacht services that we present them in categories to make things easier to find. In the first section we cover dockage, haul out, fuel, and laundry facilities. In separate sections we will cover chandleries, communications, sailmakers, riggers, and, finally, other technical yacht services, which includes everything from carpentry to refrigeration. To help you find your way around, we will always start at IMS and follow the coast to CrewsInn. This way you can easily find things on our Chaguaramas sketch chart. TTSA and the TTYC have facilities, but are not in Chaguaramas Bay, so are dealt with in their own areas.

IMS, Industrial Marine Services (VHF: 68) is a haul-out facility. They have a 70-ton marine hoist with room for about 130 boats on the hard. They have all the necessary services, including showers, toilets, washing machines, technical services, and a restaurant. They sometimes offer great long-term deals.

Peake Yacht Services (VHF: 69) is both a marina and haul-out yard. Their stern-to dock can accommodate about 17 boats. A small hotel called The Bight has 10 rooms and an indoor/outdoor restaurant and bar close to the dock. Other facilities include toilets, showers, laundry, and a brokerage. They also rent locker rooms and air conditioners if you need to stay cool. You can tie your dinghy on either side of the marine hoist dock. On the east side, tie to the small floating dinghy dock. On the west side, tie inside the yachts or pull your dinghy up on the beach, but don't put it on the grass.

The Peake office and yacht brokerage is upstairs in the hotel building. The laundry, toilets, and phones are on the other side of the same building.

CREWSINN

WILLIAM

PEAKE

POWER BOATS

SKINNER

HUMMINGBIRD

TARDIEU

CORAL COVE

TROPICAL

MARINERS HAVEN

IMS

Trinidad

VIEW OF YARDS

IMS

Peake

Power Boats

CrewsInn

Peake has a 150-ton marine hoist that can handle yachts with as much as a 31-foot beam and 15 feet of keel below the straps. One advantage of using this lift for smaller yachts is that you do not need to remove your forestay or backstay. A 60-ton hydraulic trailer transfers the boats to the storage area and can pack them in close together to accommodate about 350 on the hard. A special long-term storage area for boats being left is well fenced and has extra security. The boats can be pressure washed as soon as they are hauled. You can work on your own boat or use the complete line of services offered by the yard. Several contractors' offices are in the yard. A special area is set aside for sandblasting.

William Marine, between Peake and Power Boats, is to be an attractive new marina with two docks and a well landscaped services area ashore. Many shore offices and shops are planned, but as this facility was very new when we went to press, we do not have details.

Despite its name, Power Boats (VHF: 72) now deals more with yachts than with small power boats. It is both a haul-out facility and a marina with room for about 30 boats. They have the only general fuel dock in the area, with diesel, gasoline, and water. It opens 0800 to 1800, except Saturday and Sunday when it opens 0600-1800.

One of their marina docks starts just east of their travel lift. These are generally good and very convenient, but in the very rare event of a bad southwesterly surge, they can become rough and even dangerous. A similar dock faces the main bay to the west of the restaurant and grocery. The rest of their docks are tucked away in the creek that bounds the eastern side of the yard. These are well protected. Services include toilets, hot and cold showers, a good grocery store, restaurant, launderette (the cleaning ladies can do it for you if you are short of time), and rental apartments.

On the haul-out side, Power Boats has a 50-ton travel lift, as well as a tractor-trailer designed specifically to haul multihulls. They can store about 250 boats on the hard. Since many yachts are left here during the hurricane season, advance booking is essen-

Trinidad

tial. Don Stollmeyer, the manager, is very helpful and all kinds of repairs can be arranged through a system of subcontractors. Power Boats works with these contractors and takes responsibility that the work is properly done. They also own a gelcoat stripper that makes easy and clean work of dealing with osmosis problems and is far preferable to sandblasting or grinding. Power Boats can erect plastic covers to keep your boat dry. Those anchored out are welcome to leave their dinghies on the dinghy dock east of the travel lift. They request that you register with the office when you come ashore, and they will give you a pass to gain access through the main gate. There is a nominal charge for this. Do not put dinghies on the dock in front of the restaurant and grocery. Power Boats is the home of many shops and subcontractors' workshops. A big plus to being in Power Boats is their Power Boats Convenience Card that enables you to buy from their restaurant, Boater's Shop and Grocery store and have everything put on your bill.

Hummingbird Marine (VHF: 68) is just across the creek. Harold LaBorde, a famous Trinidadian sailor who has circumnavigated several times on boats he has built, is the owner/operator of this dock facility. There is alongside space for about 10 boats and 14 stern or bow-to spaces. Being in a narrow creek affords good protection, but in a really bad southerly (this happens maybe twice a year), things can get bad and signs warn you of this. Facilities for tenants include water, electricity, token operated laundry facilities, fax, phone, ice, a work shed, and a BBQ stand. Additionally, Harold is the port officer for the Ocean Cruising Club. Voyagers, his bar, is open all day.

Tardieu Marine (VHF: 68) borders Hummingbird to the east. Run by Heather and Derrick, their two docks have a capacity for 16 boats. Services include water, electricity, ice, toilets, and showers. Telephone lines are available at the dock, as is cable TV. Their office is upstairs in the small building at the head of the docks.

Sherrie's Laundry is on the ground floor at Tardieu. You can do it yourself or have it done and she will iron. Sherrie also has a couple of sewing machines in the shop where they mend and make garments. You can buy their clothes or have them custom made for you with your own material or with theirs. Open Monday through Saturday.

Coral Cove Marina (VHF: 68) is both a marina and haul-out yard. Three docks with fingers for alongside berthing will accommodate about 40 boats up to 90 feet long, with special areas for multihulls. All docks have electricity, water, and cable TV. Other facilities include phones, token operated laundromat, hot and cold showers, and a swimming pool. There are 14 hotel rooms with air conditioning and cooking facilities, if you don't want to stay on your boat while work is being done.

Coral Cove has a hard for about 70 boats with a 60-ton marine hoist. You can arrange to have the marina do your work, or do it yourself.

John Lanse is the director of Tropical Marine, a small marina that can take about 20 boats. It has a long dock at the western end with the dinghy dock at its head. All other berthing is stern-to along the sea wall. Water and electricity are available. Master's Laundry will do your wash inexpensively, and they pick up and deliver. Several technical yacht services are based here, as well as a snack bar.

Across the bay to the southeast, CrewsInn Hotel and Yachting Centre, (VHF: 77) is the largest docking facility to date. They offer by far the fanciest marina with 68 to 70 slips with water, telephone, cable TV, and metered electricity. A separate dock for superyachts is just south of the marine hoist dock. They regard all slips as hotel rooms, providing laundry, dry cleaning, food service, and use of the pool and other facilities. Their shower and laundromat are the best and most luxurious, with hot showers included. A daily newspaper gets dropped on your boat before breakfast. They have a beautiful air-conditioned reading room and book swap. As befits this standard, exterior work on boats involving loud power tools or excessive dust is not allowed. CrewsInn arranges fuel bunkering for large yachts alongside the commercial dock.

CrewsInn boasts the largest marine hoist in the region at 200 tons. When work is to be done, they use a giant converted bauxite shed with 2.7 acres under cover and 80 feet of vertical clearance. This enables them to work even in the rainy season and, in most cases, without removing the rig. Their Southern Caribbean Boatworks do all the work on the hard. You do not pay for lay-days while they work on your yacht, and the hotel will accommodate you while your job is being done.

COMMUNICATIONS

You don't have to be worried about being out of touch. Trinidad has excellent e-mail and communications wherever you are. Rates vary and you will often have to juggle the benefits of distance and deals to find the place that feels right for you.

Island Surf Café is in the Mariners Haven compound and convenient for those in IMS. As you walk into Mariners Haven, you come to a guarded gate, and just beyond this is a car park to your right with the ferry dock for Bay View in Gaspar Grande. If you walk in here you will come to Island Surf Café. Their specialty is unlimited e-mail access for a reasonable monthly fee. They

also do photocopies, laminating, and faxing.

The large Royal Bank on the left side of the road as you walk down to Peake has two e-mail stations that open during banking hours. Their impressive air conditioning system will keep you cool as you surf.

Nichole's Ocean Internet Café has branches in Peake, Power Boats, and Tardieu Marine. The Power Boats branch is upstairs over David Morand's (Nichole's husband) woodworking shop down by the dinghy dock. This branch opens 0800 to 2000 weekdays and 0830-1630 on weekends. The other branches open 0800-1630 Monday to Friday and 0830-1230 Saturday.

In any of their branches you can bring your own computer or use theirs. You can make overseas calls, have your mail sent here, make photocopies, or swap books, and they offer computer services and scanning. They also sell plenty of coffee to keep you going.

Cyber Sea is in Coral Cove Marina, upstairs on the same floor as the office. They offer internet access and secretarial services, as well as a book exchange and a daily courier service to Port of Spain. They also have a small stationary store and sell magazines.

The Mariner's Office at CrewsInn has internet access, office services, and full communications, including phone calls. (See also Carenage.)

CHANDLERIES

Chandleries in Trinidad are excellent. If you cannot find what you want on the shelf, it can be brought in, usually within a few days and in this case you can often save paying duty on the item. The three general chandleries are Peake, Budget Marine, and the Boaters Shop. However, there are many more specialized yacht shops that may stock the special item you are looking for. We mention all these and what they sell.

IMS

GIMS is a small chandlery stocking tools, zincs, resins, and most things you will need for a haul out. You can also find turnbuckles and rigging parts at Trinidad Rigging.

Mariner's Haven,

Echo Marine, owned by Michael and Peter, is an outlet for specific products, some at wholesale prices. These include Caribe Inflatables (they always have many in stock), Jotun and other antifoulings, aluminum and stainless stock in sheets, tubes, angles, and other shapes, along with Delrin tubing. They sell refrigeration systems and components, including space age insulation, and if you don't have enough power to run them they stock Phasor/Kubota Generators.

Echo carries several brands of watermaker and they also make their own excellent high output systems that are about half the price of other makes. Echo also stocks the best, Lloyds approved, European, stainless chain at an excellent price, along with stainless anchors and swivels.

On the east side of Mariner's Haven, Brian de Montbrun's Marc One specializes in polyester and epoxy supplies, along with a variety of cores. Those doing an osmosis job might want to discuss their Duratec Vinylester system of protection. Marc One

Trinidad

Chaguaramas: plan of boatyards and marine services

TROPICAL MARINE
Marina
Master laundry
snack bar

SERVICES
Convenient Car
Electropics
EchoMarine (branch)
Irena Trans Travel
Kiss Energy Systems
Shiloh
Yacht Maintenance and Repair

CREWSINN
200-ton Travel Lift
Marina
Laundromat
Lighthouse Restaurant
Mariner's Internet Office
Customs
Immigration (village upstairs)

UNDER COVER BDG.
Dockyard Electrics
Goodwood Marine
Nau-T-Kol
Soca Sails

THE VILLAGE SQUARE
YSATT
Apadoca's
Boater's Enterprise
Econo-car
Hi Lo Supermarket
Republic Bank
S.O.S unisex hairstyling
Travelsure
The Inn Place
Trump Tours
Video rental

TARDIEU MARINE
Marina
Ocean Internet Cafe
Sherrie's Laundry
Coffee and Roti Shop

SERVICES
Alpha Upholstery & Canvas
Chaguaramas Metal Works
Coastal Machine Shop
Corsa Marine
Engines Engines
Gittens Engine Services
Lennox Stewart (carpentry)
Marine Doctors Sign Lab
Marine Warehouse
Rick's Pizza
Stuart Electronics
Webster's Canvas Works

WILLIAM MARINE
Marina

SKINNERS YARD
Budget Marine
Budget Marine Rigging
Mechanics Coop
Chris (inboards)
Dessie (inboards)
Jeff (outboards)
Errol (glasswork)
Formula 3

CORAL COVE
60 ton travelift
Marina
Laundromat
Joe's Pizza
Hotel

SERVICES:
Coatings Specialist
C.E. Tang Yuk
Lazzari & Sampson Travel Service
L.P. Marine and Industrial Supplies
Nadpat Corrosion Control
Navtech Electronics Limited
S.G.I. Distributors
Trinidad Detroit Diesel
William H. Scott

CALYPSO MARINE
Pirogue building
& rental

HUMMINGBIRD MARINE
Marina
Voyager's Bar

IMS
70-ton travelift
Laundromat
Restuarant

GIMS Chandlery
Dynamite Marine
Ocean Sails
Trinidad Rigging
Unity Metal Shop

POWER BOATS
50-ton travel lift, hotel
Fuel Dock
Marina
Sails Restaurant
Roti Hut
Laundromat
Supermarket
Ocean Internet Cafe (services C)
European Yacht Connection

SERVICE A
Awon's Marine Services
Anthone Penn
Barrow Sail Loft
Boaters shop
Brian Huggins
Caribbean Marine
Fotress Woodworking
Mark's Car Rentals
Upholstery Shop

SERVICE B
Mark De Gannes
Ian Keiser
Lawrence Placid

SERVICES B2
Clinton Brewster
Ozia Kamba Griffith

SERVICES C
Ship's Carpenter
Yacht Maintenance

SERVICES D
Dion
Rawle Walker

MARINERS HAVEN
Island Surf Cafe
Echo Marine
Eswil
Marc One
Vickers Distributers

PEAKE'S
150-ton travelift
Marina
Bight Restaurant, Hotel
Ocean Internet Cafe (upstairs B)

BUILDING B DOWNSTAIRS
Ali's Machine Shop
Billy's Rigging
Fluid Hose & Coupling
John Francois Woodworking
Propeller & Marine
Serge's Electrical Workshop
UPSTAIRS
Calypso Marine Canvas

CHANDLERY BDG
Antoine Shipwright Services
KNJ Marine Services
Peake Chandlery
West End Retailers
& Ancill's Marine Painting

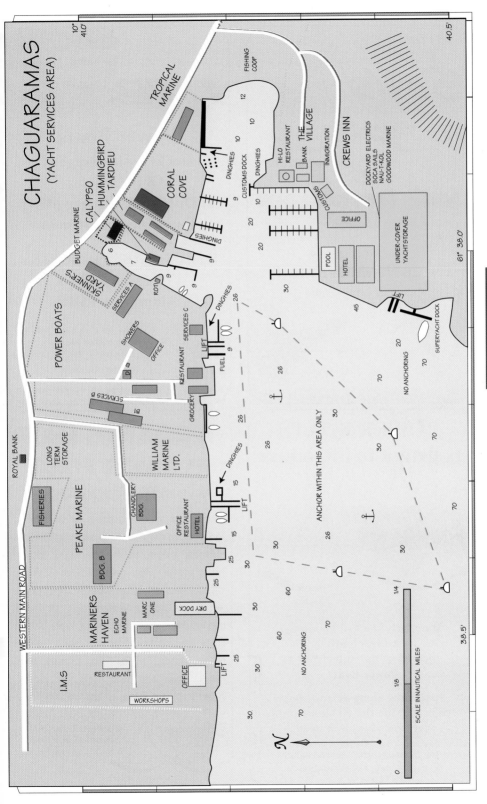

CHAGUARAMAS
(YACHT SERVICES AREA)

Trinidad

73

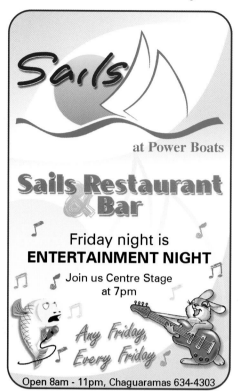

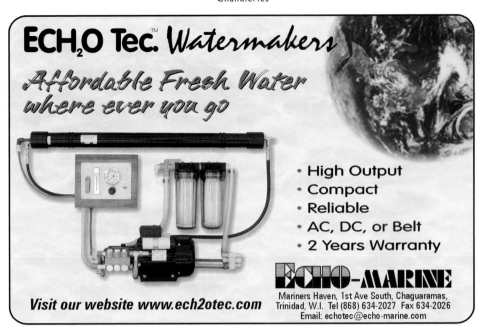
also carries all kinds of acrylic sheet, including Lexan, and they can replace the crazed old glass of your hatches. Brian also sells some yacht hardware – things like cleats and hinges, as well as inverters and power tools.

Eswil is on the west side of the dry dock. They stock hydraulic hoses and fittings, lubricants and industrial pumps, and motors. On your way out of the compound is Vickers Distributors, which carries a curious selection, including some tools, galvanized plumbing and shackles, oils and several household pots, pans, and containers.

Peake

Just north of Peake yacht docks, is their chandlery, one of the largest in Trinidad. They have a truly magnificent selection of hardware, including a vast range of stainless screws, nuts, and bolts. You will find just about everything you may need for your boat, from water pumps to paint. They offer the Rod Gibbon line of teak accessories, which are very reasonably priced. If they don't have your item in stock, they can order it for you. Floor manager, Willie Pinheiro, is a keen sailor and knowledgeable about boat systems.

Also at Peake, Fluid Hose & Coupling offer an extensive inventory of hydraulic, fuel, water, and exhaust hoses for the marine

and industrial market. They have Airquip, Parker, Gates, and Alpha Goma fittings, as well as others, and can custom make to your specifications. Serge's Electrical Workshop (VHF: 69) over in the western workshop can supply deep cycle batteries.

Power Boats

Power Boats owns Boaters Shop (VHF: 72) which is in their contractors building. It is a small chandlery, but they have most of the things you need during a haul out, as well as some general yacht hardware, and it is well used by those hauled out in Power Boats. They are the agents for AB dinghies and have a good range in stock (though they will not be on display).

Caribbean Marine (VHF: 72) is a couple of doors down, and in this electrical shop you can find batteries, wire, and electrical fittings.

Skinner's Yard

In Skinner's Yard, facing the main road, is Budget Marine, the largest Caribbean chandlery, with stores in St. Maarten, Antigua, the Virgin Islands, Grenada and Trinidad. Two floors are stocked with a huge selection of both general and technical items, many of which are featured in their large

Trinidad

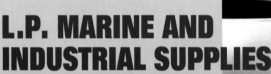

mail-order catalog. If you cannot find what you need, you can be sure that almost anything can be shipped in, often within a few days, whether it is a catalog item or not. The staff is exceptionally friendly, helpful, and knowledgeable.

Tardieu Marine

Look for Marine Warehouse, run by Kurt Kasson. He has chain, solar panels, batteries, bottom paint, resins, and epoxies in stock and specializes in buying anything you need out of U.S. catalogs and bringing it in fast, usually at 10 to 20 percent lower than catalog prices. He can have it sent by Fedex at half their normal rates.

In the same compound, Corsa sells some marine hardware, fishing, and snorkeling gear.

Coral Cove Marina

C.E. Tang Yuk carries electrical and plumbing fittings and is the agent for Sea Recovery water makers and Northern Lights generators. They will install and service

these and they keep a good stock of spare parts. They also have ropes, pumps, and tools.

Next door, the Marine Shop owned by Bhalvan Harry, is a chandlery with hardware both for small power boats and larger yachts. They also sell folding chairs and other accessories. Seachoice and Anchor are among the product lines they stock.

L.P. Marine and Industrial Supplies is both a technical chandlery and the agent for Volvo Penta, Johnson pumps, and GM generators, offering service and a good supply of parts. They carry cutlass bearings, Morse cables, Petit paints, Perkins, and Borg Warner parts, Racor filters, VDO instruments, GPSs, and much more. They also have a larger store in Carenage that will supply additional items.

Coral Cove also has a William H. Scott store, the Chaguaramas branch of the giant hardware store in Port of Spain. Here you will find power tools from Porter Cable, Makita, Dremel, and Bosch. You can rent tools by the day. They have general hardware, plywood and lumber,

Trinidad

wooden boat repair materials, and household paints and they deliver. If you need anything you don't see, ask, they may well have it in the bigger town store.

Also at Coral Cove, S.G.I. Distributors is an interesting combination of enterprises. On the one hand they sell Craftsman tools, AC Delco, and Die Hard batteries. On the other, they are the TT Post office for the area as well as agents for Fedex and Western Union money transfer. You can also have your film processed here or get some stationary and floppy disks. Talk to Sheldon Blanc.

Tropical Marine

Shiloh is a supplier of fiberglass cloths, resins, and epoxy products. Kiss Energy Systems (formally Dougbuggers) produces a neat little windmill that looks like the Southwest Marine ones, but is a bit quieter. While here, go next door and check out which electronics Electropics

has in stock, or talk about ordering.

CrewsInn

Goodwood Marine usually has some electronics in stock and much more you can order, plus they keep an excellent stock of Profurl parts. In the same block, Dockyard Electrics stocks batteries and all kinds of electrical wires and fittings.

SAILMAKERS, CANVAS AND CUSHIONS

IMS

Ocean Sails has a 2000-square-foot loft on the south west side of the yard, run by Michael Pegart who has 17 years of sailmaking experience backed by extensive cruising. He can repair and build any size sail, put a UV cover on your roller furling jib, or make you an awning or complete boat cover. He carries a supply of sail hardware.

Heliconia,
Chaguaramas
National park

Peake

Upstairs in the western workshop building is Calypso Marine Canvas (VHF: 68), owned and operated by Riad Shakeer. Whether you need cushions, biminis, awnings, or dodgers, Riad will make sure you get a good job. If your bunk cushions have become a little squishy, think about getting new ones here. They have fine high-density foam, and for extra comfort will laminate a thinner layer of soft foam on the top of it. They stock closed cell foam for cockpit cushions, a wide selection of fabrics, including Sunbrela, Strataglass scratch proof vinyl window, and Nautilex marine vinyl. They are agents for Sunair retractable awnings – motorized as well as manual. They do all their own pipe bending for biminis and dodgers, in both aluminum and stainless, and can also cover your steering wheel in imported leather.

Power Boats

The Barrow Sail Loft (VHF: 68), upstairs in the contractors building at Power Boats, is operated by Kent Barrow. They build new sails for boats up to about 50 feet and staysails or mizzens for larger yachts. If pushed, they can build a whole sail in just three days. They have a computer controlled laser cutter and offer excellent sails for somewhat less than you will pay anywhere else. They are a North Sails agent and anything they don't build themselves can be ordered through North. Barrow Sails also repairs sails and makes biminis and dodgers, including the stainless tubing frames and hardware to go with them.

Next door you will find David Mahabir at the Upholstery Shop (VHF: 72). He can make bunk cushions out of a variety of foam densities and fabrics. His work is good and prices reasonable, whether it is cockpit cushions out of closed cell foam, sail covers, hatch covers, or a custom cover for your inflatable to protect it from UV degradation.

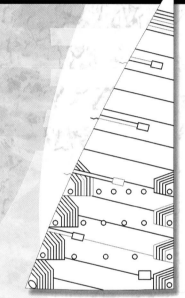

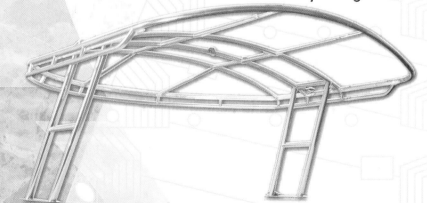
Trinidad

At CrewsInn the giant 2.7-acre yacht dry storage area, which used to be a bauxite shed overshadows the new hotel

Tardieu

Webster's Canvas Works makes biminis, dodgers, awnings, and sails covers, as well as interior and exterior cushions. They can also supply foam and fabrics. If you want to compare prices, go right next door to Alpha Upholstery & Canvas, run by Carlos Fensom, who has been doing this work for about six years. He can cover cushions and make dodger and bimini tops in a selection of different materials. He often makes covers for dinghies, winches, and BBQs.

CrewsInn

Soca Sails (VHF: 68) is run by Mark Loe who has extensive racing and cruising experience, and has been involved with sailing since he was a youngster. With a loft of over 5000 square feet and seven pits, they can handle all kinds of repair jobs in all materials. They are the agents for Doyle Sails as well as Andersen winches, Frederiksen hardware, and Stamoid fabrics, a new lightweight awning material that lasts longer. Talk to them about building you some good sun protection, be it awnings or fold down biminis. They also represent Furlboom, a new boom furling/reefing system.

RIGGING SHOPS

The rigging shops in Trinidad are also excellent. This is a good place to buy a new rig or overhaul your old one. You will get good service from all the shops below.

IMS

Trinidad Rigging is owned by Jonas Romell, who has a full rigging service and keeps a broad range of rigging parts in stock, including swages and Norseman terminals, turnbuckles, spinnaker poles, booms ready to cut to length, winch pads, tracks, and kicking strap systems. He can do swages up to 16mm and can order you a new rig if you need one. He works a lot with Selden and Norseman. Jonas is happy to come to work on boats, and is often out doing so, so the best time to catch him in the workshop is from 0900-1000.

Peake

Peake has a big service building well to the west of the chandlery. On the east side of this building, next to the big paint shed (more like a construction shed these days), you will find Billy's Rigging (VHF: 69). Billy and his team can tackle any kind of rigging work. Owner Bill Wray has over 40 years experience in this field as well as being a Lloyds qualified surveyor. He is an agent for Harken and Stalok, and has a swaging machine for lifelines and a cold header machine for Navtec rod rigging. They can repair winches, masts, booms, roller furling gear, or have terminals X-rayed and evaluated as well as putting together a whole new rig. They often do big yacht rig overhauls and repaints. They can also be contracted to do jobs anywhere else in the area.

Skinner's Yard

Budget Marine, as well as being a chan-

dlery also has a good rigging shop; Budget Marine Rigging, which is run by Niels Lund, a civil engineer from South Africa with 15 years rigging experience. They stock a complete selection of rigging wires and terminals and can do swaging of wire from 4 to 16 mm. They splice all kinds of wire or rope or combinations and they do rig surveys. They keep an excellent stock of fittings and wire on hand and can bring anything they do not have in at short notice. They can handle anything from a simple repair to a whole new rig.

TECHNICAL YACHT SERVICES

In this section we describe many of the marine services available and where you will find them. Keep in mind that all the contractors we mention are not restricted to the yard where their workshop is and will work in any of the yards or on your boat. We list them by their location.

IMS

IMS has a paint and glass repair shop to handle most of the normal haul-out jobs in their yard. IMS also makes excellent paints, including epoxies and antifoulings, as well as a new poly siloxane, which renders a very tough topside finish and has the advantage of easy application with brush, roller, or spray. Their Ameron antifouling comes in a copper base for glass and steel boats or a tin base for aluminum hulls and many find it effective in this environment. Their representatives in the yard can give you the best advise on preparation and application as well as help you do it.

On the southwest side of the yard, Dynamite Marine is seriously good at project management. Anyone thinking of doing a large refit in Trinidad should consider using them. For an agreed monthly fee their staff will choose and organize contractors, making sure jobs get done right and they will look after your project as if it were their own. On several occasions they have rescued people who have started on projects and met with disaster. They know all the contractors and which ones are the best. On big jobs they will more than save you their fee. If you just want someone to keep an eye on your boat, they will also do this.

Dynamite has a department that constructs temporary plastic covers for yachts in dry storage. This is an inexpensive way to store your boat under cover and can save time when you have paint jobs and repairs on deck. They were the first to do this, and still do the bulk of this work, visiting all the haul-out facilities. Recently they have added a small machine and metal working shop with a TIG welder. Here, Dexter can fabricate and repair in aluminum or stainless.

Dynamite also has Bay Island Yachts, the Caribbean brokers, where Linda will help you sell your boat or find a new one.

In the same building, Roger Brown has Unity Metal Shop under the sailmaker. He has a TIG welder, can do neat work, and is reasonably priced. His unit is mobile so he can work on your boat.

Peake

Peake has their own team of glass workers and painters to handle most jobs in their yard. They build fiberglass boats so are very experienced at fiberglass work and can handle any size repair. Many other contractors are also based here.

In the Chandlery building, Antoine Shipwright Services is run by Arthur Antoine, who has many years experience in traditional boat building. He can do interior and exterior repair, from planking and caulking to new teak decks. He also does cabinetry and often makes louvered doors. He can supply teak, mahogany, cedar, cypre, and applematte. These last two are fine looking local woods, similar to oak and ash, cut or milled to suit.

Arthur shares this workshop with Ancil's Marine Painting & Services. Ancil (known as "South") is proficient in Awlgrip application, having taken a course from them. He and his team do the complete job, from surface preparation to final coat in Awlgrip, Imron, clear polyurethanes, or varnishes.

Upstairs through a passageway next door are the offices of KNJ Marine Services Ltd. Fanny Wray is a project manager and she speaks Spanish as well as English. She has worked with yachts for many years and will organize any kind of work for you and make sure it is well done while you leave your boat in storage. She works on small jobs as well as large and will find people for repairs, maintenance and general boat care, varnishing, hull polishing, osmosis treatment, mechanical repairs, electric and electronic work, and upholstery cleaning and fumigation.

Peake has a big service building well to the west of the chandlery. Several shops are on the ground floor of this building. On the west end is Propeller & Marine Service, run by Christopher MacLean who does propeller reconditioning and re-pitching, precision shaft straightening, and MIG and TIG welding. If your boat vibrates excessively while under power, your solution may be right here.

Next door is Ali's Machine Shop (VHF: 68). Intiaz Ali can manufacture or repair almost anything out of stainless steel, bronze, brass, and even titanium. He'll work on stainless steel shafts with diameters of more than 6 inches, stretching to 40 feet long, or custom made toggles to fit your particular need. He stocks a wide selection of metric bolts and nuts in stainless steel.

Serge's Electrical Workshop (VHF: 69) is in the same building. He does boat wiring and motor and generator rewinding, as well as supplying and installing deep cycle batteries.

Next is a woodworking shop where John Francois does repair and remodeling of interiors, will lay new teak decks, make furniture with beautiful inlays, and do fiberglass repair. He started learning from his father, a traditional shipwright who designed and built a few boats here in Trinidad, both sail and power, including Harold La Borde's circumnavigating vessel, *Hummingbird*.

Power Boats

Power Boats doesn't do any boat-work themselves, so they probably have more contractors around than the other yards. A Power Boats contractor has to be good and keep the majority of his customers satisfied. On in-house jobs, Power Boats, like the other yards, takes a commission from the contractors. They also stand by the quality of the work of their contractors and if you have a problem with one of them, they will sort it out. In some cases they will even pay to have a problem fixed. Their approach works: they have one of the highest customer

Trinidad

Preparing to leave CrewsInn

satisfaction ratings in the industry.

The contractors are in several locations throughout the yard. Some have big offices where it is easy to meet with them, others just have a room and it is easier to contact them through the Power Boats office; still others work out of their homes and just come to the yard by day.

The contractors building is the long building that lies alongside the fence adjoining Skinner's yard building on the east side of the compound. Starting at the western end downstairs: Fortress Woodworking does all types of joinery work and has laid many a teak deck. Owner Neville Boos, who has been in the business for years, has built up a special supply of excellent woods including deck-grade teak, mahogany, purple heart, and cedar, as well as veneers and plywoods. They are good people to contact if you have a large complicated job, and they will happily cut up pieces of wood to your specification for your own project. Talk to Neville Boos who has his office upstairs where you can see some samples of their work. They may also have a few pieces of furniture for sale.

Beyond Fortress is a cubbyhole with several rooms off it. Several contractors use this as their boatyard base. Awon's Marine Services is headed by Gerald Awon who has many years experience in various types of finishes. Gerald is the top man for really high quality finishes where cost is not the major factor. He is much in demand for big yachts undergoing refits. He has a lot of experience with gelcoat, is excellent at matching colors, and has often re-gel-coated whole yachts, including nonskid decks. He also does excellent topside and interior varnish or paint spraying, using a high-volume/low-pressure method of spray application that greatly reduces the waste of costly paint.

Anthony Penn, a Rasta, is one of the best brush varnishers. You often see him in this area putting great finish on interior pieces he has brought out from the boat. Brian Huggins also keeps a room here. He does osmosis work, fiberglass repairs, and spray painting.

Next door, Caribbean Marine (VHF: 72) is run by David Laughlin and Brian

Sellier. Their specialty is DC power and diesel injectors. They can test, diagnose, charge and sell batteries, dispose of your old ones, and check out your charging systems. They repair alternators and chargers as well as DC motors and wind generators. Solar panels are also available, as well as monitoring instruments. They will tackle any kind of electrical job on a yacht and you can also walk in for good advice, and buy many electrical fittings. If you need your injectors tested, they can do it on the spot.

Ship's Carpenter is in a pretty building on the waterfront. It is run by David Morand, a Canadian with 23 years experience in marine woodwork. He has supervised several complete refits, including a 1953 Rhodes 45 that he did in Trinidad. David has extensive sailing experience, having sailed from his native country. Before arriving in Trinidad he worked at CMO in Venezuela for a couple of years. He always has teak on hand (and is willing to sell you some for your own job), as well as marine ply and decorative laminates. He does good interior

or exterior work and can tackle any carpentry or cabinetry job.

At the back of this building is Alan Dowden of Yacht Maintenance Services. Alan is an invaluable resource. He does excellent spray painting and antifouling jobs, as well as major and minor fiberglass repairs and osmosis treatment. Alan and his team will look after your boat if you are going away, keeping it aired out and charged up. He is very reliable, pleasant to work with, and his prices are reasonable. He works in both the Chaguaramas and Carenage areas.

A few contractors have rooms in another building well to the west of the yard. They are usually out on jobs so it is best to contact them through the office. Clinton Brewster has worked for some years around the yard as a day worker and has now become a contractor. He is good at hand application of paints and varnishes, he does reliable underwater prep and antifouling jobs, and can take all the antifouling off the bottom of your boat. He polishes hulls and stainless steel and can repaint your engine. You will find him per-

Trinidad

sonable and easy to get along with, and for the most part he does all the work himself, only hiring someone else when necessary. This helps keep the cost down and also brings a personal touch to the work.

Ozia Kamba Griffith is also in this building. He, too, does bottom preparation and painting, cleaning and polishing of topsides and decks. He also does West epoxy system bottom repair.

Also on the west side of Power Boats is another contractors building. In it you will find Mark de Gannes who works in aluminum and stainless steel. He fabricates and repairs tanks, pulpits, bimini and dodger frames, davits and tuna towers, and shafts, using TIG or Argon welding. Mark does excellent work, and will often fit in a small job quite quickly, but he does get booked up for big jobs, so contact him as early as possible.

In the same building, towards the waterfront, is Ian Keiser, a qualified OMC mechanic who can repair your outboard motor whatever the make or problem. Next door Lawrence Placid has a workshop and is a good general mechanic.

A couple of offices are between this contractors building and the main office. The first belongs to Rawle Walker who is on the bottom of a two story building. Rawle is a fiberglass and spray painting man and he also makes hard tops out of glass.

In a container close by is Dion. Dion rents all kinds of tools which is very handy when you have a big job. He also does sandblasting and underwater surveys and jobs.

Power Boats visiting technicians

Many good people work from their homes and visit the yards by day to work. All the following can be contacted through Power Boats for whom they are official contractors. One is Steve Ramsahai (Son), an excellent glass man. I should know as he built my new boat. He is very careful, never rushes, and does it right. He works with both regular solid glass and all the new cores.

Ricky Denoon is a cheerful and friendly character who you will enjoy working with. He is good at bottom preparation and painting, general cleaning, and polishing. He has a mechanical bent and will remove your old troublesome through-hulls. He can also do a good job repainting your engine.

Hugo de Plessis and Pat Lawlor are both surveyors. Hugo is a glass expert from the early days and has written several books on the subject. Pat is an Irishman who does Lloyds surveying for Huggins.

Sean Dupres and Rupert Grimshaw are both riggers who will be happy to go up your mast and fix problems or fix your rig or lifelines.

Gerald Mendes and John King both do marine electrics and electronics. Gerald also works on house items like TVs, radios microwaves, and computers.

Archie Fitzgerald (Blue Flame), will get your cookers burning correctly again so you are not blackening your kettle. Richard Brooks is a diesel mechanic and fabricates in mild steel.

Junior Nicholas Thomas is a refrigeration man and comes in for repairs and instal-

lation work and he also handles air conditioning.

EYC is a new business just opened in Power Boats. It is owned by Jorn Grote a very pleasant and knowledgeable man who originally came from Germany. Jorn is an active sailor and racing enthusiast and EYC is Company that will do anything from keeping your yacht aired and the engine running to organizing a complete refit while you are away.

Skinner Yard

Two workshops can be found in the big building behind Budget Marine. Stephen De Gannes and his family operate Formula III (VHF: 68). They have been building power boats ranging from 12 to 40 feet for many years, and they built Legacy and C-Mos, a couple of very successful 43-foot sailing boats that have raced extensively in the area. They do all kinds of fiberglass construction and repair, including the larger and more difficult jobs. They can treat osmosis and do top grade Awlgrip painting.

In the same building is a mechanical shop shared by several contractors: Chris De Gannes, Dessie McIntosh, Jeff Johnathon and Errol. Errol is a good fiberglass and general man who will do anything from a bottom job to polishing topsides. All the rest are mechanics. Chris and Dessie work on inboards, Jeff fixes the outboards. Between them, they can install, recondition or repair your motor or transmission, be it an outdrive or saildrive. If you are looking for a secondhand, reconditioned power source, check them out.

*The Creek
between
Power
Boats and
Tardieu*

Trinidad

Calypso Marine

A narrow creek borders Power Boats to the east. Calypso Marine Services is at the head of this creek. They have been building fiberglass boats for over 25 years and specialize in pirogues from 23 feet to 34 feet and a 32-foot deep-vee power boat. If you want to try some deep-sea fishing on your own, you can rent a pirogue from them, complete with a bimini, for a very reasonable rate.

Tardieu Marine

Engines Engines is run by Douglas Rogers who can repair and rebuild diesels and transmissions. He can have your injectors and pumps serviced and calibrated and he can sell you a rebuilt engine.

Stuart Electronics is a firm of electrical and electronics engineers. They can deal with all these systems.

Chaguaramas Metal Works is operated by Lincoln Choy Yuen. They build fixed hardtops out of aluminum or stainless as well as bimini and dodger frames out of stainless tubing. They make fuel tanks of both materials and they repair and fabricate in all types of metals.

Kent Barrow is in the corner building and he came into metal working out of the need to have pipe frames and hardware for their sailmaking business. He builds all types of bimini and dodger frames and hard tops. He has excellent machinery for cutting and fitting pipes.

Rick's Dive World rents dive equipment and can do hull and propeller cleaning.

Lennox Stewart, master ship's carpenter and cabinet maker, is also in Tardieu and he can build or repair any kind of woodwork, including interior cabinetry. He does not mind cutting out custom wood pieces for those with their own pet project.

Larry Rogers operates Marine Doctors for all types of cosmetic restoration in metal, wood or fiberglass. He will also refurbish electrical and mechanical systems, as well as assist in locating materials and services.

Richard De Montbrun runs Sign Lab, having learned his trade in Canada. He can do boat lettering in computer-cut vinyl adhesive, airbrush or hand painted. If you want racing stripes or exotic and artistic graphics, you will have come to the right place.

Adian Gittens is a good, reliable mechanic. His Gittens Engine Services offers diesel, transmission, generator, and outboard repair and service. He works on most brands, including Westerbeke, Perkins, Yanmar, John Deere, and Ford Lehman engines, and Hurth gearboxes.

Sharida Ali is the managing director of Corsa Marine, which is the Mercury and

Mariner outboard agent for service and repair. They keep a good inventory of parts and sell marine hardware, fishing, and snorkeling gear.

Caribbean Propellers is using a high tech Prop Scan to detect micro-inaccuracies in pitch, camber and section shape that are invisible to the naked eye. Ask P.J. Williams about his free analysis and report.

Next door is Coastal Machine Shop. David Francis learned from his father who operates an industrial machine shop in the oil sector. The shop has machines that can turn, thread, cut, and machine any type of material of which he has a ready supply. He also repairs hydraulics and transmissions.

Coral Cove

Closest to the docks is Nadpat Corrosion Control, managed by Geoffrey Farrell. They have a big sandblaster and power washer and can clean any hull, as well as paint it afterwards.

Navtech Electronics Limited (VHF: 68) sells, installs and repairs Icom, Furuno, and Standard electronics as well as Nera satellite phone systems.

Coatings Specialist, next door, supply Sigma coatings with a full line for all applications, epoxies, polyurethanes, enamels, primers, nonskid, and antifouling paints.

Tropical Marine

Rainer Dobring's Electropics is a good electrical and electronic workshop. They sell, install, and repair most electronics and are the people to see for the Simrad line, including Robertson autopilots. In the field of communications, they are agents for Iridium, Stratos, and Immersat. Rainer also does customized electrical installation to European standards using the master volt line. You can wander in and look at the latest GPS systems, fish finders, and radios.

Yacht Maintenance and Repair specialize in corrosion problems, sandblasting, regalvanizing, and general maintenance.

Coastal Diving is a commercial dive group that does underwater surveys, welding, photography, and more. The main divers are Robert Stauble, Rolph Hive, and Roger Govia.

CrewsInn

CrewInn has a complete service set-up under the name Southern Caribbean Yacht Works. They undertake all work and are geared to luxury and charter yachts.

Under the big roof you will find Dockyard Electrics Ltd. (VHF: 68). They repair, maintain, and install batteries, alternators, chargers, inverters, and generators, and are also agents for Balmar alternators, Exide, Surrette, Prevailer and Rolls batteries, as well as Heart and Vanner inverters and chargers. They sell satellite telephone systems as well as doing computer repair and sales and service of navigation systems. They have a complete stock of quality marine wires and cables and can fabricate custom electrical panels. Call them and they can come to you if you can't go to them. Richard and Susan Harmer Brown are the ones in charge.

Nau-T-Kol is run by Jeff Stone. Jeff cruised here from California where he ran the same business for 20 years which has given him a good understanding of the marine field.

He and his team do marine refrigeration and air conditioning, repair, installation, and service, as well as providing new and used systems. They have recently developed a state of the art, energy efficient 12/24 volt marine refrigeration system that is quite compact. Also, in keeping with today's standards, they have a couple of machines that will recover and recycle old refrigerants so as not to release them to the air. They represent Cruisair, Adler/Barbour and Grunert.

Goodwood Marine sells, installs, and repairs Raytheon radars, Autohelm pilots, Brookes & Gatehouse instruments, Edson steering systems, C-Map navigational aids, Garmin GPSs, Profurl jib furling systems, Lewmar winches, StaLok terminals, and Auto-Prop stainless steel feathering propellers. Their stock of Profurl parts is excellent. Much of the electronics is by special order and what they don't have in stock, they can ship in just a few days, talk to David Foster.

OUTSIDE CHAGUARAMAS

Several businesses far from the yachting area are well worth knowing about. (See also *Carenage* and *Point-a-Pierre*.)

Trincity Chrome Ltd. is best known for their chrome work which is very reasonable and good quality. The mainstay of their business is chroming all the steel drums for carnival, so adding a few winches, stove parts, clocks, and compasses is no problem. They also gold-plate and bronze-plate as well as polish and lacquer brass. Allow a few weeks for having things chromed. If you don't want to ride out to Trincity, Peake and several of the other yards can arrange the work for you. Ian Taxi also often takes things for chroming. Old finishes have to be removed before chroming, which they do for you, but they cannot remove baked-on enamel.

Also in Trincity, Low Tech sells all kinds of metal stock at good prices. They have some stock you cannot find elsewhere, including square section hollow stainless steel.

Soca Sailboats not only manufactures racing boats but

Trinidad

Queen of Flowers

Coastal view north of Las Cuevas

Alamanda flowers

also carbon fiber spars, lead keels, customs rudder systems, hatches, and steering pedestals.

General Diesel is the business to contact for parts for Detroit Diesel, Allison transmissions, Cummins, Delco Remy, and other well known brands.

UA Weldequip carries several items of interest to those on yachts, including Bosch power tools, grinding and sanding disks, and they sell and refill fire extinguishers.

Cisl carries a range of modern insulating materials for all kinds of jobs, from soundproofing the engine room to lagging the exhaust pipe. They will also survey your problem and advise on a solution.

Berger produces an excellent line of paints, including a whole range for marine use, and will be happy to advise you on your particular needs.

Need new mattresses? The easiest thing to do is visit one of the upholsterers in the yard. But, for a bit of an adventure you can visit the Lensyl factory in Trincity, buy your foam from them, and have custom covers and even fitted sheets made. There are a few advantages to going yourself. They a have wide variety of different density foams and make several composite-type mattresses combining hard and soft foams. By going yourself, you can find the one that suits you the best. They also have a big quilting machine that finishes the mattresses with a cover of two thin layers of foam and fabric for extra comfort. They can do this on custom shapes. They can cut foam to absolutely any shape and angle but keep in mind, that unlike the upholsterers, they will not come to the boat to measure up. This means you would have to take along exact measurements or an old mattress for a pattern, and you would be responsible for getting the shape right.

GETTING AROUND ASHORE

In the old days the only buses to come down to Chaguaramas were the big ones for which you had to buy a ticket in advance. (Most boat yards still sell them.) But, happily, the maxi taxis have now included Chaguaramas on their routes and you can just walk outside a yard and grab one to town, or for a short hop just down to another yard. When you go to Port of Spain for the first time, take the maxi right into the terminal so you know where it is when you want to return. It is on the waterfront not far from Independence Square. On the return journey, make sure the bus you catch is going all the way back. Should you want a regular taxi, CrewsInn is the most likely place to find one. If you catch a maxi with no passengers, they too will often double up as a regular taxi.

If you want to take a tour, there are several tour agents in the area. Power Boats arranges a variety of tours, including short notice tours to steel pan and other events.

Ian Taxi works around the area and is particularly known for pet transfers with all their legal complications and for taking metals to be chromed down to Trincity.

Member Only (VHF: 68) is a name you will often hear on the radio. Owner Jesse James and his wife Sharon-Rose have targeted yachts and do an excellent job of getting them around and treating them like VIPs, while keeping prices reasonable. Jesse has several routine trips. On Friday mornings he takes everyone to the True Value supermarket – and it costs nothing! True Value pays for the transport and trucks all your shopping back to the dock afterwards. On Saturdays he runs people to the big local market at Port of Spain starting early (0630) so you get the good produce, and a half hour stop at Hi Lo in West Mall on the way back – all for an incredibly low price. Every other Wednesday (depending on demand) Jesse

does a run to Price Smart near Chaguanas. Price Smart is a special discount wholesale store that runs as a club. Jesse has a special membership that gets everyone in. He is also on hand to take people to special events, including both cultural and sports activities as well as joining local hiking groups. Most of these are announced on the net at 0800 (VHF: 68). In addition, Jesse does airport runs and a big variety of tours, including turtle watching, the Asa Wright Center, Caroni, and Nariva swamp. Jesse will always be dreaming up something new, so ask him about his schedule. He will also be happy to run you around, find parts for you, drop off work jobs, and pick them up.

Trump Tours are in the CrewsInn village and offer excursions into the interior. This is top quality operation catering to the more demanding customer. They do excellent nature tours and run free buses to supermarkets from time to time. (Listen to the Cruisers net, VHF: 68, 0800.)

If you prefer to rent a car, there are several places in Chaguaramas. Mark's rentals is in Power Boats, and Mark's also offers an airport limousine service, getting you to the plane on time for a reasonable fee in a taxi shared with others. Convenient Car Rental is in Tropical Marine and Econocar is in CrewsInn.

For going further afield when it is time to leave your boat, check out Lazzari & Sampson Travel Service (VHF: 68), upstairs at Coral Cove. They are a service minded agency that takes care of your flights abroad as well as local excursions, cargo handling, and traveling with pets. They have other offices in town and at West Mall.

Zorina Aziz will help you find the right ticket at Irena Trans Continental Travel, which is in Tropical Marine. They also do airport transfers, customized tours, and a taxi service. They open Monday to Friday 0900-1700.

Travelsure at CrewsInn will also be happy to help you. This is a full service travel agency downstairs in the Village Square.

SHOPPING

The biggest supermarket in Chaguaramas is Hi-Lo, by the dinghy dock at

Trinidad

CrewsInn. It opens daily 0900 to 2100, except Sundays when it opens 0800 to noon. You can provision pretty well here as they have a good stock of cans, frozen foods, fresh fruits and vegetables, and household cleaners.

The next biggest is the Dockside Foodmart at Power Boats. This too has most things you need, and in addition they manage to find some amazing household items, such as a big stack of stainless bowls from large to small for about $10 US. They open seven days a week and are often busiest on the weekends.

A vegetable truck visits Power Boats every Wednesday and Saturday over lunch until about 1500, after which it moves on to Peake and then IMS.

If you need more than that, catch a maxi to the giant new Hi Lo and other shops at West Mall. Both Members Only and Trump Tours offer free transportation to some supermarkets on a regular basis.

The Village Square at CrewsInn has several other shops. The Inn Place sells cool tropical wear, Apadoca's has a big range of duty free liquor (you need to clear out) and some gifts. Carla Gomes' S.O.S beauty salon offers unisex hairstyling, along with facials, manicures, pedicures, and massage. Jeannine, also in the salon, collects for the poor, so this is the place to drop off clothes, old kitchenware, or anything that someone might find useful. On the dock level is a video rental place, and back on the square you can visit the YSATT office. The Boater's Enterprise office is upstairs here, next to immigration. They publish the Boca and Boaters' Directory. You can get money from the Republic Bank with a teller machine close to the parking lot. Alternatively, if you are on the other side, try the big Royal Bank, opposite Peake.

Many marinas now have their own apartments or hotels, so there is not much need to look further afield for accommodation, but The Cove, at the western end of Chaguaramas, is an apartment hotel that rents rooms as well as self-contained cabanas by the day, week, or month. If you are having extensive work done on your boat, this may be a comfortable alternative to staying on board. Although they do not have air-conditioning, the cottages are set among overhanging trees that provide a cooling shade. Fans are provided, as well as daily maid service. There is a restaurant and bar, beach, pool, and a small minimart and boutique.

EATING OUT

Luckily, nearly every yard has a bar or a restaurant, so eating out around the block will give you enough variety to stop you going crazy on a long refit.

The Galley ($D) at IMS, is open everyday except Sunday from 1000 onwards, although they are often there from about 0800 and will whip you up a breakfast and coffee if you ask them. They serve some Chinese food as well as fish, chicken, and pork dishes, in addition to sandwiches. On Fridays they have two happy hours: from 1600 to 1700, and from 1900 to 2000.

At Peake, The Bight ($C-D) is an indoor/outdoor restaurant and bar, open from 0800 onwards, serving local fish, shrimp, steaks, and chicken. The outside patio has a pleasant ambience for dinner and the inside air-conditioned room makes a good sports bar hangout.

Sails Restaurant at Power Boats is open all day. It is a good spot to watch all the fishing and party boats coming and going on weekends. They have a daily lunch special as well as their regular snack menu of sandwiches and burgers and their dinner menu. The lunch specials are usually good. On the dinner menu the chicken is good value and the shrimp is well prepared; the steamed fish is excellent. The convenience of paying with a Power Boats card keeps many regulars coming back. They often have musical entertainment on Fridays.

Also in Power Boats, is the Roti Hut ($D). Gary and Grace are welcoming and are great cooks, and they make all of their own chutneys. You can grab breakfast here and get great lunchtime rotis under their open roof. Stop by for fresh local juice anytime. The Roti Hut is excellent value and opens weekdays and sometimes Saturdays, but only from morning till the workers leave.

Tardieu Marine also has a Coffee and Roti Shop ($D), which serves rotis and sandwiches as well as breakfast or take out. They are not open in the evenings.

At Coral Cove, Joe's Pizza ($D) is consistently good and very popular. The atmosphere is informal and friendly. If you don't want to wait for a beer, you can take one from the fridge and mention it when the waitress comes by. They serve pizzas and some pasta dishes, steak sandwiches and hoagies, as well as large, fresh salads. When you have a craving for salad this is the place come. You can call in your order for pizzas and takeout. They are open for lunch and dinner everyday except Sunday.

Coral Cove also has the Curry Bien, a roti and breakfast shop open weekdays 0730-1430 and Saturdays 0830-1400.

Tropical Marine has the Wheelhouse Bar with pool tables and they open later than most others. They have special barbecues with live entertainment some nights; otherwise they

Opposite: Trinidad main market on a Saturday morning

Friday night at Sails

Trinidad

serve light snacks and sandwiches.

Over at CrewsInn, The Lighthouse ($A-C) is the fanciest and best restaurant in the area, with a pleasant view overlooking the marina and excellent food and service. They will cook your fish or steak exactly the way you want it and, if it is a few dollars more than the others, it is well worth it.

There is also the Inn Place, a combination restaurant and boutique on the CrewsInn village square. They have a bar and serve delightful light meals and snacks. Their boutique is a good place to buy tropical wear and gifts.

EXPLORING

Chaguaramas is part of a large national park, which includes tropical rainforest and lush valleys and is home to monkeys and parrots. We write some of this up in our Exploring Trinidad section. The area includes a golf course down the Macqueripe Mail Road. This nine-hole course was built by the Americans during their stay here and is open to the public for a fee. The scenery is magnificent and during the rainy season you can see Edith Falls in the background. You may also get to hear howler monkeys.

Budget Nautique racing in Tobago

WATER SPORTS

Ever thought of diving in Trinidad? True, you don't find the pretty reefs of Tobago, and visibility is often only 30-60 feet, but the fish life is fantastic, with large groupers, huge lobsters, and massive schools of snappers and jacks.

Rick's Dive World at Tardieu is a full service PADI resort that can fill tanks as well as service and repair all types of diving equipment. Ricky Rampaul gives courses up to dive master, as well as running dive excursions to the outer islands and Tobago. He also rents equipment.

Rocky at Dive Specialist Center (VHF: 68) runs a full PADI dive shop, offering same day filling, courses, equipment repair, bottle inspection and hydro-testing. If your onboard compressor breaks down, he is the man to see. He rents as well as sells scuba equipment and fishing gear. You will find him down at Cove Bay, towards the western end of Chaguaramas, just before the road block to the military unit. If you go by sea, the dinghy dock is just after the sandy beach.

BAY VIEW MARINA

On the eastern side of Gaspar Grande is Bay View Beach Resort and Marina. A small breakwater offers good shelter for about 15 boats stern-to. Managed by Shawn Weston and owned by Kamal Mohammed, this is a quiet place to go to when you want to get away from the crowds and enjoy a more natural environment. There is a beach, trails, animal and bird life, as well as historic interest. You can even get off the boat and rent a room or whole cabana if you are tired of cramped quarters or have guests visiting. Bayview is connected to the mainland by a regular ferry. It is also within reach of all but the smallest dinghies.

If you plan to leave your yacht in the water in Trinidad, this is one of the safest places to do so; it is well protected from all directions.

SERVICES

Bay View management treat their yachting customers well. Dockage is some of the least expensive in the islands and they include desalinated water and electricity. You can use their swimming pool, and there is a safe area for kids to play and swim as well as a small minimart that sells ice. If you want to leave your boat here and go away you can arrange to do so with Ragoo the dockmaster, who will also look after it while you are gone.

The island is currently linked to the mainland by cell phone, but a proper phone link is being installed now, and

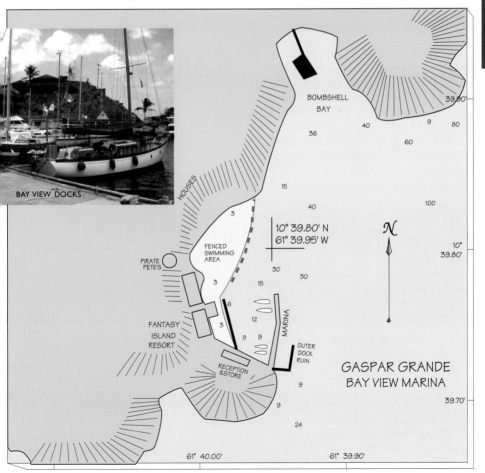

BAY VIEW DOCKS

BOMBSHELL BAY

HOUSES

FENCED SWIMMING AREA

PIRATE PETE'S

FANTASY ISLAND RESORT

RECEPTION & STORE

MARINA

OUTER DOCK RUIN

10° 39.80' N
61° 39.95' W

𝒩

GASPAR GRANDE
BAY VIEW MARINA

97

BAY VIEW MARINA

when that is finished (before this guide comes out), e-mail will be available.

A ferry runs between the resort and Mariners Haven. From Monday to Thursday they leave the resort at 0600, 0750, 0950, 1150, 1450, 1750 and 1950. They return from Mariners haven at 0630, 0800, 1000, 1200, 1500, 1800, 2000. On Fridays they run an extra ferry leaving the resort at 2150 and returning to the island at 2200. On Sundays and public holidays they leave off the ferry that leaves the island at 0950 and returns at 1000. On Saturdays they leave the resort at 0750, 0850, 0950, 1150, 1350, 1550, 1650, 1750, 1950 and 2150. They return from Mariners Haven at: 0800, 0900, 1000, 1200, 1400, 1600, 1700, 1800, 2000 and 2200. The charge is $40TT return, but it is free if you have your yacht in the marina.

ASHORE

The Lobster House restaurant serves good local food and is quite informal and reasonably priced. They serve breakfast and lunches daily and will open for dinner if requested by lunch time. People sometimes come for dinner on Friday and Saturday nights when there is a late ferry.

CARENAGE BAY

The normal route to Carenage Bay is between Point Gourde and the Diego Islands. The southern island is mined for an ingredient in the special cement that is used for capping oil wells. The northern island is a prison. You may be told that the long chute down into the sea is to take the heads of guillotined prisoners, but it is merely a drain.

Just before Carenage Bay, there is a good anchorage in Masson Bay in about 20 feet of water. This is out of any southerly chop, but can be affected in a northeasterly wind. You may have to share it with out-of-work barges, wrecks and other strange craft.

Carenage Bay is a popular anchorage in Trinidad, with easy access ashore via the Trinidad and Tobago Sailing Association (TTSA). There are many moorings off TTSA of which 15 are kept for visiting yachts. Do not pick up a mooring without prior permission – they must be arranged in advance. You will often have to wait for a mooring as they are in demand.

Otherwise, just anchor south of their

moorings and make sure you are well dug in. Do not anchor too far in the south side of the bay, as the coast guard has a station here and will consider you to be in their way. If you have to anchor east of the moorings, due to lack of space, use two anchors, since the holding is not so good here. Make sure they are well set because there has been serious damage done by yachts dragging into the moored boats. This anchorage is usually beautifully calm, but when the wind comes south of east (most often in the spring) it creates an unpleasant surge which will cause you to pitch up and down during the day.

SERVICES

The TTSA (VHF: 68) is open to visiting yachtspeople who have sailing yachts. Power boats are not accepted. It is a private sailing club, not a commercial establishment. Sensitivity is called for to keep the current excellent relationship between visiting yachtspeople and locals. The sailing Association can comfortably accommodate about 75 visiting yachts normally and up to 100 during carnival. There are not usually this many visitors, but if you find the place packed with visiting yachts, think about going somewhere else until a few people leave.

Visit the main office to register when you arrive. You will be charged a very reasonable permit fee to use the facilities. Full membership is now only open to permanent residents or citizens.

There is a small dock with electricity and water. Ashore there are showers, two card phones and one USA direct phone, a workshop and water and ice are available. If you have your own computer and server, you can plug into their line and do your e-mail. They are also a mail drop (P.O. Box 3140, Carenage Post Office, Trinidad), they will send faxes and have a photocopy machine, as well as a FedEx and UPS service. A laundromat will take care of your wash and if you don't want to do the laundry yourself, Chin's one day laundry and dry cleaning can be arranged through the office. There is a 15-ton travel lift, and

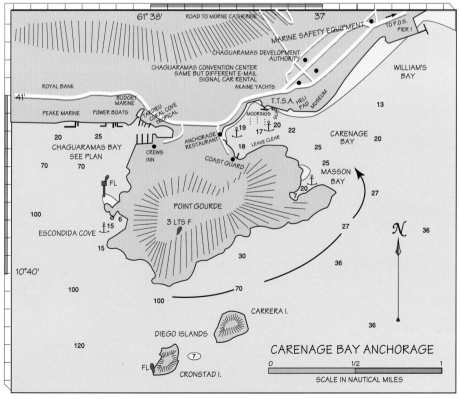

CARENAGE BAY ANCHORAGE

SCALE IN NAUTICAL MILES

although the area ashore is not huge, they do sometimes have room to store yachts. You can also haul for painting and repair. (See also the services in Chaguaramas.) You can use their dock to come alongside to take on water or get gear on and off. Arrange it in advance and make sure you do it on a weekday as it is in constant use by club members on weekends.

The Same but Different Communications are in the Chaguaramas Convention Center just a short walk away. They speak French and Spanish as well as English and offer inexpensive internet access, mailboxes, fax, photocopies, phone calls and film processing.

Signal Car rentals are in the same building and offer reasonable cars for a good price. They do listen to VHF: 68, but not all the time.

OTHER SERVICES

Marine Safety Equipment (VHF: 68) is a 15 minute walk down the road toward Port of Spain. They repair and service all makes of liferaft and inflatable dinghies. They sell RFD Survivors, and Elliot liferafts, Plastimo and Cosalt safety gear such as life rings, jackets and flares. If your dinghy needs repair, you don't have to lug it around, give them a call, they will pick it up, and if it is beyond repair they can order you a new one within a few days.

For a pleasant taxi driver call Members Only (VHF: 68) or contact Nicole Huggins through the office.

ASHORE

The legendary hospitality of the TTSA has done much to encourage visiting yachts in Trinidad. When you arrive,

Anchorage at TTSA

walk upstairs to the office, which opens at 0930, breaks an hour for lunch and reopens till 1600. Claudette Jardine or Amanda Shaw will welcome you to Trinidad and give you a package of information about the island. Before long, you will think of this as your own club. Being at the Sailing Association is a good way to get to meet Trinidadian yachtspeople. If you have young children, do not leave them unattended on the grounds.

The TTSA have a bar that opens 0900-2200. Timmy's restaurant is also on the premises. They open for breakfast at 0700 and close at 1900. You can get a good breakfast here, great lunchtime specials and snacks. Their prices are very reasonable.

Something happens almost every night to entertain the visiting yachts; pot luck night, quiz night, movie night and barbecues to name a few. Listen to the cruisers net (VHF: 68 at 0800) for details.

The Anchorage is open to the sea and the breeze, with a deck right on the water where the lights at night bring in a variety of fish especially schools of catfish. The Anchorage is place where parties are often held. They hire the premises out to organizations and those that want to good place for a fete. These are usually open to the general public with a fee at the gate, and they usually feature live bands. Although such parties nominally start about 2100 the real action usually warms up well after midnight and keeps going into the wee hours.

Next to TTSA is The Chaguaramas Military History and Aviation Museum, displaying hundreds of air and wartime artifacts as well as documenting the role of Trinidad during the war.

Pier 1 is to the northeast of TTSA. This is a restaurant, bar, pool and conference center. On some weekends they organize special functions that will introduce you to the real Trini lifestyle.

WATER SPORTS

TTSA is the home of yacht racing in Trinidad & Tobago and have races on a regular basis in both racing and cruising class. They also have a junior sailing school that uses Optimist dinghies to teach the young

ones, so if you would like your son or daughter to learn the finer points of sailing and racing, consider enrolling them in the sailing school. There are several instructors on hand and they also run an intensive program during the summer months.

Trinidad

TRINIDAD AND TOBAGO YACHT CLUB

The TTYC (Trinidad & Tobago Yacht Club) is conveniently located a short ride from town, an even shorter ride to West Mall. It is within easy walking distance of Highland Plaza and many other shops and restaurants. All yachts are welcome, both sail and power, though more of the local boats here are power and the TTYC manage most of the powerboat racing events, including the Great Race.

Like the TTSA, the TTYC, is a private club. They welcome visitors, have good docks and operate a bit like a commercial marina. You pay a small fee to be a temporary member while you are here. You can also anchor off the Yacht Club and use the facilities by paying a reasonable temporary member's fee. Berths at the TTYC are much in demand, so advance booking is usually essential. The marina is well protected and comfortable, though the outside anchorage is rolly in a southeast wind.

Expansion of the marina is a possibility in the next few years.

GENERAL SERVICES

Water and electricity (110/220 volt, 60 cycle), telephone, and cable TV are on the slips. You can hook up your computer in the office for e-mail and use the TTYC service provider. They plan to have guest computers soon. Diesel and gas are available at the fuel dock. It is open every day from 0600 to 1800. Take care coming into the fuel dock as it is shallow outside the dredged areas, at least the bottom is mud. You approach past the western wall of the marina, shaving the pier wall as closely as possible, and then head east before turning north into the fuel dock. It is dredged from time to time and has about 11 feet on the outside. The club has a reserve water tank of 12000 gallons, and a pressure pump to get it to your boat.

The office is open 0800-1800 Monday to Friday and 0800-1300 on weekends. Full office services are available as well as phone cards, and newspapers arrive every morning. Outside there are card phones and a USA direct phone. They have

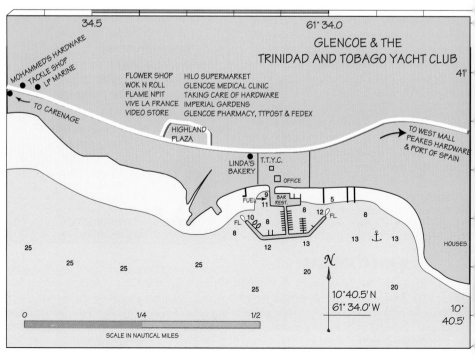

a laundromat, or you can use Chin's laundry and dry cleaning service, which picks up and delivers. The club has pleasant upstairs rooms for conferences and lounging around. One of them has a big screen TV and sitting area. Other facilities include toilets and showers.

The Yacht Club runs captains' certification courses. These are used throughout the British Commonwealth and acceptable to run private yachts up to 100 feet and light commercial craft up to 80 feet. They can be awarded to people of any nationality. Fees are reasonable and they start courses every time they get 15 people signed up. Other courses on first aid, fire fighting and safety are also available.

Aerial view of the TTYC

TECHNICAL SERVICES

Three main contractors will help with your work projects, you contact them through the marina, ask manager Jean Stampfli or one of his assistants. Henry is the woodworking man, capable of taking care of things be it some planking that needs done or cabinet work. Richard Scott does paint and fiberglass work, and Christian Northnagel will take care of your electrical problems.

Dock view from clubhouse

CHANDLERIES

A few blocks west of the Yacht Club is L.P. Marine and Industrial Supplies Limited. They are the agents for Volvo Penta, Johnson Pump and Kohler generators. This store is the best place for technical engine and electrical parts and they also have a good range of tools and some chandlery items including fenders, water and fuel tanks, glass and resin, hose and rope.

They are rebuilding the shop, but as currently designed it is hard to realize the extent of what they have, so ask. On the technical side they carry all kinds of Morse cables and steering gear as well as a huge stock of filters, prop shafts, gasket material and a ton of spares for Perkins and Volvo motors. They have just about every impeller under the sun and can rebuild any make of salt water pump in their workshop. Plus they carry cutlass bearings, exhaust hoses, VDO instruments, fish finders, GPS's, T-bolt hose clamps, fan belts and much more. On the electrical side they have wire, navigation lights, cabin lights, as well as junction boxes, control panels and breakers. If you happen to be in Tobago and need something, give them a call, they can arrange to send it up to you.

Right next door is The Tackle Shop, a complete sports fishing shop with Penn reels, Rappala lures, and a huge range of fishing accessories, plus good advice and local fishing knowledge. Almost opposite, Mohammed's hardware has building and plumbing supplies.

West Mall is in the other direction, to the east of the Yacht Club. On the ground floor, you will find a branch of C.E. Tang Yuk. They are the agents for Sea Recovery watermakers and Northern Lights generators. They can install, and service these and have a good range of spares. You will also find water pumps, ropes, stainless steel bolts and nuts as well as general hardware, and a lot of electrical hardware.

If you want to clean out your diesel tank, they have a service that recirculates the diesel, passing it through a filter, removing all the moisture and sediment from your tank. This process takes about 3 hours and is best done with 3/4 of the tank full of diesel, having previously added Biobor to kill the fungus. You need to be on a dock with power.

Further down the road toward Port of Spain you come to Peake Hardware (VHF: 69), just after the West Mall. They are full sales and service agents for Johnson outboards. The hardware store is modern and inclusive with a large range of household goods and a selection of marine hardware, including fittings, ropes, and accessories. They are agents for Stalok, Harken, Jabsco and Crosby cooling systems. They also have an excellent selection of fishing, snorkeling, and diving equipment.

Peake are also major air-conditioning manufacturers. They rent a few air conditioners to yachts at a reasonable rate and are good people to consult if you need air-conditioning or refrigeration repairs. If they cannot do the job themselves, they can refer you to someone else.

SHOPPING

Just outside the Yacht Club, Linda's is a great French bakery run by Herve from Brittany in France. It is bright and clean with several tables where you can breakfast or lunch. They bake great French breads, lots of sweet and savories and very fancy cakes. This would be a great place to come if you were throwing a party and wanted some snacks. You can also get good espresso and cappuccino coffee. They open Monday to Thursday 0800-1800 and on Friday and Saturday 0800-1900.

Over in Highland Plaza, Hi Lo has a good-sized market with everything from basic cans to fresh fruit and flowers. They will deliver if you buy enough (ask first), and they open daily 0800-1900 except Sunday when they close at 1400.

Other shops in the mall include Glencoe Pharmacy, clothing boutiques, the flower shop for silk flowers, a video store, banks, and Taking Care of Hardware, a general store with a bit of everything – tools, houseware, plumbing and electrical. The Glencoe Pharmacy also has a branch of the TT post office, which acts as agents for FedEx and Western Union money transfer.

The mall also has a medical clinic run by two doctors of general medicine and surgery. They open Monday to Thursday 0900-1900 and on Fridays 1030-1700.

Beyond this, there are several large modern shopping malls a short drive away that will satisfy most of your needs. The nearest and most plush is West Mall with a giant Hi Lo Supermarket in one building and about a hundred fancy shops in another. Among these is a branch of Lazzari and Sampson (VHF: 68), the travel agency who you will find on the Ground floor near Tang

Yuk. They have other branches in town and Chaguaramas.

EATING OUT

Skipper's at the Yacht Club is an excellent restaurant. They handle only the food, the adjoining Yacht Club Bar handles all wines and drinks. Paul Sabga runs the restaurant helped by his mother, Edna. They open seven days a week except for occasional major holidays. Their standard menu works for both lunch and dinner with everything from hamburgers to sirloin steak. In addition they have a list of daily specials. Seafood is always available. On Fridays and Saturdays they have a buffet, and on the first Friday of every month they have an Arabic night. They open at 1000 and last food orders are at 2130. They cook so well that advance booking is advisable.

Over the road in Highland Plaza, the Imperial Gardens serves good Chinese food. For fast food you have Wok 'n Roll, Flame 'n Pit and Vive La France, which is a combination Donut Boys, bakery and hot sandwich joint.

EXPLORING

If you have rented a car it may take you a short while to become familiar with the roads. The following notes should help on your first sortie to the east to visit malls, etc. When you come out of the Yacht Club and turn right there are two intersections not far down the road. For West Mall get in the left lane when the road splits into a four lane highway and turn left at the second light. This leads into a little loop that brings you

back facing the road so you can cross over to West Mall. To go north to Diego Martin (or the Starlite Shopping Center) take the big left turn which is well sign-posted and more or less opposite West Mall.

A little further down the road to Port of Spain is a flyover that will take you on the back road through St. James to Port of Spain. To visit Peake or to take the faster Foreshore Freeway to Port of Spain, turn left just before the flyover. Pass under the flyover and turn left onto the Foreshore Freeway. Ideally, to get to Peake you would turn right on the Freeway as it is just down the road. However, this is not allowed, so as you come under the flyover keep to the left lane, take the first left off the main road, turn around and come back down the same road. Now you can turn in the right direction.

PORT OF SPAIN

Port of Spain is a lively bustling city full of color. The anchorage is very well protected, even in the southeasterly winds that make the other anchorages rolly. Many boats anchor here during carnival time when all the anchorages get crowded. At other times people usually visit by maxi taxi.

You definitely need to take precautions against theft. Lock your boat up well during the day and leave someone on board after dark. During carnival people often raft up and leave one person to watch all the time.

NAVIGATION

As you approach Port of Spain two tall twin buildings stand out from afar. These are the country's financial center and were opened in 1985.

The water off Port of Spain is shallow and full of wrecks for about a mile out. It is best to stay in 30-40 feet of water until you link in with the main dredged channel. Follow this in and anchor near the small docks.

Note also the commercial fishing channel to the southeast of Port of Spain. You would not normally enter here, but in the unlikely event of a bad storm or hurricane, it might be one of the more secure spots.

REGULATIONS

Port of Spain is a commercial port of entry. Yachts should check in at Chaguaramas. However, if you have immigration problems that go beyond the Chaguaramas branch, then their office is on Frederick Street, north of Park.

SERVICES

Marine Consultants Ltd. keeps a good stock of charts and cruising guides. They are also compass adjusters and sell and service safety equipment, including flares, life jackets, EPIRBS and GPS. They are agents for Tideland, Viking and Beaufort liferafts and inflatable dinghies. They also service liferafts and inflatables.

If you want to leave your boat here and travel, or arrange for something to be shipped

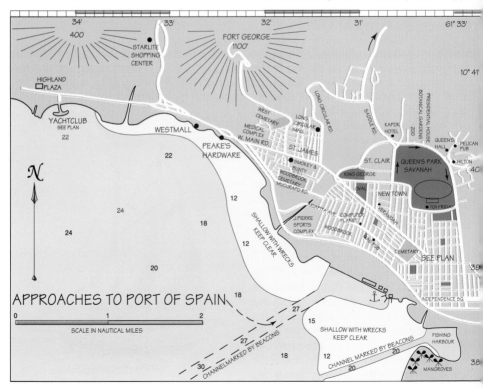

in, you will get help at Lazzari and Sampson (VHF: 68) on Pembroke Street. Lazzari and Sampson are a complete travel agent and, under the name Piarco Air Services, they handle airfreight.

B & Tees on the East side of Victoria Square is a silk-screening/embroidery place that also sells t-shirts, hats and caps. This is the place to come if you want mono-grammed or silk screened gear for your crew. You can buy items from their stock, (which is high quality, but the caps will rust), or buy your own and bring it to them to screen or embroider. Prices are significantly less here than up island.

SHOPPING

Shopping in Port of Spain is lively and fun and with lots of street traders as well as shops. They are quick off the mark, no sooner does it rain, than they are out selling umbrellas. Port of Spain is large enough to have a collection of eccentrics, homeless and beggars. The beggars here seem to be really in need, unlike those of the other islands. They actually thank you if you give them fifty cents and get excited if you give them a dollar.

The supermarkets in town are not great, most people shop at one of the malls. If you do need some stores, you will also find plenty of food down Charlotte Street along with fruit, vegetable and fish stalls that line the road.

Big general hardware stores have every-thing from tools to sinks. William H. Scott is well to the east on Independence Square. Scott carries brand names like Makita tools, Coleman, Ridgid and Stanley. They have also a good selection of lumber and ply-woods.

One the biggest, most user-friendly and reasonable hardware stores is Bagwansingh's. Unfortunately this is out of town to the east near the highway. You would not want to walk as the roads go though some of the worst of the shanty town areas. (In general you do best to stay west of Charlotte Street). The taxi fare from Independence Square is $40 each way, but the drivers are negotiable, and will wait. This huge store, laid out super-market style, allows you to pick through

Trinidad

hundreds of plumbing and other fittings.

If you lost your glasses overboard, you might want to visit Ferreira Optical on Frederick Street. They have the latest in equipment, can examine you and make new glasses at a good price. Bring in your diving mask too, and they will put in your prescription, or for those of us who need some magnification they can put in a mag-nifying lens on the bottom half of the mask.

When you have cushions made in Chaguaramas, the upholsterers will tell you to come to town and buy your own fabric. Luckily it is not hard to do, as most of the stores are packed together on Queen Street between Frederick and Henry.

Jimmy Aboud calls himself the Tex-tile King and he also owns Textile Corner opposite. Close by is Mansoor and Sons, Diamondtex (which has some good furnish-ing fabrics) and about half a dozen other stores, all packed in tight. Choosing is hard, but there is plenty of choice.

Radica Trading on Henry Street has a

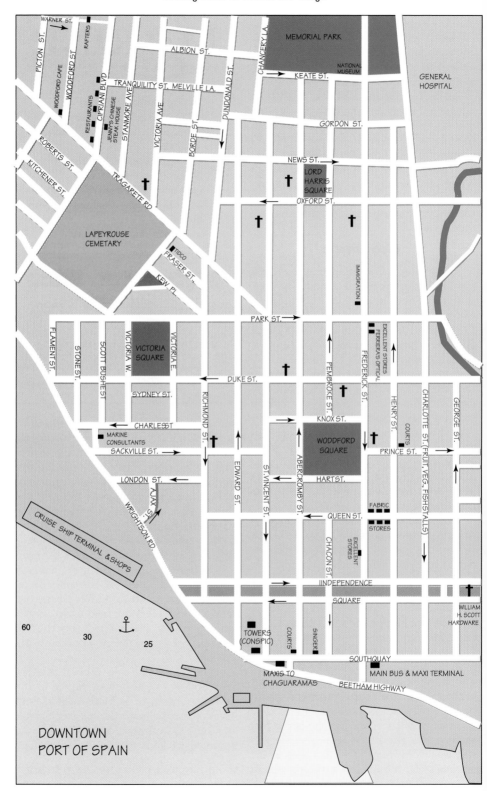

DOWNTOWN
PORT OF SPAIN

complete line of fabrics including upholstery materials, Sunbrella and real leather, foam rubber and plastic zippers of all sizes. Also nylon strapping, plastic snaps, brass grommets and stitching tools as well as 3M plastic nonskid mats in various sizes and colors.

As to general shopping, Charlotte, Frederick and Henry streets have the most shops. Charlotte Street is the best for bargain hunters, with all kinds of stores and many reasonable prices for everything from hardware to clothing. Along these streets are also several malls, each one of which contains many stores.

Excellent Stores is a good place to look for housewares, they have everything from Corel plates to plastic containers. They have stores at either end of Frederick street.

If you have been in the Caribbean a while, you will have come across Courts, the big Caribbean chain. They sell everything from appliances to furniture to sporting goods and computers, but not necessarily in every shop. You will find several branches in Port of Spain.

If you need ink for your printer, or bits for your computer, Creative Computers in the CIC building fairly high up on Frederick Street is not a bad place to start, though there are many others, and several people recommended Computer Planet on Luis Street in Woodbrook.

EATING OUT

Eating out can be as simple and inexpensive as visiting doubles salesmen who are often downtown around 1000. Doubles are a sort of crepe with curried channa (chick peas) in them. Unless you like food the hottest of the hot, don't take the pepper. Rotis are also excellent in Port of Spain and make a good lunch.

There are plenty of opportunities for more gastronomic dining. Tiki Village ($C) is on the top story of the Kapok Hotel. Just walk in and take the elevator all the way up. The air-conditioned dining room has picture windows and a bird's eye view over the city. They serve appetizing Chinese/ Polynesian dishes at reasonable prices. The Kapok Hotel is on Saddle Road near Queen's Park and as Tiki Village is popular, it is worth

Page 109:
Knowsley
House,
one of the
Magnificent
Seven

Below: Port of
Spain's twin
towers

Opposite:
Many of Port
of Spain's
older houses
have
beautiful
intricate
gingerbread

making reservations.

Phyllis Viera's Verandah ($C) is on Rust Street in a residential area. Meals are served on a spacious cool verandah. It is open Mondays to Fridays for lunch only, and on Thursdays for dinner. Parking is easy and Phyllis serves fine local food.

Rafters ($C) is in an old stone and wood building that was originally a grocery store and has plenty of atmosphere. They open daily from 1145, except Sunday when they are closed. On public holidays they open in the evenings only. Go early for lunch as it becomes very busy. Rafters is air conditioned, classy and serves such delights as shrimp flambeaux, lobster Casablanca and filet Oscar. Pub food and snacks are also available.

Outside the Pelican Inn Pub is a big sign "Open any day anytime including public holidays." Inside it has an interesting subterranean atmosphere and the feeling of a British pub. This is a popular place and it attracts a band of regulars. They serve pub food such as steak and kidney pie.

The Hilton Hotel, just to the northeast of Queen's Park, is another cool oasis when the heat of the day gets to you. Picture windows in the restaurant look out over Port of Spain toward Carenage Bay. It is sometimes called an upside down hotel because the car park is at the top and the rooms are below.

Woodford Cafe ($C) on Tragarete and Woodford St. is a delightful restaurant serving a good variety of seafood, meats and local dishes in pleasant surroundings. They are open for lunch and dinner, closed Sundays.

Thank God It's Friday (TGIF) is on the south side of Queen's Park, part of a huge new building. This is part of an American chain, bright and brash with good American style food. A bell goes every time a waiter gets tipped, and they all come sing to you if you have your birthday party here. It is very popular with both Trinidadians and visitors, especially the young crowd.

Cipriani Boulevard has quite a few restaurants, from cheap and cheerful roti joints and barbecue places to Jenny's Chinese Restaurant and Steak House ($C), which has to be one of the most elegant in town. You need to be reasonably dressed to go in here. It is good and not as expensive as the facade.

If you are into music, you need to know about the Mas Camp Pub on Ariapita Avenue and French Street. This is a serious music pub with some great Caribbean entertainers. Drop by or call them for their current program. They don't let you in with shorts, so be warned. The same company owns the adjoining Sweet Lime restaurant where you can eat before you listen. You also have a choice of quite a few fancy restaurants on Ariapita Avenue all within a block of Sweet Lime. These include the very fancy Italian restaurant Il Colosseo, The Plantation House, Chutney Rose and Red Dragon.

EXPLORING

Among other attractions, Port of Spain has the Emperor Valley Zoo. This was built in 1952 is and named after a large butterfly. It is well maintained and houses a good collection of Trinidad's wildlife species, along with a somewhat random collection of animals from other parts of the world. If you are coming by car there is parking space just west of the zoo.

The Botanical Garden, laid out in 1820, is one of the oldest in the western hemisphere. It is not as well cared for as the zoo, but it is worth walking across to look at the president's splendid house.

The Magnificent Seven is a group of eccentric and ostentatious residences built on the perimeter of Queen's Park Savannah, one on the south side, most on the west side. Six were built in 1904 when profits from cocoa plantations were high. One is now a college, another houses the offices of the Prime Minister. A few years ago there were some of the biggest buildings in town, today all the fancy modern buildings dwarf them.

There is plenty of entertainment in Trinidad. The Queen's Hall will please classical buffs with concerts and ballet. They occasionally put on classical steel band music. They are most active around Christmas and Easter. Calypso shows, popular shows and big visiting artists are either at the National Stadium in the Jean Pierre sports complex or in the stands at the Queens Park Savannah, locally known as "The Big Yard." The north stand is built every year here for Carnival and used for Panorama and the parade of bands on Carnival Monday and Tuesday.

Trinidad

NORTHWEST TRINIDAD

When the partying and sightseeing become too much and you want to get away from it all, Trinidad has several delightful and quiet anchorages within easy reach. They are often deserted during the week, but are well used for local outings on weekends and holidays.

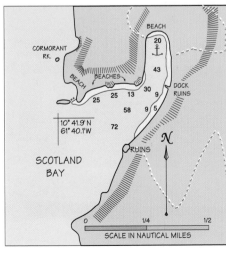

SCOTLAND BAY

This beautiful bay winds back into the hills like a fiord. It is often used as a last stop on the way to Tobago or Grenada.

During the Second World War the Americans built a large recreational center here for their troops. The ruins of these are the only signs of habitation you will see. The water is generally very deep and when it does become shallow, it does so fast. The best anchorage is right up at the head of the bay in about 35 feet of water.

This is a pleasant place to sit and enjoy the view of the hills and the ample bird life. Corbeaus wheel overhead and fight on the beach, swallows sometimes rest on your lifelines and you can spend hours with binoculars trying to figure out which birds are making all the raucous sounds ashore. When sitting palls, don your snorkeling gear and check out the reefs near the island at the entrance.

Hiking is excellent in the surrounding area, there is even a trail that leads all the way to Macqueripe Bay.

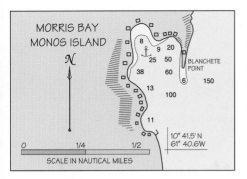

MORRIS BAY

Morris Bay has no roads, but there are many holiday homes built right on the waterfront. These are reached by boat, and the land and houses are all private. You can anchor here, but there is not much to do ashore.

Most of the bay is very deep but there is a good anchorage area up toward the head of the bay before it gets too shallow. Give good clearance to the 6-foot shoal off the south end of Blanchette Point. It is surrounded by very deep water and pops up suddenly.

Above Scotland Bay

opposite: Boca de Monos with Scotland Bay (left).

Below: Morris Bay

Trinidad

GRAND FOND BAY

***Aerial view
of Grand
Fond Bay***

This lovely bay is very quiet; there are just a few holiday homes dotted along the shore. Most of the bay is deep, but there is good anchorage in about 25 feet off the old pilings left over from World War II that are toward the head of the bay. The water shelves rapidly beyond the pilings. This anchorage seems well protected even when southeasterly winds are making boats roll in Chaguaramas.

***Grand Fond
Bay
anchorage***

You sit here surrounded by the hills and exotic songs from the birds ashore which generally manage to stay hidden in the trees. The beach at the head of the bay is covered in coconut palms, and makes a good spot for a barbecue. You can walk around the beach and find paths back into the forest.

***Aerial view
of Grand
Fond Bay***

***Grand Fond
Bay
anchorage***

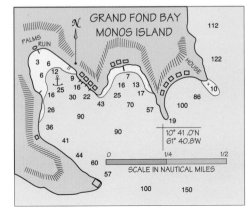

CHACACHACARE

Until about 35 years ago the island of Chacachacare was a leper colony. It was a large community, with a road running all around, busy enough to require a traffic light. When a cure for leprosy was found, the colony was abandoned. Many household and personal items were left where they were last used. Nature is about half way to reclaiming the buildings. It makes fascinating exploring, though you may need a cutlass to get through the bush from time to time.

The lighthouse up the hill is manned and you can walk up by following the road from the lighthouse dock. If you show interest, there is a good chance the keepers will invite you to take a tour.

La Tinta Bay on the west side has a pleasant beach and is popular on holidays. In 2001 Spanish speaking pirates (probably from Venezuela) attacked a yacht here, so treat this bay with a little caution.

NAVIGATION

Chacachacare Bay affords excellent cruising. There are many anchorages and you can be sure to have one to yourself, except possibly on weekends. The wind tends to blow from the southeast or the northeast so one side is often more protected and you have to be prepared for a change in wind direction. The bay is very deep, and when it shelves it does so rapidly. The distance between anchoring depth and aground may be less than 100 feet. Therefore it pays to approach any anchorage cautiously. In some places with a rapid drop off, two anchors or a stern line ashore may be necessary.

The doctors' houses lie in two secluded little bays. The shelf here is very steep, but stern-to anchoring is possible. Sanders Bay probably offers the best all-round anchorage. There is a wide enough shelf to anchor on in depths of 10 to 25 feet. Note the old sea road that runs around the rocks into Coco Bay. Coco Bay also offers a shelf where you

Trinidad

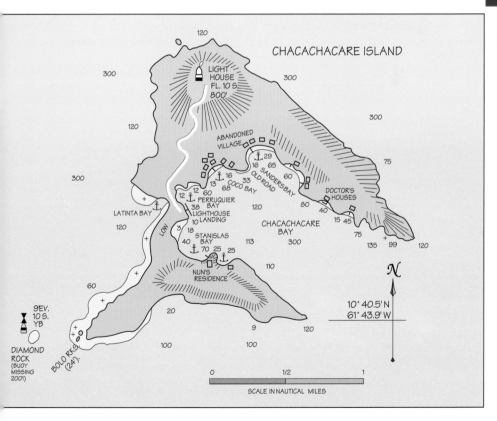

can anchor. The landing stage for the light-house is at the south end of Perruquier Bay. Two secluded beaches are north of the dock. You could comfortably anchor here with one line in the deep water and another back in the shallows. Avoid the west end of Stanislas Bay as it is shoal. At the south end the water is very deep and the holding is bad, but once hooked, you can take a line to the dock. The little bay to the east of Stanislas Bay has pretty cliffs and a good anchoring shelf. It is eight feet most of the way to the shore.

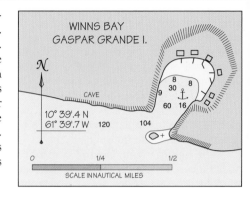

GASPAR GRANDE ISLAND

There is a very small harbor on the south side of Gaspar Grande called Winns Bay. A big fig tree grows on the small rocky island at the entrance to the bay. The bay shelves rapidly, the holding is not great and the wind can come from any direction. However, if you anchor toward the center and put a line ashore to a tree you can get comfortable enough for an overnight stop.

As on many of the islands, there is no-where to walk ashore, and there are just a few privately owned houses. This is a good place to hear kiskadees, which call to each other across the bay. Though common in Trinidad and South America, this bird is not found in Tobago. French people hear it say-ing "Qu'est-ce-qu'il dit", and English hear it saying "Kiskadee". It is somewhat raucous in either language.

POINTE-A-PIERRE

Pointe-a-Pierre is a few miles north of San Fernando in the southwestern portion of Trinidad, about 25 miles from the northern yacht anchorages. Southern Trinidad is the powerhouse behind the economy. This is the energy and production center of the country. In Point Lisas, huge plants produce ammonia, making Trinidad the largest exporter of this gas in the world. Petrotrin's giant oil refinery is in Pointe-a-Pierre. Yet, despite all this industry, much of the country is pleasant with sugar cane fields and park areas.

Lots of businesses service the oil and energy sector. Down south you will find the finest hardware stores, lots of specialized shops, and many skilled technicians. The area is a rather charming combination of brand new fancy buildings and old style houses, fancy shops and street side vendors.

A coast road runs from Point Lisas down to Pointe-a-Pierre, through Marabella and onto San Fernando. The road is lined with a multitude of shops and services.

The Pointe-a-Pierre Yacht Club is part of Petrotrin's oil refinery. Despite this it is set in a peaceful scenic bay that is well protected except from the west. The Pointe-a-Pierre Wildfowl Trust nearby is outstanding and this is an excellent anchorage from which to explore southern Trinidad. Best of all, the local yachtsmen love to see a new face, so you can be sure of a great welcome. They celebrate Guy Fawkes

Chacachacare
Anchorage

Opposite:
Chacachacare
Aerial, La
Tinta Bay in
foreground

One of the
abandoned
Chacachacare
buildings

Trinidad

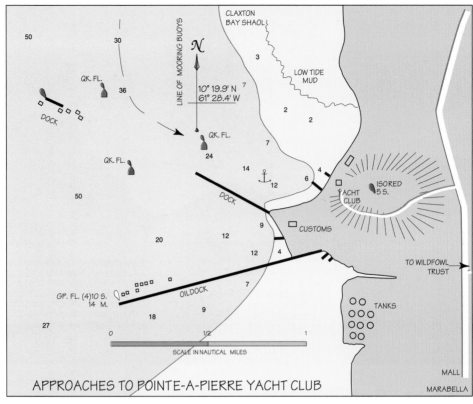

APPROACHES TO POINTE-A-PIERRE YACHT CLUB

on a Saturday close to November the 5th with an enormous bonfire, and enjoyable barbecue. No charge to come, pay for your food and drinks, visiting yachts are welcome.

Point-a-Pierre is a private club and you have to go through private land to get anywhere, you will be very welcome, but it is smart to call before you go and let them know you plan to visit. Call the commodore of the yacht club George Burnes at 658-4200 or home: 658-2222. If you cannot get him, try Jimmy Harris, currently the club Bosun. His office number is 636-0811, cell: 678-3967. You could also call active member Rod Gibbon: 650-1914.

NAVIGATION

The western shores of Trinidad are shoal a long way out, so stay four or five miles offshore or in at least 30 feet of water. Oil rigs, pipes and wrecks are features of the west coast, so it is best to go in daylight. As you come down the coast you will see Point Lisas, a huge industrial complex with chimneys, buildings and probably smoke, about five

miles north of Pointe-a-Pierre. Another good landmark is San Fernando Hill, a lone, oddly shaped hill in San Fernando, which received its strange looks from mining.

Stay outside all the navigational buoys off Point Lisas. As you get closer you can see the two long docks at Pointe-a-Pierre; the southern one is a mile long. As you come in from the north, merge with the channel into the northern dock. Follow the dock down toward the yacht club and anchor in about 12 feet off the southern yacht club dock.

REGULATIONS

Pointe-a-Pierre is a port of entry. You can anchor off the yacht club and walk or dinghy over to the customs shed, which is at the head of the docks.

GENERAL YACHT SERVICES

Point-a-Pierre Yacht club has a dock where you can arrange to take on water. The club is open on Saturday and Sunday afternoons.

Some changes are taking place. A new

ONLY 0-3' FEET DEEP

housing development is being created at the northern part of the yacht club. The present club building will stay, as will the yacht dock, but the club property will move a little south to meet the first of the large docks. When this is done a new road will lead out to the main road which will be clear of Petrotrin's operations, making access for visitors easier.

Chee's Laundry and dry cleaning is right at the beginning of Marabella, about a mile down the main road if you turn right out of the gate.

HARDWARE AND MARINE SUPPLIES

While you will not find yacht hardware, and there are no chandleries, there are good stores and you cannot find better places for buying stainless or aluminum stock. SSL Induserve Supply on Sutton Street in San Fernando is one excellent hardware store. You can buy tools here at excellent prices. They also keep a lot of hydraulic hoses and fittings, tons of fan belts, and lots of industrial clothing. They also keep an embroidery machine so they can embroider the work clothes with the company name. You can also bring your yachting hats here and they will embroider these with your name and logo at an excellent price.

In Marabella, Southern Wholesale stores on Union Road is a huge hardware store with everything from tool to plumbing with bathroom units and even fishing and snorkeling gear.

Pointe-a-Pierre Yacht Club anchorage

Tree duck at the Wildlife Trust

Samlalsingh's nearby has some of the best prices on galvanized chain. Many other big hardware stores are in the south including Bagwansingh's and Mohammed's hardware. If you want laminated glass then try Goupal Hardware at the Marabella Roundabout.

When you have a metal working project in mind, be it in stainless sheet or polished aluminum tube, you will find your material at TOSL engineering on Maharaj Avenue in Marabella. They have the largest supply of metal in the industry. You can also get good prices on stainless sheet at Point Lisas Steel Products in the Port Lisas Industrial Estate.

There are also many specialist shops where you can get special bits for projects, like bearings at the West Indian Bearings on Ciparo Street in San Fernando or welding supplies at Edoo's on Royal Road in San Fernando. Ceejay engineering in Marabella has key stock, sprockets, pulleys, chains (including stainless steering chain) and industrial electric pumps. United Bearings on Gomez Street has bearing, seals and couplings. Trinidad Hose in San Fernando have hoses for every project from exhaust hose to hydraulic hose.

Maka on the South Trunk Road in San Fernando has an excellent selection of stainless bolts and fasteners, including screws and rivets of all types.

If you have a Perkins, Leyland, Ford, GM or Mercedes engine to rebuild, visit Lenny Sumadh on Coffee Street in San Fernando. He is the dealer and has excellent prices on spares, though they will be for the industrial and agricultural versions of the engine so while the gaskets and cylinder heads will be the same, you will not get the marine bits like heat exchangers and salt water pumps.

For resins, glass and fishing gear try the General Store close to the waterfront in San Fernando, a short walk from Samson Yachts.

CANVAS AND CUSHIONS

When you need to buy fabrics you have two excellent stores close to each other in San Fernando on Cipero Street. Radica Trading has a complete line of fabrics including upholstery materials, Sunbrella and real leather, foam rubber and plastic zippers of all sizes. Also nylon strapping, plastic snaps, brass grommets and stitching tools as well as 3M plastic nonskid mats in various sizes and colors.

Opposite, Rahaman's Upholstery has an even bigger range with fabrics for everything. Ask Fariez Rahaman for a tour. He has the new "like glass" window fabric, a huge line of nalgahyde type materials including a good range of special marine quality ones. He has a big range of Sunbrella colors at excellent prices, as well as completely waterproof reinforced fabrics. He also has marine fabrics for floors and walls, even things that could work as netting on a catamaran. This is in addition to the regular furnishing fabrics, marine zips and other fasteners.

If you need foam for cushions, Vicmal is a big foam factory selling all grades of foam on the highway near Point Lisas.

To sew it all together, contact Frankie (Bones) in Dow Village, Point Lisas. He has an old fashioned shop with a big single sewing machine and a well worn chair behind it. He has no special marine experience, but he is a whizz at cushions and can make things like biminis if you bring the old one in for him to copy.

TECHNICAL SERVICES

The south has plenty of services and you can get practically anything done here except rigging and sailmaking. It is not particularly geared to yachts and it is not like Chaguaramas. The services are well spread out and you will need to rent a car and get to know the area. However, what you lose in convenience you can make up for in prices which tend to be favorable down south.

Tropical Engineering, run by Jimmy Harris is in Port Lisas. They build specialized trucks for all kinds of operations that run on hydraulics. Consequently they have good machines for rolling and shaping metals including stainless and aluminum, and they have these metals in stock. They also weld steel, but not stainless or aluminum. They work with heavy equipment and can help out with hydraulic problems and parts.

Trinidad

Perhaps best of all, Jimmy has been a yachtsman for years, knows all the businesses down south and can tell you the best person for any job you have.

Trojan Engineering are a good machine shop and fabricator. They can work well in all metals including aluminum and stainless and can also machine down your cylinder head or tackle just about any job. Talk to Peter or David.

Rod Gibbon, a yacht club member, works in wood. He is more on the factory end of things and can supply teak, balata cedar and is soon to produce local balsa core. He makes a line of teak accessories that are sold through chandleries. He can sometimes be persuaded to do custom work, depending on the project.

Superior Machine Shop and Engineering is run by Harry Stauble. He mainly does commercial work for the oil industry, but he lives in Port of Spain and comes by the boatyards in Chaguaramas a couple of times a week to pick up or drop off work. His yacht work includes pushpits, anchor rollers, chain plates, and hard top/bimini frames. Materials are no problem, he is right beside TOSL Engineering the big oilfields supplier.

Pointe-a-Pierre Yacht Club

Below: Trinidad is the world's largest exporter of amonia

Samson Boats is on the waterfront in San Fernando. Managing director Jim Wilson is very charming and has a good team of glass men. He builds a series of whaler's and dinghies and often has some already built for inspection. He builds many local fishing Pirogues, but he also tackles much larger projects, including the building of giant cats. Go visit the workshop for yourself, and talk to some of his old customers.

Tang How Bros. on Amarsingh Street in Marabella are muffler specialists. As part of this work, they have a big hydraulic pipe bender that can bend anything up to four inches in diameter. If you bring stainless or aluminum tube, they can bend it to your specifications.

For engine repairs, contact Cliff Muridali at Detroit Diesel. It is about four miles south of San Fernando.

ASHORE

The yacht club bar is open Wednesday and Friday evenings and Saturday and Sunday afternoons. Drinks are very reasonable. You will probably be made a temporary member of the Pointe-a-Pierre Club, which will enable you to use the other club facilities (open every day), including tennis courts, swimming pool, golf course and the main club restaurant and bar. The local members will make you feel right at home.

SHOPPING

If you walk to the main road and turn right you can walk or take a maxi down to the Tropical Plaza right at the beginning of Marabella. They have a big Hi Lo, a Pizza Boys, and a pharmacy that opens seven nights a week till 2100 most nights and 2200 on the others. There are also other bigger Malls, such as Gulf City in San Fernando.

EATING OUT

This is a big area with lots of restaurants. You will find many fast food and roti shops. For a fine meal at a reasonable price I recommend two Chinese restaurants. Jenny's Wok and Steak House on Ciparo Road is a fine establishment with a long bar and lots of dark wood. Soong's Great Wall on Circular Road in San Fernando is even fancier with excellent food and attentive service.

EXPLORING

The Pointe-a-Pierre Wildfowl Trust was started from within the refinery and is on its grounds. Its 60 acres include two lakes that are used as reservoirs for the refinery's emergency fire and cooling systems. It was started in 1966 and now houses a captive breeding program where birds such as anhingas and scarlet ibises have recently hatched out. The lakes attract countless birds, including many ducks, geese, herons, storks and song birds. Look for gallinules and jacanas walking on the lily pads. Caimans can also be seen in the lakes. It is a wonderful place for a picnic and a good way to get acquainted with local and migrant birds. There is a nominal entrance fee and you have to call them in advance and let them know you are coming. Speak to Molly Gaskin. It is within long walking distance, or take a maxi taxi right outside the gate heading south and ask to be put off at the wildfowl trust.

Pointe-a-Pierre is ideally situated to explore Trinidad's southern forests, the east coast beaches and the pitch lake. Rental cars are available in San Fernando.

TRINIDAD'S NORTH COAST

The northern coast of Trinidad is wild and rugged, the northern mountain range drops steeply to the sea. Close to shore it can be very rocky, but luckily most of the hazards are visible either as breaking water or as rocks. There are wonderfully scenic anchorages along this coast which are reasonably protected from the easterly winds, and well protected from southeasterlies. They are open to the north and could be untenable in strong northeasterlies or northerly swells.

LA VACHE BAY

This is a spectacularly beautiful anchorage set in the wilds, amid steep wooded hills with a view back over Les Boqets and Saut d'Eau Islands. It is also the best north coast anchorage. You would be comfortable here for a day or two on your way to Tobago.

NAVIGATION

As you approach along the north coast you can go between Saut d'Eau Island and Medine Point. Stay on the Medine Point side of the channel as there are some nasty looking rocks just below the surface (water breaks on them) just southeast of Saut d'Eau Island. Pass outside Les Boqets Islands and head over to the eastern side of La Vache Bay, below the Timberline Resort buildings.

You will see two small beaches with ruins near them. The best anchorage is off the northern of these beaches. There is a fair-sized shelf with good holding sand in 13-25 feet of water. As the wind comes from all directions in here, you may be safest and most comfortable with two anchors, holding your boat with bow or stern toward the beach.

Trinidad

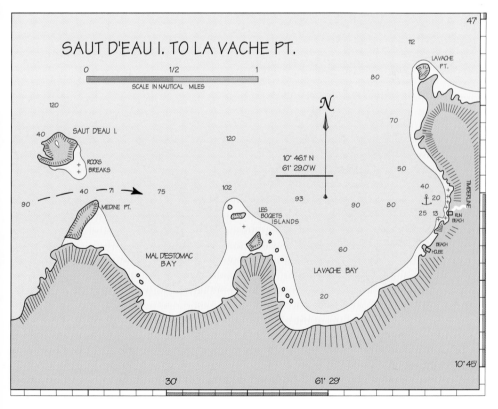

ASHORE

This is a great place for dinghy exploration among interesting caves, ledges and cliffs. In times of rain you can take your dinghy under a little waterfall dropping into the sea.

A trail leads from the ruin above the beach to Timberline Resort above. This is a great restaurant and bar perched on a ridge with spectacular views. It was closed for refurbishing in 2001, and the reopening date was somewhat uncertain so call before you go.

In a little house on the waterfront to the south of the anchorage you will find Frank McCume, who takes people on fishing trips and to explore nearby caves.

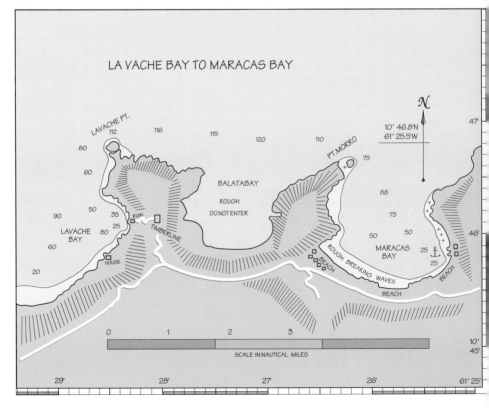

LA VACHE BAY TO MARACAS BAY

SCALE IN NAUTICAL MILES

MARACAS BAY

This magnificent bay is over a mile wide and has three white sand beaches. It is a very popular beach area for locals, especially on weekends and holidays. You will roll a little in here unless conditions are exceptionally calm, but it makes a perfectly acceptable rest stop on your way to Tobago. It has the advantage of being three miles farther east than La Vache Bay.

NAVIGATION

Pass outside the little island off Point Morro and head toward the east side of Maracas Bay. You will find a large shelf on which to anchor off the beach and close to the rocks. The holding is good in mud. Small swells come in from every direction, so a stern anchor is not much help. The wind, too, can switch around.

ASHORE

This is a popular holiday spot and if you pull your dinghy up the nearest and calmest beach, you can walk west down the road to a big car park where some little shacks sell beer and snacks.

Opposite top: Maracas Bay, the anchorage is way over on the far side of the bay

Below: La Vache Point

Page 127: View west from Chupara Point

Trinidad

LAS CUEVAS

Two anchorages lie 3 miles to the east of Maracas Bay and provide a good halfway stop for those on their way to Tobago, as well as a pleasant away-from-it-all spot for a change from Chaguaramas. You would not want to be here in a northerly swell or strong northeasterly wind. But on a regular trade-wind day with the wind east or south of east these anchorages will be very acceptable. Many Trinidadians stop here on their way to Tobago.

The village of Las Cuevas has a fishing fleet and is small. To the west of the village is a magnificent beach. Anchorage is possible here, or you can head another mile or so up the coast to anchor behind Chupara Point. This is a rugged and attractive part of the coast

NAVIGATION

Give reasonable clearance to Las Cuevas Point and head towards the village of Las Cuevas. Anchor off the fishing fleet in about 20 feet of water. Alternatively head up towards Chupara Point. Do not hug the coast

on the way up as there are under water rocks several hundred yards off the shore. You will see a white block house and an old estate house behind it. You find the best protection along the coast between these houses and the point. The closer you tuck in the calmer it will be. When leaving to or arriving from the east, you have to make a wide sweep back to the west at Chupara Point. There is a very nasty rock awash here a few hundred yards to the west of the point.

ASHORE

If you go ashore at the village of Las Cuevas, you will probably be able to buy fish almost any time any day.

Further up near Chupara Point the chances of your getting ashore are more slender. But if you do, there is a pleasant small beach with interesting rocks, and a well made pathway leads up to the main road. Just before the road a rough path leads uphill to the north. If you follow this there is quite a pleasant little walk along the headland to the light structure at Chupara Point.

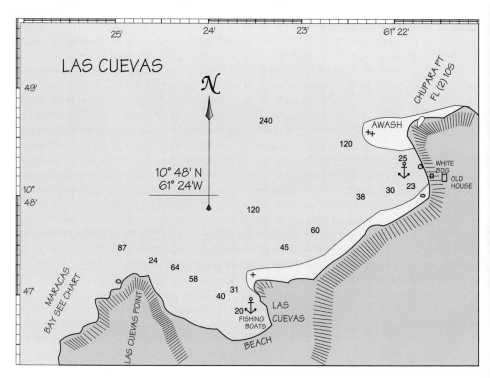

GRAND RIVIERE

Grand Riviere is a spectacular anchorage right up towards the eastern end of Trinidad. It is a place where many come to watch turtles by night. The beach is great and ashore you will find a small hotel. The anchorage is a good place to stop on the way to Tobago, though if you want to spend some ashore time here it may well be better to do it by car, as you may have a problem getting ashore in your dinghy in the swells. There is always a swell on the beach and often the waves are quite large. But the anchoring area, which is further to the northeast,

is calm in moderate easterly or southeasterly trades when you get close to shore. Avoid this anchorage in northerly swells or strong northeasterly trades.

NAVIGATION

A large rock marks the outer edge of a shoal that extends from the western side of Grand Riviere Bay to the north. A few more rocks can be seen inside this. Pass to the north

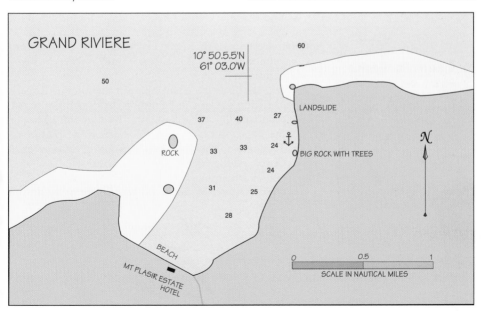

Grand Riviere

Chupara Point light structure

of all these rocks, giving the area reasonable clearance. Head over to the eastern side of the bay and find the calmest spot you can. There is a good area close by a large rock with some trees on it. There is 25 feet quite close to shore most of the way up this coast.

ASHORE

Grande Riviere is one of the best places for turtle watching as it is a long way from anywhere and so less popular. If you manage to get ashore you can eat at Mt. Plasir Estate ($C), a charming small hotel on the beach owned by Piero Guerrini from Italy.

There are many excellent hikes in the Grande Riviere area and hiking guides can be arranged through the hotel. There is one small waterfall just a short walk from the hotel. The more impressive ones are a few miles west up Matelot River. The hike up the river is very beautiful in sometimes wild country and the falls, while not high, are wide and have a big pool for swimming.

Tobago

Tobago at a glance

REGULATIONS

If you are coming from abroad, go directly to Scarborough or Charlotteville with your yacht to check with Customs and Immigration. When you leave Tobago for another country, you must go back to these ports for your clearance. You can try by bus, but in some cases they may want you to come with your yacht. If you plan to discharge any crew, you must notify Immigration of your intentions. Scarborough is about a three-hour beat from Crown Point against wind and current and about five or six hours from Man of War Bay. The procedures are easy once you arrive. If you want to avoid overtime charges (around $40US), clear in on weekdays from 0800-1600. When you clear in, let the customs officer know all the harbors you wish to visit.

Customs will charge you $50TT navigation dues for the first 30 days, and when you depart will collect $50TT a month for however long you have stayed.

Trinidad and Tobago are one country. If you are coming from Trinidad and going to return to Trinidad before clearing out, you should go by Customs and Immigration in Trinidad before you leave and get them to endorse your entry papers. At the first reasonable opportunity, show these to the Customs and Immigration in Scarborough (you can go to Scarborough by bus). If you clear into Tobago and are going on to Trinidad and leaving from there, you must notify Customs and Immigration so that they can send the papers to Trinidad with you.

The whole of Buccoo Reef is now a restricted area and yachts are not allowed to anchor here except in the case of a hurricane.

SHOPPING HOURS

Shopping hours are 0800-1200 and 1300-1630. Most shops close Saturday afternoons and all of Sunday. Most banks are open 0900-1400 Monday to Thursday, and on Fridays from 0800-1200 and 1500-1700.

HOLIDAYS

See Trinidad.

TELEPHONES

There are card phones all around Tobago. There are two kinds of cards: those which you put in the phone and which work for local calls and the ones with a long string of numbers you have to punch in, which work for international calls. Cards may be purchased at some of the banks in town, the TSTT building on the corner of Main and Jerningham Streets in Scarborough, at the tourist bureau or the Republic Bank at the airport, as well as various other locations. You cannot use card phones to make credit card or collect calls, but TSTT has a USA direct line, and there is one at the airport. See also Trinidad.

TRANSPORT

Several airlines connect Tobago to the rest of the Caribbean. There are several flights a day to Trinidad and you can link there with major airlines. There is a $100TT departure tax. Most people get around in "route taxis" which are normal size cars, or maxi taxis which are mini buses. Both have license plates that begin with an H. (Note that regular taxis also begin with an H.) The fares range from $2TT for a short drop to about $12TT, which would take you from Scarborough to Charlotteville. You flag down a taxi going in your direction, confirm the destination and fare, and share the cab with other people who are doing the same thing. Route taxis will often also act as regular taxis and are often quite negotiable on price.

There are also individuals with private cars, whose license plate begins with a P, who provide a transport service and whose prices are close to those of the route taxis.

Regular taxis are also available and typical rates for 1-4 people in $US are:

5-6 hour trips........................150
Scarborough to the airport ..30
Scarborough to Plymouth......30

There is also a national large bus system that runs throughout the island. The main bus terminal is in Scarborough, near the market. Passengers must buy bus tickets in advance. Buses will not stop at the designated stops unless you stretch out your hand to signal them.

Rental cars are available and you can drive on a USA, UK or international license. Drive on the left.

PIGEON POINT

Tobago

Tobago

Store Bay Anchorage

Page 137: Arnos Vale water wheel

Tobago is a little out of the mainstream of the other Caribbean Islands. Too far to sail in a day and too often a struggle against wind and current, it is less popular than the islands to the north. However, for the adventurous sailor the extra effort required is amply rewarded by a visit to one of the last unspoiled Caribbean islands.

This small (116 sq. miles), mountainous island has lovely beaches and green hills. With a population of only 47,000, it does not feel in the least bit crowded. Long used as a holiday place for Trinidadians, Tobago has a low key but expanding tourist industry. Fishing is important and much of the catch comes from seine netting. When anchoring in Tobago, you need to consider the needs of the fishermen. We give more details under specific anchorages where it is relevant.

Tobago changed hands more times than any other Caribbean island – between Dutch, English, Courlanders, and French – and the count is sometimes 24 times, sometimes as high as 30 times. This figure is vague because for many years no country had a firm grip on Tobago and a change in administration was hardly noticeable. (Who's counting?) Possibly spotted by Columbus in 1498, there was no permanent settlement for over 150 years. Carib raids and disease ended a Dutch settlement which was established in 1628. Later, colonists of various

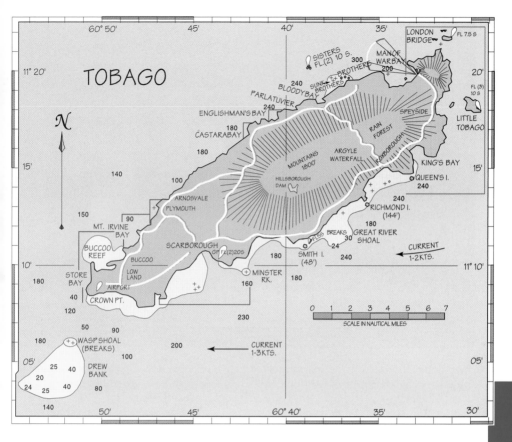

ous nationalities periodically laid waste to each other's settlements, which disrupted the pirates operating in the area. The Duke of Courland (now part of Latvia) was very persistent in trying to exercise sovereignty over the island, which had been given to him as a birthday present by his godfather, King Charles II of England.

By 1771, English colonists were using slaves to grow and harvest sugar cane. After an infestation of ants destroyed the cane, the settlers tried cotton. In 1781 the French took the island over for 12 years and made serious attempts to develop Tobago's economy, still using slave labor to grow both sugar and cotton. After the British regained control in 1793 they remained in power with only a slight interruption until Trinidad and Tobago became an independent country in 1962. Tobago was united with Trinidad in 1899, after its economy had totally collapsed and no one knew what to with it.

Today tourism is developing at an ex-

panding rate. One of the largest new projects is the Angostura-built Tobago Plantations, which includes a Hilton hotel, a golf course, lots of residential properties, and a marina which is still in the planning stage. So far, however, Tobago is not what you would call a touristy island. There are not yet any international chain stores, and with the exception of the major hotels, businesses that cater to visitors are very individualistic, and sometimes charmingly quirky.

NAVIGATION

Though just outside the "hurricane belt," Tobago has been hit. In 1847 a hurricane blew the roofs off the buildings at Fort King George. Hurricane Flora, an intense storm that struck in 1963, almost laid waste to the island's agricultural base.

Lying as it does at a slight angle to the trade winds, Tobago does not have an obvious windward or leeward shore. Anchorages are to be found in protected areas and in-

dentations all around. How well protected these are depends on the prevailing conditions. The anchorages from Crown Point to Man of War Bay will be uncomfortable to untenable in any northerly swells. Fortunately, Tobago is small enough that it only takes a few hours to get from the north to the south coast. Inside the new harbor wall, Scarborough is comfortable in nearly every condition. The best time to come is from February onwards, when the chances of northerly swells and strong northeasterly winds have diminished. If you are planning to circumnavigate the island, it makes sense to go clockwise from Scarborough, since the northern shore is generally more protected and has less current.

The tidal range is around three feet in Tobago, so when you anchor make sure there is enough water under your keel.

Although the waters around Tobago are generally clear, they may become murky after heavy rainfall or if swells have stirred up the bottom. In addition, outflow from the Orinoco River can reduce undersea and reef visibility from time to time. This happens most often during the hurricane season, from August to October.

Exploring
Tobago

Exploring Tobago

Tobago is an especially rewarding island for nature lovers. Like the other Eastern Caribbean islands to the north, it has rainforests, clear waters, and pristine beaches, but it is the only island apart from Trinidad that once was part of the South American continent. It has 210 species of nesting birds, whereas there are fewer than 80 on any other small island. Many of the birds are brightly colored and so unafraid that you can spot them from a car. After a while, if a bird doesn't have more colors than a traffic light, you hardly bother to look.

Strangely, Tobago shares several species of frogs, lizards, and birds with South America that are not present in Trinidad. This has led to speculation that there was once a land bridge from Tobago to other parts of South America that skirted Trinidad. Trinidad was part of South America as recently as 11,000 years ago, but Tobago has not been part of the continent for more than a million years.

The cocrico, more properly the rufous-vented chachalaca, is Tobago's national bird. It is a big bird that looks like a slender long-tailed turkey. The raucous cries of "cocrico" begin at dawn, continue irregularly through the day, and reach a second crescendo near dusk. The bird is protected by law, but the din, together with its habit of eating some agricultural crops and the fact that it is quite tasty, have contributed to the perception by some that it is better dead than alive. The birds are quite unwary and could quickly go from pest to endangered species if unrestricted hunting were allowed.

There are two excellent outfits that lead nature tours in Tobago. David Rooks sometimes leads scheduled nature trips you can join and he will arrange other journeys on request for four or more people. He takes groups to the bird sanctuary on Little Tobago Island, and to the 14,000-acre protected rainforest in the center of the island. He includes other stops and you will learn about local agriculture and history as well as natural history. He is an enthusiastic and knowledgeable naturalist and birder – the one who is called in when big wigs arrive. All-day tours cost $45 to $55US. Wear reasonably good walking shoes for the rainforest trip and a change of clothes during the rainy season, June to December. The walk is only a couple of miles long but the path can be slippery. He will pick people up from most anchorages or arrange transportation from Man of War Bay or Blue Waters Inn. He also sometimes gives lectures and slide shows at leading hotels.

Pat Turpin and Renson Jack operate Pioneer Journeys, an organization that specializes in exploring "the unknown Tobago." Pat's specialty is ferns and Renson is a forest warden, but they both know all aspects of their island's natural history thoroughly. Their four standard journeys each have a different focus and include visits to a cocoa plantation, the rainforest, a waterfall, and wetlands for birdwatchers. On any trip you will see a good cross section of Tobago's natural history. Prices for full day tours range from $42 to $55US, and include transport, meals, and park fees.

If you are touring Tobago on your own, the prettiest roads are in the eastern half of the island, from Castara east on the north coast and from Roxborough round to Charlotteville. The road from Roxborough to Bloody Bay is right through rainforest, much of which has been protected since 1765. Trails leave this road, including a two-mile loop trail near the summit or a hike from the top down to Bloody Bay. There is a very rough road from Bloody Bay to Charlotteville. Some of it is passable with a four-wheel drive, but it is best done as a hike. You follow the coast much of the way with occasional great views down to the sea and across to Charlotteville. You will see lots of leaf cutter ant trails, parrots and other birds, and cows which are left to graze in the road. It takes a good half day one way, so you need to get dropped off and arrange for someone to pick you up at the other end. There is not a lot of shade, so go well protected against the sun.

Two sets of waterfalls might attract your interest. The Argyle Waterfalls at Roxborough are photogenically arranged in three tiers. There are pools for swimming and falls where you

Motmot, notice the distinctive tail with its cutaway just before the tip

Opposite: Resevoir at Hillsborough Dam

When you need a cool one a rum shop is always close by

Tobago

can take a shower. They are well sign-posted and there is a small fee to get in. You do not need a guide but the trained guides are not expensive and they are knowledgeable about the local trees and plants.

Rainbow waterfall at Goldsborough is signposted off the main road. It lies on the private land of Hughford McKenna. Hugh is going to be busy for the next few years as he is secretary of agriculture, marine affairs, and the environment in the Tobago House of Assembly. However, his wife will be happy to arrange a guided tour for you, or you can also pay a reasonable fee (about $3 US per person) and she will put you on the right path. It is a delightful 15-minute walk through trees and meadows, with big stands of bamboos and small patches of bananas. The falls are magnificent in the rainy season, more of a trickle in the dry season, but at all times the pool below is delightful to swim in. If you come at a crowded time and prefer somewhere more private, they can direct you to another waterfall that is a considerably longer walk. The Mckenna's now have a bar and restaurant here, which I am sure is delightful and I hope to visit it soon.

Looking at a map of Tobago, the Hills-borough Dam stands out bright blue against the land. Although not mentioned in any tourist literature, it looked alluring, so we paid a visit. Parrots and kingfishers livened our drive along the twisty road and when we arrived we paid a nominal entry charge and signed the visitors' book. We were the only visitors in a week. We were entranced by the pretty lake and by the wildlife, including cormorants, anhingas, and herons. Best of all, we got to see several caimans, (small alligators), both swimming and sunning themselves on the bank. Take good binoculars. I am told the best bird watching is in the late afternoon.

As a break from all your driving, Richmond Great House makes a magnificent lunch or drink stop. It lies in the hills above the south coast main road, about 3 or 4 miles west of Roxborough. The gardens are replete with bearing fruit trees, including cashews and avocados. A swinging seat affords a bird's eye view over the swimming pool to the ocean in the distance. The estate house itself has been beautifully restored, with lots of antiques and Afro-art. For those who want a real night away from the boat, they have 10 rooms.

HERITAGE FESTIVAL

Tobago's Heritage Festival begins in mid-July and continues until early August. It is an annual celebration of the island's cultural and artistic history. The opening day's events take place at the cultural center in Shore Park, but then the center of activity moves from village to village each day. A boat is christened in the old way at Black Rock and then old style music, food, dances, even traditional ways of courting and marrying are re-lived, first in one village and then in the next.

SPORTS FISHING TOURNAMENT

Trinidadians are the main competitors in this tournament, owing to a lack of fueling and other facilities, but overseas visitors are very welcome and will enjoy this competition in delightful surroundings, usually with plenty of fish. It takes place in early May.

ANGOSTURA YACHTING WORLD REGATTA

A great way to visit Tobago is to join in this premier yachting event, sponsored by Angostura Rum and Yachting World magazine. The regatta takes a week, with two races on Monday, one on Tuesday, a lay day on Wednesday, and more races on Thursday and Friday. The racing is serious and to a very high standard in both the racing and the cruising class which operates under the CSA rating. Live-aboards are also catered to with a special easy course for those racing their houses. This class uses a PHRF, modified CSA or arbitrary handicap.

The parties and social life are great, and the regatta is small enough that you are bound to get to know a bunch of people, and it all takes placed early- to mid-May.

BUMBOAT RACES

Ask the tourist board for the dates of the next Bum Boat races and visit to see this spectacle, held at Store Bay. These are the local sail-powered fishing boats of yesteryear and attract competitors from as far away as Carriacou and Bequia.

opposite:
Angostura
Yachting World
Regatta

Tobago
roadside

Tobago

Fort George

**Page 144:
Scarborough
aerial**

**Scarborough
wall art**

SCARBOROUGH

Scarborough, the main town on Tobago, has had a tumultuous past. It was first settled by the Dutch Lampsin brothers and called Lampsinburg. Both the name and controlling power changed repeatedly from 1666 to 1803, when the British took the island from the French for the last time.

Today it is a lively town for its 17,000 inhabitants. People may tell you that Tobago is a calm and quiet backwater, the perfect antidote for the hectic pace of Trinidad, but if you arrive in Scarborough on a Friday or weekend you will be greeted by a whole week's worth of cheerful noise, with the population relaxing in the town's streets. Every other restaurant blasts music into the air and people are laughing, walking, talking, and selling food and trinkets from tiny stalls.

The new outer harbor wall makes Scarborough a protected anchorage and a good place to leave your boat while you explore the interior of the island.

The town is naturally divided into two areas. An older, more picturesque section, Upper Scarborough, is on hilly ground to the east of the harbor. To the north is Lower Scarborough, with a large new cruiseship and ferry dock with terminal, a modern market building, bus station, library, and shopping mall, along with an assortment of small enterprises. A large, conspicuous pink building stands out in Lower Scarborough, about a five-minute walk beyond the cruise ship dock.

NAVIGATION

Scarborough is upwind and current of anywhere you might come from, unless you make this your first landfall when crossing the Atlantic. A current of one to two knots sweeps westwards along the coast and right the way over to Trinidad. It is only about nine miles from Crown Point to Scarborough, but it can take about three hours to motor sail against wind and current to get there. If you are sailing from Trinidad, you will almost certainly have to motor sail hard on the wind so as not to be swept back to Crown Point.

If you are coming from Crown Point, stay well clear of the coastline to Lowlands Point. In addition, whichever way you come, be very careful to avoid the Bulldog Shoal. This is clearly marked by a beacon. Stay well outside this beacon and continue to the entrance beacons. You have to allow for the current that sweeps you into shallow water. Once you get past the entrance beacons, head into town.

The yacht anchoring area is inside an imaginary line (well, we have drawn it on our sketch chart, P.145), between the end of the breakwater and the end of the customs dock. You do need to leave a little room clear for the loading area just behind the sea

wall as barges pull in here. Do not anchor elsewhere in the harbor, though if you can stand the waves and roll, you can anchor outside the harbor wall.

Although Scarborough is well lit, strong currents and many shoals make it inadvisable to enter after dark without good local knowledge.

REGULATIONS

Scarborough is a port of entry. You should first visit Immigration; they are upstairs in the port building at the head of the cruise ship dock. Immigration hours are 0800-1600, Monday to Friday. They are also on duty on Saturday 0800-1200. On Saturday you will be charged for overtime.

Customs hours are Monday through Friday, from 0800-1600. And on Saturdays, Sundays, and holidays, 0600-1800. They are also often around later than the official hours on weekdays. Weekends and late entries include overtime charges. Should you arrive when immigration is closed, visit customs first and they will find an Immigration officer for you. You will pay your first 30 days navigation dues of $50TT when you arrive, and will be charged $50TT a month for any extra months you have stayed when you leave.

Tobago

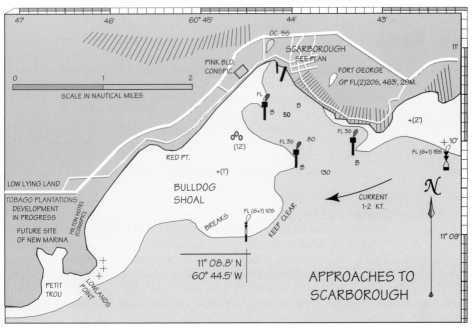

COMMUNICATIONS

Two e-mail stations will help you keep in touch. Jupiter Tech is upstairs in the Phillips Building on Burnett Street. He opens Monday to Friday 0900-1500 and on holidays, 0800-1200. You can make overseas calls here.

Andy Robert's Matrix Technology is upstairs in a building on Robinson Street, between Piggot and Main. It is well signposted. He opens daily from 0830 to 2030 and is often around later than these official hours. Andy is a good software and hardware person, so as well as doing your e-mail you can get help with computer problems.

SERVICES

Yachting is not yet big enough in Tobago for many services to have developed. Water is available at the base of the cruise ship dock, on the west side. Check with the Port Authority first at the cruise ship terminal. This is not a dock designed for yachts and is high off the water. Unless you are going to take on a large amount, it may be easier to jerry jug it. You will have to jerry jug fuel from one of the nearby gas stations (a short taxi ride away). They could also give you water.

On Carrington Street, opposite customs, there is a route taxi stand and you can use a taxi to transport provisions and fuel or arrange for a ride to other destinations. Ice is available from the supermarkets and gas stations.

SHOPPING

Supermarkets in Scarborough have a very local flavor and are well stocked with essentials, but don't expect anything too fancy. The supermarkets rarely have fresh produce, which is easily found in the market or at a street-side stand. Food Town, right opposite customs, is the closest. It opens Monday to Saturday, 0730-2000. New Port supermarket is one of the best and a little farther down the road. They open Monday to Thursday, 0800-2000, and Friday and Saturday, 0800-2100. When I looked, their frozen section was the only one with a good stock of frozen fish. Penny Sav-

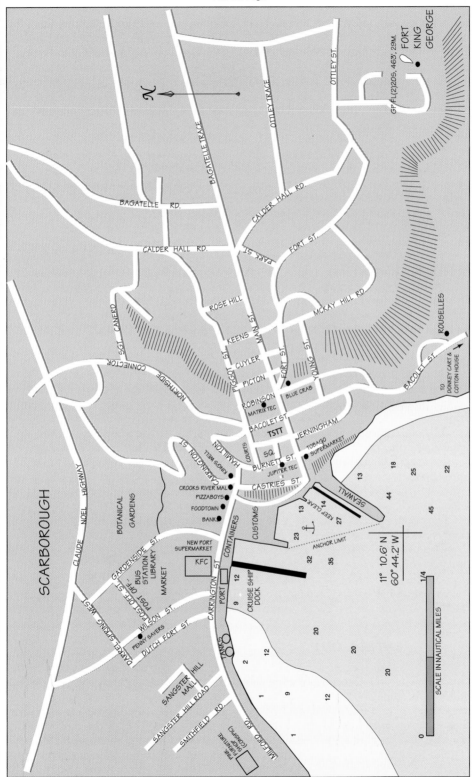

SCARBOROUGH

Tobago

FORT KING GEORGE

GP.FL(2)20S, 463', 29M.

OTTLEY ST.

OTTLEY TRACE

BAGATELLE TRACE

BAGATELLE RD.

CALDER HALL RD.

CALDER HALL RD.

PARK ST.

FORT ST.

ROSE HILL

MCKAY HILL RD.

ROUSELLES

KEENS

MAIN ST.

CUYLER

PIGOT ST.

PICTON

FORT ST.

YOUNG ST.

BACOLET ST.

TO DONKEY CART & COTTON HOUSE

NORTHSIDE CONNECTOR

SGT. CANE RD

ROBINSON

BLUE CRAB

MATRIX TEC

BACOLET ST.

JERNINGHAM

TSTT

SQ.

TOBAGO SUPERMARKET

CARRINGTON ST.

HAMILTON

COURTS

KING'S WELL

BURNETT ST.

JUPITER TEC

CASTRIES ST.

SEAWALL

CROOKS RIVER MALL

PIZZABOYS

FOODTOWN

BANK

CUSTOMS

CONTAINERS

KEEP CLEAR

ANCHOR LIMIT

13

18

25

22

13

44

27

14

13

45

23

CLAUDE NOEL HIGHWAY

BOTANICAL GARDENS

GARDENSIDE ST.

NEW PORT SUPERMARKET

KFC

PORT

32

35

LIBRARY

BUS STATION

MARKET

POST OFF. ST.

WILSON ST.

PENNY SAVERS

DARREL SPRING WEST

DUTCH FORT ST.

CRUISE SHIP DOCK

TANKS

20

20

20

SANGSTER HILL

SANGSTER HILL MALL

SANGSTER HILL ROAD

SMITHFIELD RD.

MILFORD RD.

PINK FURNITURE STORE (CONSPLO)

1

2

9

12

12

11° 10.6' N
60° 44.2' W

SCALE IN NAUTICAL MILES

1/4

0

ers is farther away on Wilson Street. They open Monday to Thursday, 0730-2000, and close half an hour later at 2030 on Friday and Saturday.

In the other direction, Tobago Supermarket, up the hill on Burnett Street, is open Monday to Friday, 0700-2000, Friday and Saturday, 0700-2100, and Sunday, 0700-1400.

The produce market behind the NIB Mall is large, with many fruits, vegetables, and fish. Vendors also sell local handicrafts, often artistically designed and well made, and usually constructed from eco-friendly materials. When you need cash, it is easy to find a bank as they are all over town.

The Crooks River Mall is on Carrington Street where it takes a sharp turn uphill. A mixture of shops sell clothing, arts and crafts, souvenirs, and jewelry. Check out the Culture House for arts and crafts and Home Zone for houseware. The Lunch Basket in this mall is a tiny restaurant where you can get a good lunch inexpensively. While in this area, take a look at the lovely old-fashioned Parker's Trading building, with its intricate gingerbread. One of the better pharmacies is in the same block.

Tobago Treasure is opposite customs and has a good collection of handicrafts.

Sports and Games is a fancy new store up on Burnett Street. Courts, block or so away, sells all kinds of household appliances, as well as a fair number of computers. Downstairs a big office store sells stationary and does photocopies.

The Cotton House is a batik studio just past the Old Donkey Cart House on Bacolet Street, where fabrics are hand waxed, painted, dyed, and made into comfortable garments. It is a good 15-minute walk from town.

EATING OUT

Scarborough has many cheap and cheerful bars and restaurants and loud music is often dished in such generous amounts that it is like eating in a discotheque. This can be fun, the prices are unbeatable, and the food is very local.

For the older at heart, there are three excellent restaurants where the fare is first

rate and the ambience delightful. Rouselle's ($B-C) is a 5-minute walk down Bacolet Street. It is upstairs and has a light airy feel. You can eat out on the balcony, or just while away some time at the bar, looking out over the sea. They offer a choice of full dinners that always include delicious soups and fresh local seafood, cooked to perfection. Lobster is often available. Open from 1800 to 2300, Tuesday to Saturday, it is advisable to book in advance.

The Old Donkey Cart House ($B-D) is a 10-minute walk beyond Rouselle's on Bacolet Street. It is set in a traditional plantation house that is over 100 years old. You sit and eat in the pleasant garden surrounded by flowers. The a-la-carte menu is about the largest in Tobago, with a choice of anything from lobster to pasta.

The Blue Crab ($B-C) is right in town on Robinson Street. It has a view over town to the bay. They are open for lunch everyday except Sundays, and will open for dinner by request. Expect good local food. Seafood is always available.

King's Well Inn ($D) is on Carrington Street. The food is local and inexpensive and if you wish you can sit outside and watch life on the street.

Fast food has now also come to Scarborough. A big Pizza Boys/Donut Boys is right opposite Customs and you can get food here all day long. It is handy for breakfast. If you prefer Kentucky Fried Chicken, their big building is near the market.

EXPLORING

The hilly part of Scarborough is capped by the ruins of Fort King George, which is set in an immaculately kept garden of flowering trees and shrubs. Nearly a dozen huge old saman trees add class, as well as shade, and support generations of epiphytes. The combination of the tended gardens and the magnificent views makes this a perfect place to relax. As for the rest, some buildings are in good repair, but the hurricane of 1847 blew the roofs off many structures. On the grounds is a local art gallery and The Tobago Museum at the fort is open from Monday to Friday, 0900 to 1630.

Hilton Hotel at Tobago Plantations

There is a small admission fee ($3TT adult, $1TT child).

There is also a botanical garden in town. Some areas of the garden are very pleasant, though they lack the drama and views found at the fort.

TOBAGO PLANTATIONS

A few miles along the coast, west of Tobago, a large tract of low-lying land is being extensively developed by Angostura. The first stage of the development, which includes a golf course and an elegant Hilton Hotel, is complete. Those who need a touch of international luxury will find everything they want here, including fancy restaurants and huge suites. The second stage of development is going ahead, with many luxurious homes for sale.

A marina is planned for the third phase. This will include not only property with private docks, but also a public facility for visiting yachts. It is unlikely to be finished during the life of this guide, but we will post updates on doyleguides.com. In the meantime, a visit to the hotel and building project is interesting, especially for those who might like a house in Tobago with minimum worry and upkeep.

STORE BAY

The western side of Tobago is low lying, with picture perfect, white sand beaches separated by rocky outcroppings. Much of the hotel activity on Tobago is concentrated around Crown Point, which also has the airport. Store Bay lies to the north of Crown Point and is the main anchorage.

NAVIGATION

If you are arriving from the north, stay well clear of Buccoo Reef to the north. If you are sailing from Scarborough, stay well clear of the shallow water on the western end of the south coast.

Store Bay is well protected, except in times of northerly swells. A cable supplying Tobago with electricity from Trinidad runs into Store Bay. The cable is well marked with a yellow sign ashore which is lit at night and by three yellow buoys that flash orange. The cable carries 33,000 volts, probably enough to turn your boat into something resembling Chinese firecrackers and simultaneously put all the lights out in Tobago.

Anchor to the south of all this, the bay is large; there is plenty of room.

Do not anchor close to the Crown Point Hotel or coastline to its west. There is a good diving reef all along this shore, which drops to about 45 feet. This reef is protected by law, anchor outside it.

SERVICES & COMMUNICATIONS

The Clothes Wash (and internet) Café is a great new institution for yachts. They open every day from 0800 to 2300. You can use the coin operated laundry machines while you relax, do your e-mail and enjoy their coffee and soft drinks bar. You can lounge around, reading magazines or books from the book swap. Roger or Lisa will help you in any way they can, and Dave will be there when you run into a computer problem. They all give good local advice. You can also drop your laundry off if you would prefer them to do it for you and they will take care of dry-cleaning.

Cyber Café is across from the airport.

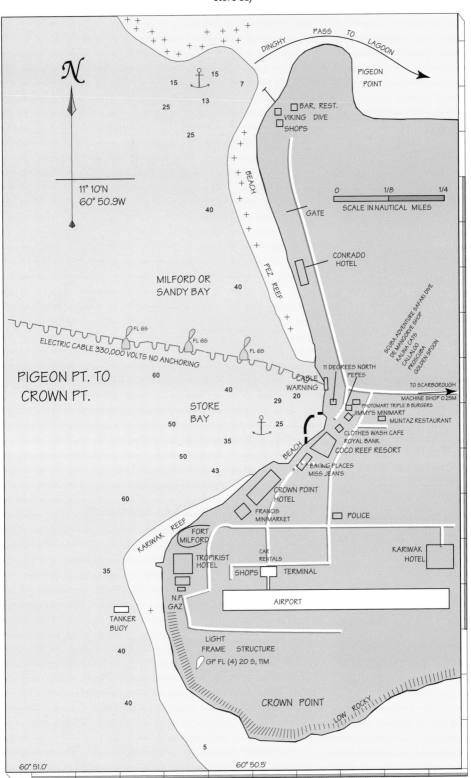

N

11° 10'N
60° 50.9W

DINGHY PASS TO LAGOON

PIGEON POINT

BAR, REST.
VIKING DIVE
SHOPS

SCALE IN NAUTICAL MILES
0   1/8   1/4

GATE

CONRADO HOTEL

MILFORD OR SANDY BAY

FL 65   FL 65   FL 65
ELECTRIC CABLE 330,000 VOLTS NO ANCHORING

PEZ REEF

BEACH

PIGEON PT. TO CROWN PT.

STORE BAY

CABLE WARNING

11 DEGREES NORTH
PEPES

TO SCARBOROUGH

MACHINE SHOP 0.25M

PHOTOMART TRIPLE B BURGERS
JIMMY'S MINIMART
MUNTAZ RESTAURANT

CLOTHES WASH CAFE
ROYAL BANK
COCO REEF RESORT

EATING PLACES
MISS JEAN'S

CROWN POINT HOTEL

FRANCIS MINIMARKET

POLICE

BEACH

KARIWAK REEF

FORT MILFORD

TROPIKIST HOTEL

CAR RENTALS

SHOPS   TERMINAL

KARIWAK HOTEL

N.P. GAZ

AIRPORT

TANKER BUOY

LIGHT FRAME STRUCTURE
GP FL (4) 20 S, 11M

CROWN POINT

LOW ROCKY

SCUBA ADVENTURE SAFARI DIVE
DE MANGROVE SHOP
KALINA CATS
CALLALOO
PROSCUBA
GOLDEN SPOON

Tobago

60° 51.0'

60° 50.5'

15   15
7
13
25
25
40
40
40
60
40
29   20
50
25
35
50
43
60
35
40
40
5
60
50

149

ELECTRIC CABLE

Aerial of Store Bay showing the location of the electrical cable.

Page 148: The public beach at Store bay

Selling t-shirts at regatta

This is a dedicated e-mail facility and has a big bank of machines. They open Monday to Friday from 0900-1900, on Saturdays till 2000 and on Sundays from 1500-2000.

The nearest gas station is about a mile down the road towards Scarborough. You would need to take a taxi. For cooking gas, go to NP at the west end of the airstrip.

TECHNICAL SERVICES

David Francis and his wife Wendy were just about to open the Francis Marine and Industrial Machine Shop. His location is on the main Scarborough road near the Sunshine hotel. It is about a quarter of a mile (easy walking distance) down the Scarborough road on the right hand side. He does all kinds of machining and fabrication and will help with mechanical and other problems.

SHOPPING

In Crown Point a lazy holiday attitude is widespread and there are plenty of shops and restaurants. The Royal Bank is on the main road just past the Coco Reef Resort. You will find another bank at the airport.

You can top up on provisions at Jimmie's Mini Mart on the main road open everyday from 0700 to 2300 or Francis Supermarket at the Crown Point Beach Hotel. They are open 0800 to 1800 except Sundays, and have some pharmaceutical items as well as a good selection of basics. Francis Supermarket sells ice and stocks beer and soda in cans, rather than bottles, especially for people on boats. Good fresh vegetables are available from a truck that parks just outside her shop every day except Sunday.

Two bigger supermarkets, Penny Savers and View Port are about a mile down the main road towards Scarborough. These are local in style, not the gleaming modern markets you might have got used to in Trinidad, but they have most basics. You will need to top up on fresh produce from vendors.

Boutiques at the airport include The News Stand for books, Karri for a wide range of handicrafts, including leatherwork, batik, pottery and carvings, and Native Instincts for gifts. All accept credit cards. Most of the larger hotels have small shops.

Many local vendors offer local crafts and paintings in the tourist facility behind the beach. More tourist shops can be found down the main road after the Coco Reef Resort, these include De Mangrove shop and Photo Mart who will develop your pictures.

EATING OUT

The restaurants range from local small buildings on the beach to more elegant hotel verandahs. Miss Jean's Local Dishes is the first of a series of small restaurants that serve big portions of down home food at very low prices. They are in the public area behind the beach. Sylvia, Esmie, Joicy and Alma all have restaurants in the same area. They are great for lunch, but tend to close about 1900, so if you want dinner go very early. This is a good place to try out Tobago's national dish; crab and dumpling.

Triple B Burgers is on the main road past the Coco Reef Resort, their fast food makes a change from local meals.

When you are ready for a bigger night out, the large hotels are happy to have guests and several good restaurants can be found. The newly opened Coco Reef Resort ($A-B), the fancy red roofed structure to the northeast of the beach, has a breakwater and it's own beach which makes dinghy access easy, they have two restaurants and bars.

The Bay Restaurant ($C) at the Crown Point Hotel is arranged around a pool with a view of the bay. They are open all day, handy for breakfast, lunch or dinner.

The Kariwak Village ($B) is back from the beach, but has a pleasant dining room and pool shaded by lush garden plants. They have a set four-course dinner with a choice of main courses and fresh seafood is always available.

Muntaz ($C) is an excellent Indian restaurant a short walk away. They serve traditional East Indian rather than Trinidad Indian cooking. The ambience is acceptable, the cooking good.

Eleven Degrees North ($B) is a very elegant restaurant with a good chef and pleasant patio ambience. Just opposite, Pepe's ($C) will also turn out a good meal at a fair price.

Other restaurants in the area include the Jimmie's ($C) Golden Spoon ($C) and the Callaloo ($C).

EXPLORING

While you are walking around, look at the remains of Fort Milford just past the Crown Point Hotel. These ruins are in a tidy small park overlooking both Store Bay and Milford Bay. Benches under the almond trees offer yet another shady spot to sit and relax. The British built this fort in 1777. It was built on the site of an early Dutch redoubt that occupied the site from 1642 to 1660.

For going further afield, you can rent a bike at the roadside or you can rent cars at the airport and on many of the surrounding streets.

Tobago

WATER SPORTS

Goran who runs the Viking Dive Shop (VHF: 71) is a yachtperson who has sailed all over the Caribbean and he will go out of his way to help people on yachts. He has an outlet in a small tourist shop right outside the Crown Point Hotel. His actual facility is down at Conrado Hotel.

Proscuba and Scuba Adventure Safari Dive are both on the main drag at Store Bay. Proscuba is run by Marco and Sharon Priester from the Netherlands and between them they speak Dutch and German as well as English. They are a Padi Shop and sell and service dive and snorkeling gear.

The western end of Tobago is a popular area for diving. The easiest dive to do on your own is the reef right off the Crown Point Hotel. It is a pleasant reef with lots of small fish that starts in shallow water and drops to about 45 feet. Watch out for current at the western part. However, currents are strong for the more exciting dives, which are best done as drift dives with the local dive shop. One dive, called Flying Reef, is off the southwest coast. This is an undulating reef at 60 feet with plenty of hard and soft corals. You are likely to see turtles, stingrays, eels, lobsters, barracudas, and nurse sharks. The Shallows (on Drew Shoal) is an advanced drift dive in up to 90 feet. You dive over a coral bank richly textured with drop-offs and changing contours. You are likely to see black-tipped sharks, hammerhead sharks, barracudas, turtles, groupers and stingrays. Mt. Irvine Wall off Mt. Irvine Bay is a wall dropping to about 60 feet. There are amazing underwater caves and tunnels that you can swim through and you will see lots of lobsters, eels, and a variety of reef fish including snappers and groupers.

PIGEON POINT

Pigeon Point is about a mile north of Store Bay. This anchorage is beautiful with the reef on one side and Pigeon Point on the other. It can roll somewhat, especially at high tide, but it is more protected from the north than Store Bay. It should be noted that Pigeon Point beach is the only privately owned beach in Tobago. This anchorage is part of the Buccoo Reef Restricted area and sometimes they allow yachts here and sometimes they do not. They look more favorably on those with holding tanks.

This anchorage has the advantage of being well protected and having a dinghy dock where you can easily get ashore. You will have to pay a fee to be here, but it is reasonable. The disadvantage is that is a long walk down to Store Bay for all the shops and facilities. It would work very well if you were also renting a car.

NAVIGATION

Eyeball your way in, favoring the Buccoo Reef side. Anchor just south of the reef in about 15-18 feet of water. Try to choose a patch of sand, as there are a few soft and hard corals that could be harmed, especially in the shallower depths. There is also a dinghy passage around Pigeon Point into Bon Accord Lagoon.

SERVICES

Club Pigeon Point welcome yachts and requires you to register with them if you anchor off their beach. The office is downstairs behind the main restaurant and marked administration. They charge TT$100 per boat per week for a couple plus TT$25 for each additional person. This allows you full use of the facilities and use of the inner part of the dock (the narrow part) for your dinghy. Dinghies must not be left on the beach. They provide toilets, showers and garbage disposal bins. The office can help you with phone calls and faxes and if you are using their car park for your rental car, you must discuss it with them first. Water is for sale and available on the dock. Check out the depths carefully and remember the 3-foot tides. You need to take water at a time you will not conflict with the commercial tour boats that come and go. Discuss it with the management.

Pets are not allowed on Pigeon Point so do not bring them ashore. The gate normally closes at 1900, so if you expect to come in late you need to make arrangements with security so that you will be able to get back to the car park.

Aerial of
Pigeon Point
showing the
southern half of
Buccoo Reef.

BUCCOO REEF AND BON ACCORD LAGOON

ASHORE

A cluster of small buildings houses the facilities at Club Pigeon Point. You will find a couple of restaurants and several boutiques for clothing, handicrafts, block-outs and other essentials. This is a daytime facility and everything closes at night.

Down the road towards Crown Point, the Conrado Hotel has a bar and restaurant and boutique. Local craft vendors' facilities have been put in opposite the hotel, but were unoccupied in 2001.

WATER SPORTS

Buccoo Reef is great for snorkeling, and one of the advantages of the Pigeon Point anchorage is that you are within swimming distance of the reef. It should be noted that this whole area is a national park and fishing or collecting shells or corals is forbidden.

David Byrne's Wild Turtle Dive Safari is based here and can take you diving. It is a Padi dive shop and they limit their diving to 8 people per trip. They have two covered dive boats that carry oxygen.

REGULATIONS

Buccoo reef is one of Tobago's national parks. All the marine life is protected and fishing is not allowed, nor is removing or harming corals, shells or other sea-life, anchoring your yacht here is not allowed. Buccoo Reef offers miles of good snorkeling with lots of fish and it is easily explored by dinghy. You should be very careful when you anchor your dinghy not to damage any coral. Watch out for the current.

Bon Accord Lagoon, also a national park, is the most protected anchorage in Tobago but is also restricted and can only be used in the case of a hurricane. The beach on No Man's Land is quite delightful and very popular for daytime picnics on weekends. Both No Man's Land and the lagoon are easily accessible by dinghy from Pigeon Point or Store Bay.

NAVIGATION

This is all a restricted area; we only give navigation instructions in case you need to shelter from a hurricane.

Finding your way into the deep area inside Buccoo Reef is no problem. Approach from the south when the light is good and follow the outer reef, keeping a safe distance off. The false channel is quite narrow and easy to identify. The next channel is the real one. If visibility is not good, go to the southern of the two large reef marker buoys (Pigeon). Head slightly to the right of the next (northeastern) marker buoy (Buccoo). Before long you will see breaking water ahead of you on the north side of the entrance channel. After that, eyeball your way in.

Having said that, both of these buoys were missing in May 2001. One was parked in Milford Bay. This caused some confusion during the first race at race week when they were indicated as course markers! They should be back in place soon,

but one has been out for six months at thi point. This is a good illustration of how dan gerous it is to rely on local navigational aid in the Caribbean.

The channel into the lagoon is a littl less than four feet at low water and abou six to seven feet at high water. This is a comfortable channel for yachts drawin up to five feet and a possible channel fo boats with six-foot draft. While slightl deeper draft boats can make it in, it doe not leave any room for error. Since ther is lots of coral and some swell, the en trance should not be undertaken lightl Unless you know the area well, go in on a rising tide.

The long twisty channel into the la goon is marked by green stakes (mainl iron pipes with sticks in them) which yo leave close on your port side. There is als one obvious starboard stake right near th end, pass outside the murky colored wa ter marking the sand spit, but do not g too far over toward the other side as that too, is shoal. Inside the lagoon there is a vast anchoring area, with about 10 feet o water.

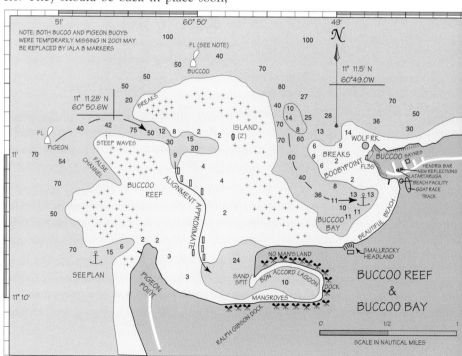

BREAKING

8-14 FT

Approach to Buccoo

ASHORE

Bon Accord Lagoon is a large mangrove area, and quite a few birds use the mangroves for roosting at night. There are two small docks where you can get ashore. The Ralph Gibson dock allows you access to the road. Tie your dinghy up in the mangrove trees so you won't be in anyone's way.

BUCCOO BAY

Buccoo Bay is a pleasant, quite well protected anchorage, and on most days of the week Buccoo is a peaceful waterside village. This all changes on a Sunday night at 2200 when they have what is known as Sunday School. People come from all over the island for an all night fete of drinking, merry making and music so powerful you can hear it to Pigeon Point. Drinks and food are available all evening long to keep you going. Buccoo village also hosts another famous national event, an annual goat race, which takes place on the Tuesday following Easter Monday.

Buccoo has a gorgeous beach and

there are several boatmen here who make their living taking people out to Buccoo Reef or arranging picnics on No Man's Land.

NAVIGATION

The approach to Buccoo is not quite as bad as it looks on the charts, but you should approach in sunlight when you can see the shoals. You would not want to enter in large swells. More people seem to run aground here than elsewhere so if you are not a first rate reef navigator, give it a miss.

If you are coming from the west, pass outside Buccoo Reef, staying outside the buoys.

A good place to start your approach is outside Buccoo Reef on the eastern side opposite the small sand island. Stay close to Buccoo reef and head for the rocky area that interrupts the beach. You can keep track of your position by noting when the low island lines up with Pigeon Point and later when Rocky Point and Booby Point line up. (See also Mt. Irvine Bay sketch chart.)

Try to eyeball your way past the 8-14 foot patch. If you find yourself in it, it is

probably best to edge back out into deeper water. Look for the 2-foot patch that breaks, even in moderate seas. This should be well to your east, but it is part of the shoal patch you have to avoid. Eyeball your way past this, staying way over on the Buccoo reef side of the channel in water 30 to 50 feet deep. As you get past the shoal area, ease around and head toward the village, passing over water that is mainly 11 to 13 feet deep. Anchor in about 13 feet between Booby Point and the small rocky outcropping on the beach opposite.

There is a good little dock for leaving your dinghy.

ASHORE

Esse's, just down the road on the right, is a small mini market and general store. Local vendors also sell fresh produce right by the roadside.

Right next to La Tartaruga is the New Reflections, a boutique with an unusual but attractive loose pebble floor that sells all locally made items of clothing, arts and crafts.

Drop into Hendrix Hideaway ($D). Hendrix is a real character, and usually several locals gather here to chat and joke. Hendrix will keep you amused and serve you food. A simple snack is always available, but for more elaborate meals give him notice and the longer it is the better the food will be.

Happy Lil Vibe ($D) is connected with the Miller Guest House and opposite the dock. They serve light lunches from 1100-1300 and dinner every day from 1930-2100. They usually cook just a couple of dishes with a choice of meat or seafood. Owner's Cecil and Cindy will welcome you.

Buccoo's fanciest restaurant is La Tartaruga ($C closed Sunday and Monday). It is in a pleasant modern building right by the dock. It opens for dinner only and serves good Italian food.

The Seaside Garden Café serves meals to order and they keep a couple of sociable parrots. Zan's Village Inn ($D) is owned by Vernon Brizan. They are open all day and can cook you a meal, but will need a couple of hours notice. They also rent very cheap rooms.

You will probably want a rental car or taxi to take you to Shivan's Watermill, which is on the road between Buccoo and Crown Point. Well worth the effort for a special night out in this elegant restaurant, one of Tobago's best.

MOUNT IRVINE

MOUNT IRVINE BAY

This is a prosperous and attractive resort area with a good public beach. The anchorage inside Rocky Point is gorgeous with interesting rocks and a beach backed by a thicket of coconut palms and trees. You can scramble over the rocks to lovely small beaches on the point. The reef here is very good for snorkeling and diving with an abundance of sea life, both large and small. The Mount Irvine Hotel, which overlooks the bay, is built on the site of a sugar plantation that was owned by Charles Irvine in the second half of the 18th century.

NAVIGATION

The approach is easy. Anchor in the northeast corner off the bay, behind the local fishing boats. Keep well away from the reef.

ASHORE

The public beach facility ashore, on the northern side, boasts the Surfers Restaurant ($C) open everyday 0730 to 2300. You can get good local food here including Bake & Fish. The staff may also be able to arrange for to have your laundry done. The restaurant is often lively on Sunday afternoons with a calypso singer from 1600-1800. Next door the Ocean View Arts and Crafts Shop is a local cooperative that

Windsurfing at Pigeon Point

Opposite: Buccoo Village

Chart inset: Mt. Irvine beach

Tobago

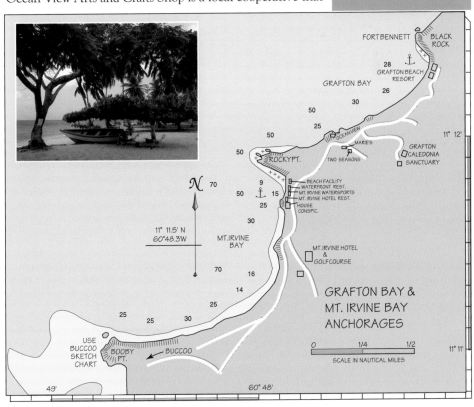

GRAFTON BAY &
MT. IRVINE BAY
ANCHORAGES

stocks locally made handicrafts, fabrics, t-shirts and a few jams and sauces. Mt. Irvine Water Sports Center has a phone that can be used for a small fee. The bus to Scarborough passes about every half-hour.

Just down the road the Mt. Irvine Bay Hotel is one of Tobago's fanciest hotels and has the island's oldest golf course. For a fee you can enjoy this or play tennis. Equipment for both sports is available. The Mt. Irvine Bay Hotel also has elegant restaurants. The Sugar Mill ($B) is built by the side of the pool with a panoramic view of the bay beside a well-restored sugar mill that is over 200 years old. Le Beau Ravage ($A), with a French trained chef, offers fancy cuisine, blending French knowhow with local produce.

There is another local bar about a 10-minute walk in the direction of Plymouth, which sits atop a rocky hill overlooking the ocean. It is called appropriately enough the Ocean View Bar ($D) open everyday, 0800 to 2200 serving drinks and local food prepared by Pearl Legerton. Across the road is Marie's Place open Monday-Saturday 0800 to 2000 and on Sunday 0900 to 1700. This is a new two-story structure with a restaurant

on the top floor and a very well stocked and laid out market and boutique on the ground floor. Right next door to this is the Two Seasons Restaurant, ($C-D) run by Sue, and specializing in local food and pizza, as well as having fresh baked bread on sale. On Friday nights stalls are set up to sell snacks on the little green opposite the Two Seasons from about 1800.

Also of interest in this area is the Grafton Caledonia Bird and Wildlife Sanctuary, accessible via a road that branches off the main road. This used to be an estate, but, when the nearby forest was wrecked by Hurricane Flora in 1963, birds sought food nearer to human habitation and the owners adopted these feathered orphans - feeding, watering and protecting them. Motmots are among the many colorful birds that can be seen on the nature trail. The best time to come for bird watching is early morning or at sunset. There is no charge, but visitors are not allowed at night.

WATER SPORTS

The Mt. Irvine Water sports Center is right on the road. Kay Seetal will probably greet you and you may get to meet

Bertrand Bhikarry. They can arrange any kind of trip for you from hiking to diving. Bertrand owns two stables and offers horse riding. From his nearby stable the riding will mainly be coastal, but he also has property in Argyle from where he arranges forest rides and hikes and bird watching trips. If things are not too busy, they will probably help you out with phone calls both local and international.

There are good dives along the coast. Arnos Vale Reef is an easy 30-foot dive, with lots of rocks encrusted with hard and soft corals and sponges with lots of reef fish. Englishman's Bay has rocks and walls dropping to 80 feet. These are well encrusted with marine life and support angelfish and parrotfish; turtles are sometimes seen.

GRAFTON BAY

Grafton Bay was used as one of the overnight anchorages during the annual Angostura Yachting World Regatta held in the early part of May. Although usually rolly, one can reduce this with the use of a second anchor to hold the bow or stern into the swell. The best place to anchor is close under the north point behind the fishing boats in about 30-feet of water. Landing your dinghy on the beach can be a wet affair; it is best to do this right up on the north end of the beach.

NAVIGATION

The approach is easy, The Grafton Beach Hotel and the larger pink Le Gran Courlan hotel beside it are easy to identify.

ASHORE

The Grafton Beach Hotel has several shops selling crafts, gifts, books, film, clothes and pharmacy items. There is also a beauty salon and car rental agency. Out on the point, what is left of Fort Bennett is surrounded by a little park with great views up and down the coast. A pleasant spot to sit for a while, doing very little. The hotel has a restaurant.

GREAT COURLAND BAY, PLYMOUTH

Plymouth is a delightful small town set on a hill above a long pristine beach on which turtles lay their eggs. One can sit for hours anchored close to Pelican Rock watching the antics of the seabirds. In the spring and summer when the laughing gulls are here, they badger the poor pelicans mercilessly, trying to steal the pelicans' fish by sitting on their heads and pecking at their bills. The pelicans have learned to keep their beaks underwater and spin in circles to get rid of the gulls before they lift their beaks to swallow their catch. We woke at dawn one morning to the sound of a

floating flowers and leaves, Parlatuvier

Opposite: Mount Irvine Bay

Tobago

Barrel of Beef

**Great
Courland Bay**

**Chart inset:
Fort James**

**Kelvin carving
bamboo**

heavy downpour. When we came on deck the source of the noise turned out to be tiny jumping fish that were so plentiful all the water in the bay was boiling. A flock of about a thousand seabirds, mainly gulls, pelicans and roseate terns crisscrossed the bay snatching at the fish and calling to each other.

Plymouth was the first English capital of Tobago and the site of a very early Dutch settlement in 1628. Later the Duke of Courland established a settlement here. The Swedes captured the Duke and imprisoned him for a short time. While he was safely out of circulation, the Dutch grabbed Tobago. When he was free, the Duke got his godfather, Charles II of England, to give him a hand and the Dutch were expelled. After this the English kept a garrison of 50 men at Fort James but the French outwitted them. Twenty-five French soldiers sailed into Courland Bay at night, sneaked close to the fort and made an enormous racket the next morning, giving the impression that there were hundreds of soldiers. The leader of the French force sought out the English commander and told him his position was hopeless, as there were thousands of French soldiers poised to attack. The English commander, who had not yet had his first cup of tea, surrendered on the spot.

The indefatigable Duke of Courland claimed sovereignty again in 1682 in a joint venture with an Englishman, John Poyntz. Poyntz's role was to attract settlers and as part of his mission he wrote and published a description of Tobago that was so enticing that it is believed to have inspired Daniel Defoe to write Robinson Crusoe. Crusoe is quite a popular figure on Tobago. His cave has been identified, car rental agencies are named in his honor and a dive shop commemorates Man Friday.

Both the ruins of Fort James, now surrounded by a park, and a famous tombstone bring tourists to Plymouth. The large tombstone, for 23-year old Betty Stiven and her baby, dates from 1783 and states mysteriously that "she was a mother without knowing it, and a wife without letting her husband know it, except by her kind indulgence to him."

NAVIGATION

About 200 yards southwest of Pelican Rock is a sunken rock, two feet underwater, called Barrel of Beef. It is part of a chain of rocks that extend from Pelican Rock. The rest of them are about 10 feet deep. Keep well clear of this area and approach Plymouth from the beach side.

Anchor off the dock in about 25 feet of water. Do not anchor off the Turtle Beach

Hotel; fishermen seine net here and you will be in the way.

If there is a surge, you may find you can make yourself more comfortable by using a stern anchor to keep your stern to the seas.

ASHORE

There are several small supermarkets down the main road. Check also Price Right on the road to Arnos Vale. If you want to do a large provisioning, it is only a short ride by bus, taxi or route taxi to Scarborough.

Out on the fort you might find some handicrafts. Kelvin sometimes hangs out here, busily carving Bamboo into art and if Calypsonian Rafael Davis is around he will royally entertain you.

There are only two restaurants in town. When I wandered into TJ's (right by the gas station), Anton told me they serve the best

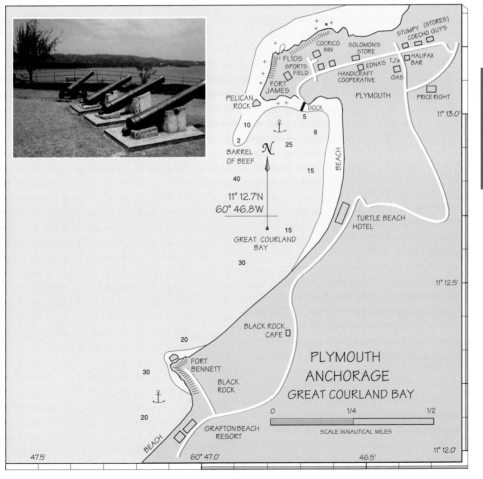

food in Tobago, with great local dishes including fish, pork and crab. Since Anton is the barman he might be biased, but both he and Kurt, the chef, were cool guys and you will enjoy a meal here. They are open all day every day.

The Cocrico Inn also serves good local food at a reasonable price.

If you wander down to the Rex Turtle Beach Resort you will find a well-stocked boutique and a choice of places to eat. The Kiskadee ($B), has something special every night with entertainment that varies from a brass band, fire eating and limbo to folk dancing and a one man band. On different nights they have barbecues, buffets, set dinners and a la carte menus. There is also a coffee shop/beach bar where you can while away the hours, buy snack type meals, and listen to a steel band, (usually Saturdays). Tuesdays at 1730 David Rooks gives a nature talk on the various tours available in Tobago, including the rainforest and Little Tobago.

Just north of Plymouth is Adventure Farm, open everyday except Saturdays. It is a 12-acre estate that specializes in organic fruits. For about US$3 they will take you on a guided tour and point out the different trees, flowers and wildlife. Many of the trees and plants are labeled, and feeders scattered around bring the birds in close. They sell refreshments and a variety of fresh fruits.

A little further along the same road is the romantic Arnos Vale Hotel ($B) which is built out of an old plantation in a heavily forested hill that slopes to the sea. The restaurant is cool and breezy, in a large colonial room with antique furniture and a muralled wall. It overlooks the sea, and birdfeeders attract a large variety of birds in a daylong show. It is within walking distance of Plymouth and the snorkeling is reputedly good enough to be worth taking your gear over.

WATER SPORTS

Turtle Beach Hotel has a water sports shop for renting windsurfers or small sailboats, or for water skiing. They also have a dive shop; Tobago Dive Experience, and are well placed for good dives up and down the coast.

PLYMOUTH TO MAN OF WAR BAY

Once you have rounded Barrel of Beef in Plymouth, you can sail east along the shore all the way to Bloody Bay, and a quarter of a mile offshore clears all dangers. If the wind is east or south of east Tobago gives some protection from the seas and the sailing is usually very pleasant. After Bloody Bay you can pass between the Sisters and the Brothers. The two off-lying sunken Brothers are a danger, though you can often see one of them breaking. If you cannot see it, stay at least halfway over to the Sisters from the Brothers that you can see.

Several small anchorages lie between Plymouth and Man of War Bay. These can be wonderful calm overnight anchorages, or they can be so rolly it is impossible to land a dinghy on the shore. The only way to know is to go and look. If they are rolly, or conditions are not settled, it is better to consider them as daytime anchorages. We have not included Bloody Bay as this is poorly protected in most conditions.

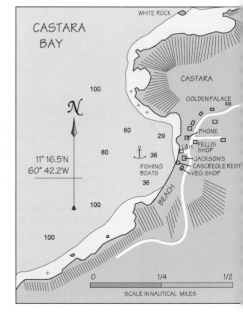

CASTARA BAY

Castara is a small fishing village set on a lovely beach with steep hills to the south.

NAVIGATION

The approach is clear of shoals. If you are coming from or leaving to the east, pass outside the conspicuous White Rock.

The best protection is tucked right up in the northeast corner off the beach, but this area is used for seine netting, so it is better to anchor outside the fishing fleet in about 36 feet of water. Landing on the beach can be risky if there is a swell.

ASHORE

Castara Beach

Loris and Hazel's L&H shop is right behind the beach, they open daily from 0800-2100. If the shop looks closed, shout up at the restaurant upstairs. If what you need is not here, try Jackson's Grocery, Fellis Shop or the Vegetable Shop. There is a card phone opposite Fellis store.

L&H ($D) also have a restaurant upstairs over their shop serving local food.

On the beach is the Cascreole restaurant ($D) where you can get excellent local fish and chicken. Tourists tend to come here and they have a curious eating platform built into the palm trees. They told me that soon they would rebuild the restaurant.

Tobago

ENGLISHMAN'S BAY AERIAL

If you walk up the hill on the road out of town heading east, you come to Ernest McKnight's Golden Palace ($D). Here you can get good rotis, chicken and chips, plus snacks.

ENGLISHMAN'S BAY

Scooped out of the rocky, forested coastline with a flawless golden beach at its head, Englishman's Bay makes a spectacular anchorage. The calmest and best spot is off the beach tucked up close to the eastern shore. Here you will find a large shelf of sand about 25 feet deep. If you see a small boat with a seine net anchored in the middle of the bay,

be prepared to move while they fish. You will be out of their way tucked down in the southern part of the bay. Return when they have finished, because, should a swell come up in the night, the southern part of the bay could be very bad. If there are fishermen around and the southern part of the bay is too rolly to be tenable, carry on to Parlatuvier Bay or to Man of War Bay.

ASHORE

Englishman's Bay is all part of Englishman's Bay Estate, which is a nature preserve and a low-key development for nature lovers. The scenery here is gorgeous, so walks in any direction, on or off the road, are rewarding. There is a picnicking and barbecuing facility at the western end of the beach that you are welcome to use. There is also a hut with a snack bar and boutique called One Stop Shop run by Ula.

WATER SPORTS

The snorkeling along the rocky eastern side of the bay is good, there are walls dropping to 80 feet. These are well encrusted with marine life and support angelfish, parrotfish and all the usual reef fish. In addition you are likely to see turtles. If there is any swell running, the water may be murky.

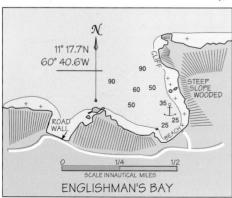

ENGLISHMAN'S BAY

ENGLISHMAN'S BAY

PARLATUVIER BAY, BELOW:

PARLATUVIER BAY

The northeast coast gets progressively higher, steeper and wilder as you sail from west to east. The black rocks that edge the sea give way to a band of light colored grasses in the dry season. Above are vivid green shrubs, dull yellow bamboos and big patches of waving balisiers. Interspersed among these you will see the glint of silver thatch palms.

Parlatuvier Bay is considerably more protected than the previous anchorages and it, too, is very picturesque with a long white sand beach and a small fishing vil-lage. There is a long and high concrete dock on the north side of the bay. Water is avail-able on the dock and a lower section can be used to tie up your dinghy.

Anchor off the fishing fleet in about 40 feet of water. It is unwise to anchor in the south side of the bay as it is used for seine netting.

ASHORE

You can buy essentials at the Chance Variety Store. Mr. and Mrs. Chance also run a guest house and are happy to see visitors. There is a card phone opposite their shop. A

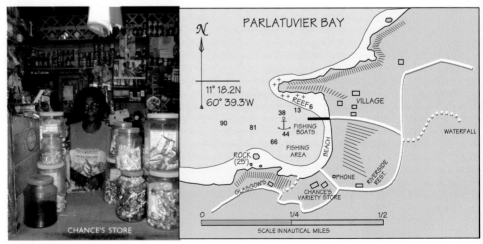

CHANCE'S STORE

little ways up the road and sitting high up on stilts, is the Riverside Restaurant ($C-D) open everyday for lunch and dinner, a very local and entertaining establishment. You can ask them for information about hiking in the area; several waterfalls are a hike away in addition to the one mentioned below. A dive shop had been set up below the restaurant.

Parlatuvier's delightful small waterfall makes a great destination for a short walk. Follow the road that leads off the dock, cross over the main highway and continue on a grassy track. You will quickly come to a river. Follow the river upstream, the surrounding country is lush and green with large bamboo stands. You will shortly come to the waterfall. It is in three tiers with pools ideal for swimming. A few years ago it was used as a water source and the top tier is dammed. You will see the remains of old pipes

Glasgow's bar is on top of the hill at the southern end of the bay. You can take a shortcut by using a path that goes uphill from the end of the beach. Glasgow's has a spectacular view of the bay and is great place to take a drink. Otherwise there is not much to do except watch the fishermen or laze on the beach.

MAN OF WAR BAY AND CHARLOTTEVILLE

Man of War Bay is a spectacularly beautiful natural harbor. Nearly two miles wide and a mile deep, it is surrounded by steep convoluted hills of tropical forest with many small valleys and dainty beaches. If you are lucky enough to come during the dry season when glowing yellow trees light the hills, you may have trouble putting your camera down.

Charlotteville is a pleasant sleepy town on a long beach in Man of War Bay's southeastern corner. Until the 1930's when a decent road was built, most of Charlotteville's business was conducted by sea. It was a thriving agricultural area and by 1865 several small estates were joined into a 1100-acre

Tobago

PARLATUVIER FALLS

holding owned by the Turpin family. As in many other parts of the Caribbean, diverse plantings were all given over to sugar cane production in the early years of slavery. Cotton, cocoa and bananas have since risen and fallen in prominence.

Fish production in the bay has always been good and a fishing cooperative has been set up to market the catch, which comprises about half Tobago's total. Much of the fishing is done by seine net. Spotters on the hills look for arriving shoals of fish and direct the fishermen below to encircle them. On a bountiful day hundreds of good-sized fish are netted.

One or two adventure cruise ships now visit Charlotteville. The government has plans for a big Cruise Ship facility here, which may run against the feelings of the local residents who have not been consulted. Many of us hope the beauty and ambience of Charlotteville will not be ruined.

NAVIGATION

Avoid the western side of Man of War Bay, which is rough and has at least one sunken rock. The eastern side of the bay is well protected, though it would be uncomfortable in a northerly swell. Since fishing is vitally important you cannot anchor off the beach areas where seine netting is done.

When you think about anchoring in Charlotteville, get in the mindset you are going to be in deep water. The best anchorage is outside the fishing fleet, anywhere north of the gas station. The holding is good but it is 60 to 70 feet deep so you will need lots of anchor line. If you anchor further north up outside Pirate's Bay you might be able to find water more like 40-50 feet deep. However, make sure you anchor outside a line between the end of the Charlotteville dock and the northern headland of Pirate Bay. Our last guide showed an anchorage in much shallower water in the very north end of this bay. However, having yachts anchor there has created a few problems with fishermen and locals, and questions of pollution

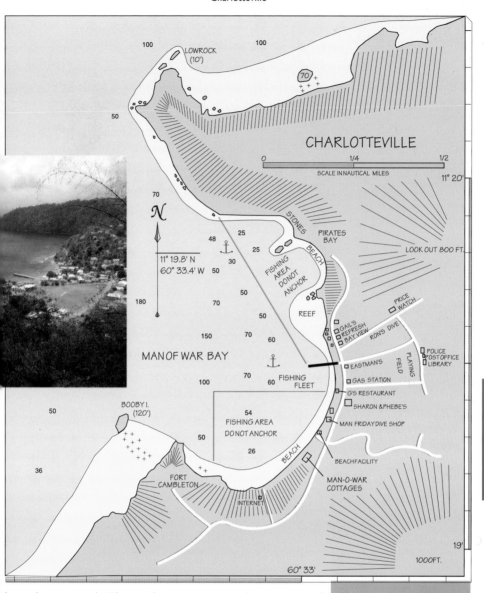

CHARLOTTEVILLE

0   1/4   1/2
SCALE IN NAUTICAL MILES

11° 20'

11° 19.8' N
60° 33.4' W

N

LOWROCK
(10')

100   100

70

50

70

48   25

25

30

50

50

50

70   60

70

60   FISHING
FLEET

100

54
FISHING AREA
DO NOT ANCHOR

50

26

STONES BEACH

PIRATES
BAY

LOOK OUT 800 FT.

FISHING
AREA
DO NOT
ANCHOR

REEF

180   70

150

MAN OF WAR BAY

BOOBY I.
(120')

50

36

FORT
CAMBLETON

BEACH

INTERNET

PRICE
WATCH

GAIL'S
REFRESH
BAY VIEW

RON'S DIVE

PLAYING FIELD

POLICE
POST OFFICE
LIBRARY

EASTMAN'S

GAS STATION

G'S RESTAURANT

SHARON & PHEBE'S

MAN FRIDAY DIVE SHOP

BEACH FACILITY

MAN-O-WAR
COTTAGES

19'

1000 FT.

60° 33'

Tobago

have been raised. The anchorage area we show is out of everyone's way and will help foster good relations with the local community. Instituting moorings here instead of allowing anchoring is a strong possibility, and as the water is deep it would be very helpful. If this happens appropriate charges will be instituted.

Make sure you are anchored well clear of any reefs including the one that extends to sea between town and Pirate's Bay.

REGULATIONS

Charlotteville is a port of entry and may have a customs and immigration station soon. In the meantime you can sail in

Charlotteville waterfront views

here, anchor and hoist your yellow flag. Walk to the police station and ask the officer in charge (if you are lucky it will be acting Sergeant Dillon who is very helpful) if he would be so kind as to call the customs and immigration authorities in Scarborough to let them knows you are here. They will probably instruct you to come to Scarborough to clear by bus, but they have been known to tell you to wait while they come up. If you have a boat with a phone, the best thing is to call customs and immigration in advance and tell them when you will be arriving. (Customs: 868-639-2415, immigration: 868-639-2681.)

SERVICES

You can jerry jug diesel, gasoline and kerosene from the gas station, which also sells ice. (If they are out there is a fishing place opposite that sells ice and smoked fish.) The dock has a small, low section on the north side where you can tie up your dinghy.

For laundry, local information and rooms for a night ashore contact Sharon at Sharon and Phebe's Restaurant.

For e-mail, walk down the beach, past the Man of War cottages and right on till you see a road leading up from the beach. Shenda's house is second on the left and you will see an internet sign outside. You can do e-mail here from 0900-1600, Shenda's sister Shenelle is usually in charge.

On the far side of the playing field next to the police station and post office is a large, modern and air-conditioned library. Here you can sit and cool out for a few hours and enjoy a wide variety of reading material.

Route taxis leave for Scarborough in the mornings.

SHOPPING

Charlotteville is a sleepy seaside village where no one is in a hurry and it is easy to make friends. Bay View Shopping is run by the Greenidge family and right at the head of the town dock. You can stock up here on most essentials. They open every day from 0700-2030. Check out also Price Watch further down the same road.

For fresh fruits and vegetables just walk down the waterfront and look at the outdoor stands and little mini-shops. Mineta's often has fresh produce among others. Anytime you hear the sound of a conch shell, come in to buy fish. This is a great place for fresh fish.

For souvenirs, check out Maurice's handicrafts in the open stand behind the dock. He works with calabash, seeds and bamboo, all ecologically sound.

EATING OUT

Eating out in Charlotteville is entertaining, low key, local and very inexpensive. Sharon and Phebe's ($D) is the fanciest restaurant with a delightful ambiance, neat tablecloths and a lovely view of the bay below. Sharon was the first person in Charlotteville to take a positive attitude towards yachts and she is fond of her yachting customers. The original restaurant was a cute, tiny wooden building. In 2000 it burnt down and the new even fancier restaurant was built in the same spot, this time in less flammable concrete.

Sharon and Phebe's is open everyday from 0900 onwards, though if you want dinner come before 2030. They serve excellent local food and the fish is delicious. On Sundays, when there are enough yachts in the harbor, they offer a yachty special with even lower prices for both drinks and meals from about 1800.

Yachties all love Gail. Gail's ($D) opens for breakfast at 0830, and then again for dinner at 1900. Gail has a warm effusive personality and will make you feel like a good friend within a few minutes. She cooks up an excellent meal every night, and likes to change her recipes often. She usually just does one meal a night, but if you don't want what she has prepared, she will cook up something else. I have not yet eaten here, but everyone says the food is excellent, and you cannot but help have a good time. To find Gail's turn left as you come off the dock.

Eastman ($D) is very close to the dock. He opens from 0800-2000. You can come in here for some fresh local juice and he has snacks (fish'n chips or sandwiches) any time. He will also cook you up a good local meal, such as crab and dumpling, the Tobago national dish, or fine fish, shrimp, local meat meals if you give him a little notice.

Marilyn Gray runs G's Restaurant ($D) right opposite Sharon and Phebe's. This tiny establishment has just three tables. She is open 0830-2100 and serves a menu that changes daily but often includes lobster, shrimp, fish, chicken, goat and beef. She also does rotis.

Jane at Jane Quality Foods, bakes both cakes and bread. She is open daily except Saturday from 0900-2300. She also does rotis and daily local meals. Eat them on a wooden bench under a seagrape tree.

ASHORE

I can think of nowhere in the Caribbean where such beautiful walks are so easily available. The easiest is the path over the hill to Pirates Bay. The hillsides are a wild garden of balisiers and tropical trees with precipitous views of the reefs, beaches and sea. In the other direction the hike up to Fort Cambleton will reward you with photogenic vistas of the bay. Visit the Lookout as well; take any transport as far as the Lookout road, and hike up to the Lookout. Apart from the panorama you will see anis, motmots, yellow tails, tanagers and parrots.

There is an excellent (at least four hours one way) hike along an old west coast road till you join the proper road again just north of Bloody Bay. You can of course just walk part of the way, it is all in beautiful countryside. Take the road past Fort Cambleton and keep going.

Sharon at Sharon and Phebe's can help

Tobago

you organize a variety of other tours or hikes. You should also talk to Pat Turpin down at Man of war cottages, she is very active in the environmental movement and can arrange excellent tours.

For the music minded, Vanley Perry, who lived in Trinidad for 17 years and made pans (steel drums) for such famous groups as Angel Harps, Silver Stars and the Blue Diamonds, will be happy to demonstrate how pans are made and played. Vanley leads a steel band group called Booya-ka who play at Sharon and Phebe's and Blue Waters Inn.

WATER SPORTS

This is another excellent area for diving. There are many sites with miles of underwater rocks and reefs. Since the current can occasionally be strong, most dives are done as drift dives. One of the many sites is St. Giles Island, a vast area of reefs and rock from 20 to 60 feet deep. Huge building-s zed rocks provide walls, crevices and caves that keep turning up unexpected surprises; a six-foot nurse shark complete with three remoras, sleeping in a cavern; a broad passageway where half a dozen giant-sized queen and French angelfish swim up as if to say hello; a huge tarpon disappearing into the distance. The massive brain corals are impressive as are the colors of the sponges, which glow brightly in shades of green and blue.

Man Friday Diving is located just beyond G's Restaurant, and is run in a pleasantly laid back manner by Bjarne from Denmark. Wander over and chat with them. They will be happy to pick you up from your yacht. Ron's Water sports, run by Ronald Tiah is another good operation, you will find him down the road that runs back from Bay View Supermarket.

CHARLOTTEVILLE TO KING'S BAY

Much of the coast at the eastern end of Tobago rises steeply from the sea. These inaccessible cliffs and the many offshore is-lands provide safe nesting areas for seabirds, whose on-the-ground nests are easy prey for many mammals. The nearby sea-permarket is exceptionally well stocked because Tobago lies at the edge of a continental shelf and an upwelling of deep water brings nutrient concentrate from the seabed. The result is an abundance of frigatebirds, laughing gulls, boobies, terns and tropicbirds.

The east coast of Tobago can be rough if the wind is strong and the current is ripping through. On the other hand, on a calm day, the passage between Speyside and Little Tobago can be very pleasant. The east coast also has one of Tobago's nicest little anchorages; Anse Bateau.

There is a little group of islands off the northeast tip of Tobago. London Bridge is the one with the dramatic hole going all the way through. The Melville Islands are a little farther along. They include the 72-acre St. Giles Island and were given to the government in 1968 by Charles Turpin as a nature preserve. Frigatebirds, boobies and many other seabirds nest here, and you cannot land without permission from the wildlife warden.

NAVIGATION

The southwesterly equatorial current hits Tobago and divides; pushing westwards down the south coast and northwards along the East Coast. This northerly current is usually at its worst on the eastern side of little Tobago, so it pays to pass between Little Tobago and Speyside. The current is affected by the state of the tide. It is generally strengthened on the falling tide and weakened on a rising tide. At full or new moon, when tides are higher, their effect on the current is stronger. On a falling tide around new or full moon you can get up to four or five knots sweeping up inside Little Tobago. At other times you can get as little as one knot.

The first decision is whether to go inside or outside London Bridge and the Melville Islands. Outside is safer and easier, but it takes you farther north, and out into stronger current. It is the only way to go if you plan to sail, or have any doubts about the inside passage. If you have a rea-

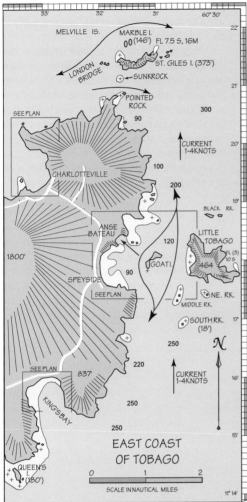

MELVILLE IS.
MARBLE I.
OO (146') FL 7.5 S, 16M
LONDON BRIDGE
ST. GILES I. (373')
SUNK ROCK
POINTED ROCK
90
300
CURRENT 1-4 KNOTS
SEE PLAN
CHARLOTTEVILLE
100
200
BLACK RK.
ANSE BATEAU
120
LITTLE TOBAGO
FL (3) 10 S
464
1800'
GOAT I.
90
SPEYSIDE
SEE PLAN
NE. RK.
MIDDLE RK.
SOUTH RK. (18')
250
N
220
SEE PLAN
837'
CURRENT 1-4 KNOTS
KING'S BAY
250
250
EAST COAST OF TOBAGO
QUEEN'S I. (180')
0   1   2
SCALE IN NAUTICAL MILES

22'
21'
20'
19'
16'
15'
11° 14'
60° 30'
33'   32'   31'

Rock and South Rock.

Going north with the current behind you presents no problem. I would suggest passing outside the Melville Islands and London Bridge, admiring the scenery and the birds as you go.

ANSE BATEAU

Anse Bateau is a quite delightful anchorage and generally excellent - much calmer and more protected than one would expect looking at the charts. It is the only good anchorage on the east coast, and was so good that in the early days it was used for careening sailing boats.

Anse Bateau is the home of Blue Waters Inn and it is set on its own amid steep wooded hills. There is a pristine beach with excellent snorkeling, diving and exploring. From the cockpit you can enjoy the views outwards toward Goat Island and Little Tobago.

Here you are close to all Tobago's major nature attractions, including the rain forest, the waterfalls and the Little Tobago bird sanctuary. This is an excellent place to anchor for a few days in comfort and organize a car or tours to see the best of Tobago.

NAVIGATION

You need to take care approaching and anchoring in Anse Bateau. There is an extensive reef off the southern headland. Most of the water over this reef is 12 feet deep, but there are a few six-foot patches. Approach on a line between the house on Goat Island and the main building of Blue Waters Inn. Come in good light so you can see the shallow parts.

The approach is over coral about 14-16 feet deep. The hotel is planning to have moorings and they also have buoys to demarcate the swimming area, which look like moorings. The anchoring area between the demarcated beach area and the reef is very small. The best thing to do is call Aquamarine Dive Shop (VHF: 16) for instructions.

Once the moorings are put in, you should use them. Under no circumstances

sonable motor, the inside passage can save time. There is plenty of water between St. Giles Islands and Pointed Rock, but the presence of a nasty sunken rock in the middle of the fairly narrow channel makes it challenging. I would only attempt this passage in reasonably calm conditions. If you can see breaking water on the sunken rock, going inside is no problem. Even if you cannot see it, you should be OK if you stay close to the northern coast of Tobago and then when you get near Pointed Rock, pass it as closely as you safely can.

As you come down the east coast pass outside Long Rock, inside Little Tobago (sometimes called Bird of Paradise Island), either side of Goat Island, inside Middle

Tobago

should you anchor on coral, which is easily damaged.

SERVICES

You will find yourself welcome at Blue Waters Inn, manager Dave Harriston used to manage the Secret Harbor Hotel for the Moorings and likes to encourage yachts, as does the hotel owner Glen Tucker, a power boat enthusiast.

Blue Waters Inn and Aquamarine Dive stand by on VHF: 16. They will have moorings, which you should use. They charge $10 US a night, but you can apply this to your restaurant bill and enjoy their showers. They will also tell you where to dispose of well-wrapped garbage.

There is room for one boat at the head of the dock with electricity and water. You can also come into the dock to take on water or fuel, which they sell. This is currently the only yacht fuel dock in Tobago. Ask at the dive shop. Check out the depths at the head of the dock carefully, it is about 8 feet deep at the end and shelves quite quickly to about 5 feet.

Register with them when you come ashore. Other facilities include water at their dock, a garbage service, toilet and shower facilities, full communications including e-mail, and rental cars or taxis. They can usually sell you ice, both block and cube. Keep in mind Blue Waters Inn is a low key, quiet establishment very much into ecotourism. Aquamarine, a full service dive center is on the premises.

REGULATIONS

The Blue Waters Inn has won the Prime Ministers award for environmental management, and we need to live up to their standards. The anchorage is quite different from the other anchorages we are used to as the wind is onshore and will push anything that comes from your yacht onto the pristine beach and into the clear shallow water.

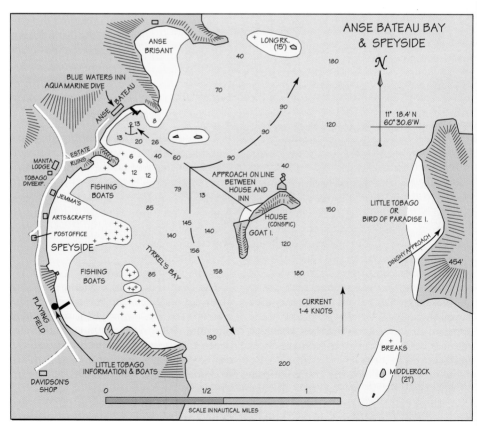

ANSE BATEAU

If you have a holding tank, use it. If you do not, use the toilets provided ashore. You must of course be particularly careful here not to throw anything over the side or pump your bilges.

Use the moorings, or get advice from Aquamarine (VHF: 16) on where to anchor. It is easy to damage the coral here.

ASHORE

If you run short of food you can try your luck in Speyside, at the Arts and Crafts Center (yes, it sells some food) or better yet at Davidson's Shop. You will enjoy the walk over the hill and through the old sugar mill ruins to Speyside. If you only end up with a bag of beans and a can of spam, don't despair, for you can always eat out.

The Blue Waters Inn restaurant is called The Fishpot ($B) and overlooks the beach. It opens from breakfast to dinner every day. Lunches are informal and inexpensive, dinners are more elaborate and advance booking is requested. Seafood is always on the menu and you can often get lobster. Their Mot-Mot grill ($D) is informal, under a thatched roof, and serves fresh grilled seafood and meats. The Shipwreck bar features local and Caribbean cocktails.

On the road to Speyside you will find the Manta Lodge whose aim is to encourage scuba divers, birdwatchers, artists and nature lovers. They have a boutique, dive shop, The Reef Bar and a restaurant ($B).

In Speyside, don't miss Jemma's ($C-D). You dine in a quaint tree house that is propped up on stilts around a large old almond tree hanging out to the surf line. A perfect atmosphere in which to enjoy her excellent Creole cooking, featuring chicken, fish, shrimp and lobster. Jemma opens for lunch and dinner, except on Fridays and Sundays when she closes at 1700 and Saturday when she is closed all day.

EXPLORING

Dinghy exploration here is good, both around the islands and to Anse Brisant.

While you are anchored here a visit to Little Tobago Island should be on your agenda. You can do this by dinghy, or take one of the many little boats that ply the route.

Little Tobago is also known as Bird of Paradise Island because in 1909 its owner, wealthy British newspaperman William Ingram, imported 50 of these birds from their

Tobago

Anse Bateau beach

native New Guinea. At that time beautiful feathers were in high demand for ladies' hats and Ingram wanted to protect the Bird of Paradise from the hatters. The birds did well for many years and after Ingram's death his son deeded the island to the government with the stipulation that it be kept as a reserve. But Hurricane Flora, having no respect for deeds, blew almost all the elegant birds out to sea in 1963 and the few stragglers that survived soon died out. The government of New Guinea has offered to give Tobago some new birds, but local naturalists are of two minds about the proposal. Many native birds now thrive and breed on Little Tobago and might be displaced.

A trip to Little Tobago with a local guide will be the most rewarding way to see it. This is easily arranged at Anse Bateau with either Frank's or Top Ranking, both have offices out in the car park. Even if you find your own way along the trail that goes up the hill from the small beach, you cannot miss getting good views of red-billed tropicbirds that are here during their nesting season from December to April. In season sooty terns, much prettier than their name suggests, brown noddies and brown boobies can also be seen nesting on the rocks below the lookout. A forest ranger fills bamboo water troughs every day and these are used by many land birds. Blue-gray tanagers, white-tipped doves, Caribbean elaenias, and bare-eyed thrushes come to drink while you are just a few feet away. Little bananaquits hop right in the drinking water for some vigorous bathing. Blue-crowned motmots are a common sight.

Early planters destroyed most of Tobago's dry forest, but

on Little Tobago it was not cut because the island is too dry for farming. Beautiful white orchids, called virgin orchids, grow from many tree trunks.

WATER SPORTS

This end of Tobago has some of the best diving in the Caribbean with many dive shops in the area. I suggest you go with Keith Dawant's Aquamarine Dive. They have been here forever, know the waters and the currents very well, and operate very professionally. Keith also does fishing trips in the area and the fishing is excellent.

The eastern end of Tobago has extensive reefs, clear water and spectacular diving and snorkeling. Occasionally the visibility drops for a few days because of currents coming up from the Orinoco River.

Keep in mind that currents are strong so dives are always drift dives. If you snorkel outside the protected bays, it is probably best to drift snorkel. Take your dinghy, and hang off it on a line. Let the current take you where it will and when you are done pop back in and hope the motor starts.

We will mention just a few of the many dives in this area. The Alps is out on the reef near Middle Rock. The dive starts in a most non-alpine way on a long flat area about 40 feet deep with all kinds of coral formations and small reef fish - a pleasant coral garden to get you really relaxed. Then there is a passage through a steep canyon in the rocks. On the far side the current sweeps you into a curious crater-like depression which forms an almost perfect circle - a kind of mini-amphitheater a couple of hundred feet across. Inside this area huge tarpon normally cruise, more curious than frightened by the divers. The crater was formed by the scouring action of breaking waves, and if you look above, they create a pattern of disturbed bubbles on the surface. On to the far side of the crater more large tarpon and pelagics roam, in addition to large and very tame angelfish.

Black Jack Hole is a dive in a large bay with about a 45-degree slope. The dive is normally done at 45 feet deep, though

Tobago

KING'S BAY

you can go down to 80 feet. There are two walls and an abundance of hard and soft corals. The dive got its name because towards the end of summer you sometimes see something quite amazing; the bay becomes alive with hundreds of large dark crevalle jacks. It is also just out of the fierce northerly current and this attracts big pelagics such as black-tipped sharks.

Coral Gardens is an easy and pleasant dive, amid a profusion of soft and hard corals, reef fish, banded coral shrimp and sponges. Tobago has some exceptional brain corals, but here is the largest of them all. Rising some eleven feet high and spreading sixteen feet in diameter, it is reputed to be the second largest in the world.

There is also always the chance of diving with manta rays, an unforgettable experience, which has put Tobago firmly on the dive map.

KING'S BAY

King's Bay is well protected, though you can get a swell in a southeasterly wind. The water in the bay is very deep and then shelves fast. If you don't have enough anchor line to be in the deep water, you can use two anchors, one in shallow water, and one out in deeper water to hold you in place. The best anchorage is off the eastern end of the beach in 40-60 feet. For more privacy you can anchor off the eastern shore a little to the south.

ASHORE

Apart from the small beach facility there is not much ashore. While you are here you might take a walk to the King's Bay Waterfall. It is an attractive 20-minute walk, though the falls are a mere trickle if you go in the dry season. Land near the beach facility and follow the road back. Turn left at the main road and look for the waterfall sign on your right.

For a meal or drink, wander back and check out Liz's café, restaurant and bar on the main road. It is not always open, so have a backup plan, or pass by and book in advance.

SOUTH COAST BETWEEN KING'S BAY AND SCARBOROUGH

There is no particularly good anchorage along this coast, so you might as well stay out in deep water and take advantage of the prevailing westerly current to sail down to Scarborough. Take care to stay outside the Great River Shoal as you approach Scarborough. Pass well outside Minster Rock, which is buoyed.

KING'S BAY

CRUISING GUIDE
TO BARBADOS

Barbados at a glance

CUSTOMS

There are two ports of clearance; Bridgetown and Port St. Charles. Customs details are given under *cruising information* and the sections on the two ports.

PUBLIC HOLIDAYS

January 1

January 21 – Errol Barrow Day

Good Friday and Easter Monday. Easter is March 31, 2002; April 20, 2003 and April 11, 2004. For dates later than 2004 check links on doyleguides.com.

April 28 – Heroes day

May 1 – Labor Day

Whit Monday – May 20, 2002; June 9, 2003 and May 31, 2004. For dates later than 2004 check links on doyleguides.com

August 1 Emancipation Day

First Monday in August – Kadooment Day

November 30, Independence Day

December 25 and 26

CURRENCY

Barbados dollars, which are pegged to the US dollar at a rate of two Barbados dollars to one US dollar (you will get more like 1.98 by the time the bank takes a commission). Most Bajans will be very happy to accept payment in US dollars, travelers' checks or credit cards.

TELEPHONES

Card phones are placed all over the island. You can buy cards from Cable and Wireless and selected shops. The Barbados telephone numbers works just like the USA. The area code to call into Barbados is 246, and from any other country you treat it just as you would an American area code. From the USA you dial 1+246+seven digit number. To dial the USA from Barbados, dial 1 plus the ten-digit number. To get other countries dial 011+country code+ the number.

ELECTRICITY

Electricity on the island is 110 volts, 50 cycles.

TRANSPORT

Buses are the mainstay of the Barbados Transport system. Some are government operated public buses and some are privately operated minibuses. The main bus station is in town off Fairchild Street close to the market and river. A smaller one is near the main Post Office. In general if you are heading north go the to Post Office bus terminal, for everything else go to the Fairchild Street Station. Bus fares are $1.50 Barbados, no transfers. The mini buses leave from their own part of the terminal.

To catch a bus when you are out of town, look for a bus stop. It is illegal for buses to pick you up anywhere else, though a few of the mini-buses will do it.

Rental cars are also available. You need a local license, which costs $10 Barbados and is available from the rental company or the nearest police station. They will need to see your regular driving license.

Taxis are also plentiful. They are not metered and rates are negotiable especially for sightseeing tours. Typical taxi rates in $Barbados are:

Bridgetown to the airport	$30
Bridgetown to Fort St. Charles	$40
Tour hourly rate	$32
Short ride	$7-10

PLANNING YOUR CRUISE

Introduction

*B*arbados is 21 miles long by 14 miles wide. It is a civilized, orderly country with a gentle topography of rolling hills and green fields. Under British rule for over 300 years, it is often called Little England. Barbados became independent in 1966 and is today a stable parliamentary democracy and active member of the Commonwealth. It is a relatively affluent country. The driving force for the economy is tourism, and this has fueled many other light industries, including printing and light manufacturing. The second largest money-earner is in the overseas financial sector.

The majority of the 260,000 inhabitants are of African descent; the rest came mainly from England and India. The island has many British traditions, though these are well mingled with African influence.

Geographically, Barbados is an anomaly in the Eastern Caribbean. Ninety miles to the east of St. Vincent, it is way outside the arc of the other islands and straight to windward. It is the only island in the Eastern Caribbean that is not volcanic. It is the top of a buckle in the seabed that got pushed above the surface during tectonic plate movement. At a later period it was largely submerged, then rose again giving it a heavy limestone capping. As a result the island is relatively flat (the highest hills are about a thousand feet) and it has spectacularly beautiful white sand beaches.

In the days of sail, especially in the days of square rigged ships, it was very hard to reach from the rest of the island chain, which helped it stay outside the battles between the British and French that characterized the history of most of the other islands.

Left to their own devices, English-speaking Bajans evolved the most distinctive accent in the region. It is a pleasant friendly sound, thick enough to cut with a cutlass. After you have spent a while here you will recognize a Bajan anywhere else in the world as soon as he speaks.

Bajans count among the finest seamen in the Caribbean. Their fishermen venture far out to sea in all conditions. For their yachtspeople, visiting any other destination and getting home involves serious windward work in the open ocean, with seas that often seem rougher than they do in the island chain. There is often a foul current to deal with as well. I am always amazed at the casual way Bajan Yacht crews turn up for races throughout the Caribbean and they think nothing of beating their way back afterwards, a trip that would give most of us considerable pause.

Missed by Columbus, Barbados narrowly escaped being named after a Catholic saint. The word Barbados came from the Portuguese for the "bearded one," a name given to it by a visiting Portuguese explorer Pedro a Campos, who stopped by in 1536 and was impressed by all the fig trees with their thick aerial roots that give them a bearded appearance.

Barbados was claimed for England in 1625 by one Captain John Powell and colonized two years later by his brother Henry with a party of 80 settlers and 10 slaves. They called their settlement Jamestown and it was in the area that is now Holetown. The island was uninhabited when they arrived, though archeological evidence shows that it had been inhabited both by Arawaks and Caribs from South America.

During the early years of settlement, Barbados had many small farmers, but around 1650 the advent of sugar brought about a sharp change. Smallholdings were bought up by the richer landowners, who imported slaves and created an immensely rich plantocracy, which survived for several centuries.

The first legislative assembly was formed in 1639 and it opposed Cromwell when he took over England and beheaded King Charles I. Cromwell sent over an invasion force, but the Bajans managed to negotiate a surrender in which they accepted governance by a governor and a freely elected assembly, and they were given freedom from taxes without local consent.

Of course, freely elected in those days meant elected by the landowners, not the slaves and indentured workers, who lived in very impoverished conditions. Although slavery was abolished in 1834, power to the people only became a reality in the 1930s and '40s, long after sugar had become a far less profitable industry. It happened as the result of class struggle, with labor unions, serious unrest, and street riots. One of the leaders of the 1937 labor disturbances was Clement Payne, now one of the country's national heroes.

As the sugar industry declined, tourism evolved to take its place. The island is flat enough that a large airport presented no special feats of engineering and, unlike square-riggers, jet planes have no problem getting here. Barbados's quiet beauty, dreamy beaches, and pleasant climate make it natural for tourism and Barbados was the first of the eastern Caribbean islands to develop this industry on such an intensive scale.

As a result, there is plenty to do here, with many types of restaurants and shops, lots of nightlife and plenty of roadside attractions. The people are very welcoming - they understand the value of visitors and treat them well. While the south and west coast are heavily built up to cater to this industry, if you head to the northeast or center of the island, you soon get away from it all.

Barbados is a landfall for over 300 yachts every year between November and March. Most arrive in modern conventional craft, but they have their share of the oddballs too. Bombard arrived here having drifted over on his inflatable dinghy, the raft Ra arrived here as did the world's smallest gondola. Someone even crossed in a converted factory boiler and a Frenchman claimed to have swum across, towing his rubber raft behind him.

It is well worth visiting Barbados, but from a yachting perspective it can be a challenging trip from the other islands. For Europeans, it makes a lot of sense to make Barbados your first landfall as you come across the Atlantic. However you get here, you can be sure of enjoying your stay.

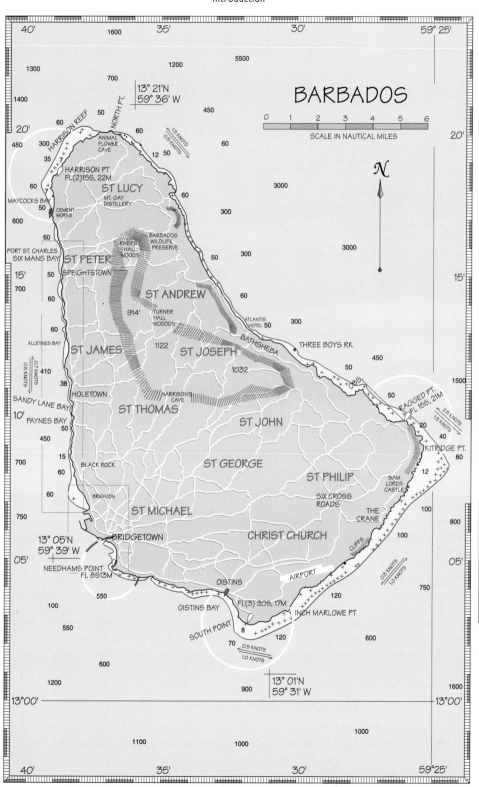

BARBADOS

0   1   2   3   4   5   6
SCALE IN NAUTICAL MILES

N

13° 21'N
59° 36' W

HARRISON REEF
NORTH PT.
ANIMAL FLOWER CAVE
1.5 KNOTS
0.5 KNOTS
12   50
60

HARRISON PT
FL(2)15S, 22M

ST LUCY
MT. GAY DISTILLERY

MAYCOCKS BAY
CEMENT WORKS

3000

BARBADOS WILDLIFE PRESERVE

TURNERS HALL WOODS

PORT ST. CHARLES
SIX MANS BAY
ST PETER
SPEIGHTSTOWN

3000

ST ANDREW

914'   TURNER HALL WOOODS

ATLANTIS HOTEL 50

ALLEYNES BAY
0.5 KNOTS   0.7 KNOTS
410
38
ST JAMES
1122
1032
ST JOSEPH
BATHSHEBA
THREE BOYS RK

RAGGED PT.
FL 15S, 21M

SANDY LANE BAY
HOLETOWN
HARRISON'S CAVE
ST THOMAS

2.5 KNOTS
1.5 KNOTS
20
40

PAYNES BAY
50
ST JOHN
KITRIDGE PT.
60

450
15
60
BLACK ROCK

ST GEORGE
12

SAM LORDS CASTLE
ST PHILIP
SIX CROSS ROADS

60
BRIGHTON

100

ST MICHAEL
THE CRANE

100
CHRIST CHURCH

13° 05'N
59° 39' W
BRIDGETOWN

CLIFFS
100

NEEDHAMS POINT
FL 8S13M
AIRPORT
0.5 KNOTS
1.0 KNOTS
750

OISTINS
120

OISTINS BAY
FL(3) 30S, 17M
INCH MARLOWE PT

SOUTH POINT
8
120

70   0.5 KNOTS
1.0 KNOTS
600

13° 01'N
59° 31' W

13°00'

Cruising guide to Barbados

Cruising Information

WEATHER

Barbados has a very pleasant climate throughout the year. Temperatures are about 70-86° F (21-30°C). The two seasons are the dry season (roughly February to June) and the rainy season (July to December). However, Barbados is low enough in elevation to be relatively dry even in the rainy season.

The winds are northeast to southeast year round from 10 to 25 knots. During the winter months high-pressure systems to the north can generate a strong northeasterly breeze of 25 knots or more. It is quite possible to sail in these conditions, but it can be a bit rough. Locally, strong winter winds are known as Christmas winds.

The high-pressure systems that create these strong winds are countered by cold fronts that come southwest from the USA. These never get as far as Barbados, but their presence further north can create pleasant sunny weather with light winds.

Cold fronts and other storms to the north sometimes create northerly and northwesterly swells which can make anchorages uncomfortable and landing a dinghy on the beach hazardous.

Hurricanes are a possibility throughout the Caribbean from June through to November with August and September having by far the highest number of hurricanes. Barbados last received a direct hit along with Grenada in September 1955, but if you are visiting during these months you need to pay attention to weather forecasts.

You can get the local weather on the Caribbean Broadcasting Corp, 900 on the medium wave band. Listen after the 0700 news. You can also call the airport for weather (428-7101). On the short wave the most popular forecast is the Caribbean Weather net at 0830 local time on 8104 kHz USB.

CUSTOMS AND IMMIGRATION

There are two ports of entry to Barbados, Bridgetown Harbour and the new Port St. Charles about ten miles north of Bridgetown on the west coast. Clearance is easier up in Port St. Charles as it not a commercial port. However, customs have a strange rule that you have to clear out of the same customs station you clear into. So if you decide to go clear in at Port St. Charles, you will have to return there when you want to leave.

In either case you must proceed directly to the port of clearance and contact them for directions of where to berth. **You may not anchor and dinghy in.** (See also Carlisle Bay and Port St. Charles sections.) Once berthed you will need to visit Customs, Immigration, Port Authority and Health officials. When berthing in Bridgetown Harbour, lay out lots of fenders and take care, as at some states of the tide their big fenders will be at your lifeline height.

Fees

Customs charges are Bds $25 for clearing in and $25 for out, with an anchoring fee of $8.33 making a total of $58.33. Overtime fees are extra and start at 2200 hrs.

Cruising permits

Once you clear into Bridgetown Harbour you can go and anchor in Carlisle Bay. But if you want to visit any other areas, including Port St Charles from Bridgetown, or Bridgetown (and Carlisle Bay) from Port St. Charles you will need permission from customs and port authority, and will have to give them your schedule.

Other anchorages lie along the west coast. At this point customs are reluctant to give you permission to visit these. However, you can ask, and if you can get someone from the yacht club to vouch for you, you may get permission.

There are plans to open up more cruising areas and marker buoys are being placed at several locations where there are sandy areas big enough to permit anchoring. A chart showing these authorized anchoring areas will soon be available from the Barbados Port Authority.

Firearms

If you have firearms on board you must declare them and the Customs officers will hold them for you until your departure

Arriving Crew

If crew are joining the boat and flying in, it is necessary for them to have a letter from the captain stating this, it is further recommended that the captain meet the crew at the airport with the ships papers.

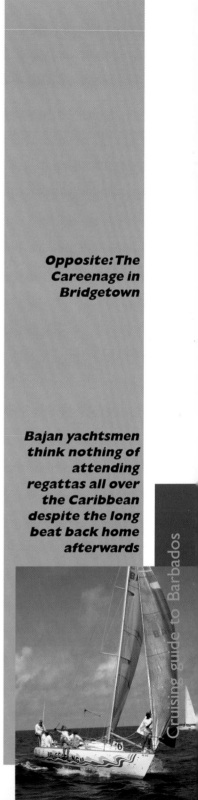

Opposite: The Careenage in Bridgetown

Bajan yachtsmen think nothing of attending regattas all over the Caribbean despite the long beat back home afterwards

Cruising guide to Barbados

Transshipment

Imported ships supplies can be transshipped duty free to your vessel under customs supervision.

Visas

Visas are required for citizens of China, Taiwan, Pakistan, non-commonwealth African countries and all South American countries except Argentina, Brazil and Venezuela. If you are dropping crew off in Barbados they will need a ticket to a country where they have right of domicile.

Pets

Barbados is rabies free and animals are not allowed to enter the island without stringent quarantine procedures. Yachts with pets aboard must remain at anchor with the animals kept on board. Under no circumstances are you to bring your pet ashore.

Clearing out

You must clear out of the port you cleared into, only the captain need go with the papers, unless discharging crew, in which case the crew should also see immigration, and they will need a ticket back to the country where they live or have right of abode.

Fishing

Non-commercial trolling and hand-lining for fish, for your own consumption are OK except in designated marine parks.

Anchoring regulations

Over 50% of the shallow waters around the island have coral reefs. These are vital to the tourist industry and yacht anchors are seen as a major threat. Anchoring (collecting or otherwise damaging) coral is forbidden. Penalties of US$25,000 and possible imprisonment are in place for anchoring on a coral reef. In a recent case a mega-yacht was given a huge fine and compelled to leave it's anchor on the reef (so raising it would not cause further damage).

Buoyed anchoring areas may be in place in the future; in the meantime you are responsible for making sure you anchor in sand not on coral. All areas not clearly visible as sand bottoms should be considered as coral reefs. You must also get permission from customs and port authority.

MEDICAL

Barbados has excellent medical services and hospitals. When other islands run out of medical options their patients are often sent here for care. If you need medical attention, contact the Barbados Association of Medical Practitioners (429-7596, bamp@ sunbeach.net), for dental recommendations the Barbados Dental Association (228-6488).

SPECIAL EVENTS

The Barbados Sailing Association has a full program of racing. It is done under the CSA rating system and includes the Around the Island Race in January, the Mullins Beach Bar Race and the BYC race in February, and the Mount Gay Rum/Boatyard Regatta in late May or early June.

The Mount Gay Rum/Boatyard Regatta is perhaps the best known internationally. It takes place shortly after Tobago Race Week, making for (with luck) a one-tack journey to Barbados from Tobago. It is a relatively small regatta (about 20 yachts), but rates as one of the friendliest in the Caribbean. Although Bajans never seem to have a problem beating to Barbados, they realize that for lesser mortals it involves considerable effort, so they reward this by being superbly welcoming. They have five races over three days, with both racing and cruising classes and even supply lunch between races. Those that make the effort to get there rate it among their favorite events.

Sailing to Barbados

Because Barbados lies well to windward of the other islands, it is the island least visited by yachts. However, it is by no means impossible to reach by sail. Bajans visit the other islands and get back as a matter of course.

A few years ago finding Barbados could be a challenge, as it is relatively low lying, and the ocean currents are variable. When I first came to the islands, I heard stories that the old schooner captains would always carry a pig on board. Pigs have a highly refined sense of smell, which is why the French use them for hunting truffles, (despite the difficulties presented

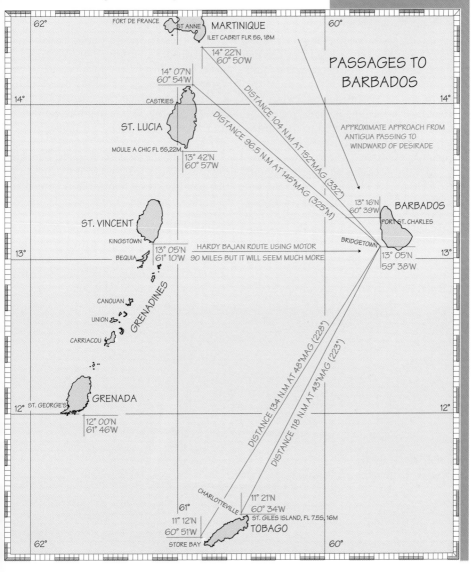

PASSAGES TO BARBADOS

62°

FORT DE FRANCE

ST ANNE MARTINIQUE

ILET CABRIT FLR 5S, 18M

14° 22'N
60° 50'W

60°

14° 07'N
60° 54'W

14°   14°

CASTRIES

ST. LUCIA

MOULE A CHIC FL 5S,22M

13° 42'N
60° 57'W

DISTANCE 104 N.M AT 152°MAG (332°)

DISTANCE 96.5 N.M AT 145°MAG (325°M)

APPROXIMATE APPROACH FROM
ANTIGUA PASSING TO
WINDWARD OF DESIRADE

13° 16'N
60° 39'W   BARBADOS

PORT ST. CHARLES

ST. VINCENT

KINGSTOWN

BEQUIA

13° 05'N
61° 10'W

13°   HARDY BAJAN ROUTE USING MOTOR   BRIDGETOWN   13°
              90 MILES BUT IT WILL SEEM MUCH MORE

13° 05'N
59° 38'W

CANOUAN

UNION

CARRIACOU

GRENADINES

GRENADA

12° ST. GEORGE'S   12°

12° 00'N
61° 46'W

DISTANCE 134 N.M AT 48°MAG (228°)

DISTANCE 118 N.M AT 43°MAG (223°)

CHARLOTTEVILLE

11° 21'N
60° 34'W

61°

ST. GILES ISLAND, FL 7.5S, 16M

11° 12'N
60° 51'W   TOBAGO

62°   STORE BAY   60°

in stopping several hundred pounds of porker from eating the truffles before you can get them in the collecting bag). The idea was that if Barbados did not show up when expected, they threw the pig over the side and sailed a short distance away. The pig would then smell the land and head in the right direction, giving the captain a new compass course.

Luckily, the era of GPS has replaced porcine navigation and finding Barbados is now no problem.

Although St. Vincent is the closest island to Barbados, this is a tough place to begin from as Barbados is directly to windward. Some Bajans do go back by this direct route, usually with considerable help from the iron topsail. Most people favor leaving from the north end of St Lucia or the south end of Martinique. The distance from the southern end of Martinique to Bridgetown is about 110 miles but it gives you a few miles to windward compared to the northern end of St Lucia, which is 98 miles from Bridgetown. (Distances shown on our planning chart are between offshore waypoints and so a bit shorter.) In either case, you have a chance of making it in one tack, or at least getting pretty close. The trick is to head up as high as possible to allow for the current, which will generally be against you as it sets to the northeast, though its strength can vary enormously.

If you are in Trinidad, it probably makes more sense to cruise to Tobago and then set off from Charlotteville in Tobago's northeast corner. The distance is 120 miles to Bridgetown (130 if you start from Crown Point), but you should make it in one tack if the wind is not north of east.

If you wish to explore South America, Barbados makes an excellent starting point, giving you a fair sail down to English-speaking Guyana. This was one of the old trade routes plied by sailing schooners.

For those arriving from the east, Barbados has a light at Ragged Point with a 21-mile range, near the easternmost tip. It is usually reliable, but you should never rely solely on one navigational aid.

Reefs extend nearly one and a half miles from Barbados's eastern point. A barrier reef protects much of the south coast and has water deep enough for fishing boats behind it. You need to give this coast good clearance in passing, as you might not only lose your boat, but be fined for damaging the reef to boot.

In the old days, according to Barbados folklore, Sam Lord used to lure ships onto this reef by setting lights ashore to make it look like a safe harbor. He would then salvage the cargo.

You also need to keep well off the eastern coast, as it is rough, with big breaking waves hitting the shore, and the northern and northwest coasts, which also have reefs well over half a mile offshore.

EXPLORING BARBADOS

The west and south coasts of Barbados are very built up. If you head to the north and east of the island you can get into a pleasant rural setting. The area around Bathsheba is one of my favorites. The beach is very wild, with big surf breaking in and surfers are often out taking advantage of it. The hills behind Bathsheba are attractive, as is the low coastal road to its north. The Atlantis Hotel in Bathsheba overlooks the fishing boat anchorage and makes an excellent lunch spot.

If you visit only one site in Barbados, I would recommend Harrison's Cave, a remarkable natural attraction that is unlike anything you will see on the other islands. The standard tour is an excellent introduction. You don a hard hat and sit in an electrical train that whizzes you through various parts of the cave, stopping at major attractions and allowing you to get out and take a look. These include giant cathedral-like areas decorated by a magnificent array of stalagmites and stalactites, underwater streams, waterfalls, and pools.

You would get a much better idea of the scale of the cave if you hiked through it. This is not something you would be allowed to do on your own, but organized hiking groups do occasionally get to visit and you could ask if they know of anything that is being organized when you visit.

Barbados has many well-organized attractions. These include the Barbados Wildlife Preserve in St. Peter. You can roam freely around in the same four-acre enclosure as most of the animals do. African green monkeys are the main inhabitants. These monkeys were imported to Barbados, St. Kitts & Nevis, and Grenada many years ago. This is a good place to view them. You will also see the large red-footed tortoise and imported exhibits include toucans, parrots, and wallabies. There is even a caiman in the pond.

Turner's Hall Woods is a good place to see what Barbados would have looked like had its forest not all been cut down to grow sugar. This 50-acre site was more or less left unchanged and includes lots of large trees of the dry forest type, including sand box, silk

Above: Fishing Harbour

Opposite: Holetown Church

cotton, cabbage palm, and trumpet trees. When the settlers came, most of the island was covered with this kind of forest. This is one of the best examples left in the islands.

Welshman Hall Gully, maintained by the National Trust, offers a great walk through a large deep ravine. It includes a massive pillar four feet in diameter that was supposed to have originally been a giant stalagmite and stalactite that joined together. The area has been intensively cultivated in the past, and it is now being allowed to slowly return to a more natural state. A good path takes you for about half a mile through several distinct areas. At the end of the walk are ponds with lots of frogs and toads and there is a good view to the coast. You have a chance of seeing wild monkeys here.

Birders like to visit the Graeme Hall Swamp, surrounded by mangroves. It attracts lots of water and shore birds, including three endangered species of Caribbean ducks. There is a relatively small area you can walk through; the rest is for the birds.

Gardeners will enjoy Lazaretto Gardens, just outside Bridgetown, Andromeda Gardens near Bathsheba, and the Flower Forest in St Joseph.

History buffs will discover several museums, including the Barbados Museum at the Garrison, Sunbury Plantation House in St. Philip, the Hutson Sugar Museum near Holetown, and Tyrol Cot Heritage village just north of Bridgetown. They can also visit Sam Lords Castle in the southeast part of the island.

If you like the idea of joining others for walking or running, join in with the hash house harriers (see barbadoshash.com for their next meet). The National Trust also organizes a five-mile walk every Sunday starting at 0600 or 1530. If you prefer to go on your own, the Barbados Nature Conservation Commission has developed a number of trails, and you can contact them for more information.

If you are planning to visit several na-tional sites in Barbados, contact the Barbados Tourism Authority (888-barbados) about the new Heritage Passports that can save lots of dollars on entry fees.

Barbados also has every kind of tourist activity, including four golf courses and several riding stables.

Keep your eyes open for free publications giving you a current calendar of nightlife. Groups to watch out for include the Merrymen, an excellent band and one of the most famous in the country and the Red Men who play good country western and rock and roll on the bar circuit.

Cruising guide to Barbados

ANCHORAGES IN BARBADOS

BRIDGETOWN AND CARLISLE BAY

Bridgetown is the capital of Barbados and the island's biggest city. It is attractively built around the mouth of the Constitution River, so you get views of the water and boats. You can follow the river mouth up into the town with about 7-foot of draft; it is full of other boats with permanent berths. To stay here you have to apply to the Barbados Port Authority to rent one of the limited berths here. Most visiting yachts anchor instead off Carlisle Bay just southeast of the river mouth. This is a scenic anchorage with a lovely sweeping two-mile beach that is home both to the Barbados Yacht Club and the Barbados Sailing and Cruising Club.

It can get a little noisy here on the weekends with shore side businesses having loud music till the early hours.

Architecture in Bridgetown is an inter-esting blend of very old and modern. A square that used to be called Trafalgar Square has a statue of Nelson that predated Nelson's Column in London by some 36 years. The square has now been renamed National Heroes Square, and Nelson was turned round so he no longer faces down Broad Street. There is a move to relocate him elsewhere, so check him out while you have the chance. Bridgetown has excellent shopping and restaurants and it is relatively compact, making it easy to walk around.

REGULATIONS

(See also *customs and immigration* under *planning your cruise*.)

You must proceed directly to Bridgetown Harbour for clearance. Before entering Bridgetown Harbour contact them on VHF: 16 *Signal Station Port Control*. They will direct you in. Once tied up go to the Customs and Immigration offices in the building at the south side of the harbor. You will also have to deal with the health officer who is stationed here as well. Officers are on duty until 2200, after that you may have to

194

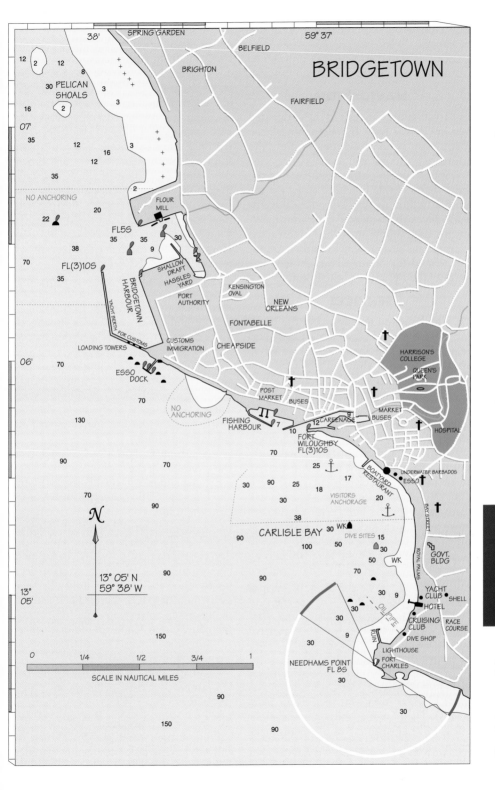

BRIDGETOWN

SPRING GARDEN
BELFIELD
BRIGHTON
FAIRFIELD
38'   59° 37'

12
2   12
8
30 PELICAN
SHOALS
3
16   2   3
07'
35
35
12   16
12
35
2
NO ANCHORING
20
FLOUR
MILL
22
FL5S
35   35
30
38   9
FL(3)10S   SHALLOW
DRAFT
35   HASSLES
YARD
BRIDGETOWN
HARBOUR   PORT
AUTHORITY
70   FL(3)10S
YACHT BERTH
FOR CUSTOMS
LOADING TOWERS
CUSTOMS
IMMIGRATION   CHEAPSIDE
06'   70
ESSO
DOCK
70   POST
MARKET
BUSES
NO
ANCHORING   FISHING
HARBOUR
130
90
70
70
70
90
70
130
90

KENSINGTON
OVAL
NEW
ORLEANS
FONTABELLE

HARRISON'S
COLLEGE
QUEEN'S
PARK
†
†
†
†
MARKET
BUSES
9
12 CARENAGE
7
10
FORT
WILOUGHBY
FL(3)10S   HOSPITAL

25
30   90   25
17
18
VISITORS
ANCHORAGE
30
38
CARLISLE BAY
90   100
90   90
70

BOATYARD
RESTAURANT
UNDERWATER BARBADOS
ESSO
†
20
†
BAY STREET
30 WK
DIVE SITES 15
50   30
50   WK
GOVT.
BLDG
ROYAL PALMS
YACHT
CLUB
SHELL
30
9   HOTEL
30
CRUISING
CLUB
RACE
COURSE
DIVE SHOP
9
LIGHTHOUSE
30
FORT
CHARLES

N

13° 05' N
59° 38' W

13°
05'

150

OIL PIPE LINE
RUIN
NEEDHAMS POINT
FL 8S
30
30

0   1/4   1/2   3/4   1
SCALE IN NAUTICAL MILES

90

150
90

90

Cruising guide to Barbados

195

stay in the harbor until the next morning for clearance.

Once cleared in you may proceed to Carlisle Bay to anchor.

NAVIGATION

You may only anchor in the designated area in Carlisle Bay. If you anchor off the yacht club with the local yachts, the coastguard will tell you to move.

When moving around, beware of the shoal that extends out from shore on the southern side of the bay just off the government offices, this is marked with white markers that flash yellow at night. This area also encompasses several wrecks fairly close together used for diving. They include the wreck of the Berwyn and the Ellion.

SERVICES

The Boatyard Restaurant at the north end of the bay welcomes yachts. Co-owners Sean Defreitas and Shane Atwell are active members of the Barbados Yacht Club and The Boatyard co-sponsor the excellent Mount Gay/Boatyard regatta in early June.

They have ten moorings that will accommodate yachts up to 60 ft. Currently there is no charge for use of the moorings, but should a charge be instituted it will probably be redeemable in the restaurant and bar. Their location is convenient should you want to dinghy up into town. You can call them on VHF: 16. The Boatyard plans to finish a 309-foot dock, with a 32-foot L at the end well before Christmas 2001. You will be able to tie your dinghy here (there is no other dinghy dock in Carlisle Bay) and you will be able to come alongside to take on water. In the meantime you can beach your dinghy. There is sometimes a surge that breaks on the beach so be cautious when coming ashore. There is a designated swimming area that you should avoid.

The Boatyard offers several facilities including showers, toilets, restaurants and shops (see our restaurant section for more details). Their internet and communications office will help you do your e-mail, make phone calls and send faxes. They also offer a laundry service, basic procurement, water and information. Register with them upon

arrival so they can issue you the appropriate passes. They open seven days week from 0900 till late at night.

At the other end of the beach is the Barbados Yacht Club, (VHF: 16), an imposing old colonial building with a long tradition of sailing. It is very much a proper yacht club with large high ceilings and walls decorated with old and new photos and paintings of ships and the sea. It is a smart establishment, the Bajan equivalent of the Royal Yacht Squadron, but more fun with good sailors. However, they do expect a level of decorum, and it is not the place to slop around in a ratty old t-shirt, torn shorts and flip-flops. However if you treat their establishment with respect, you will be welcome.

Visiting yachts are given a one-week complimentary membership that entitles them to use the facilities like bathrooms, restaurant and beach bar. Check in with the office upon arrival. There is no dinghy dock but the beach is secure although the swell can sometimes make landing and launching exciting and wet. They have an active sailing and racing schedule from Optimists and Topper dinghies to yacht races; their big yearly event is the Mt. Gay Boatyard Regatta in early June.

South of the Barbados Yacht Club, on the other side of the big hotel with the pier, is the much more informal Barbados Sailing and Cruising Club, generally known as the Cruising Club. You will be very welcome here, even in your oldest t-shirt. They are closed on Tuesdays and Thursdays. Other days the bar is open 1630-2200. If club members are around at other times you can get to use the showers. They also hold a barbecue every month. While there, check out their photo album with photos of early voyagers including Colin Mudie and John Guzzwell.

On Broad Street, close to the wharf, are a couple of internet stations.

You can take on fuel at the fishing Harbor just north of the Careenage. As you enter there are two T docks on your right, the first one you come to is Esso and the next one Texaco, (VHF: 68). Both only sell diesel at the same price. There is about 13-foot of depth in the harbor but it is small, with not much space to turn around in. They are

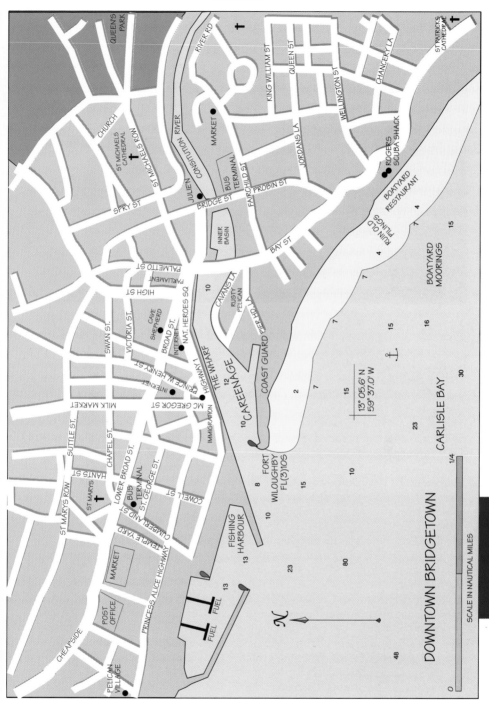

open 0900 to 1700 Monday to Friday and 1000 to 1500 on Saturdays. These docks do not sell water or ice. The least crowded time is in the afternoon. Large yachts would do better to take on fuel at Port St. Charles.

Otherwise you can carry fuel, water and ice by jug from one of the nearby gas stations; Esso next to the Boatyard and Shell opposite the Yacht Club.

Willie Hassell is a well-known Barba-

dos yachtsman who often cruises the Grenadines. He does a lot of commercial diving work in the islands and in Barbados he and his son Michael run Willie's Diving and Marine Services, which is located in the south end of the inner Bridgetown Harbour, also known as the Shallow Draft Harbour. They have a 45-ton Travelift with a draft capacity of 7-feet and limited storage space. They can arrange for most repair and mechanical work. Most of the dock space here is taken up by local charter vessels. In the case of impending storms it is made available as a refuge for fishing boats and visiting yachts.

The Port Hole Marine Supplies just at the gate is a small shop of marine essentials run by Derrek Johnson who is also a diesel mechanic.

Carter's Fishermans Corner (VHF: 06) is the only big marine store. It is on the western end of the wharf. They carry fishing supplies as well as navigation lights, switches, ropes, bilge pumps, resins, fastenings, some electronics, safety gear and a variety of other marine basics. They are also agents for Harris Paints, a local manufacturer who produce a variety of marine paints including antifouling.

Just outside of town in an area known as Wildey, is McEnearney's, the Ford dealership with a marine department that handles OMC Evinrude, Johnson outboards. They have parts and a service department as well as new outboards of all sizes. They have some Ford and Kubota parts as well as Boston Whaler dinghies, Apex inflatables and kayaks. Contact Alex Mckenzie at 426-2471 or cell: 231-2199, he is a sailor and will be happy to be of assistance. The Yamaha dealer is Star Products on Baxters Road in Bridgetown.

William Ince's DI Manufacturing in Guinea, St. John represents Mercury, John Deere, Yanmar and Mariner.

Val Knowles used to operate a Boatyard in Carlisle Bay. He now has Knowles Marine (246-435-3068) and runs a consulting business for visiting boaters and can help you find anything or get anything fixed.

From a yachting point of view, Barbados is well known as the home of Doyle sails[1], the largest sail manufacturer in this end of the Caribbean. The Doyle Loft is a huge success. They export most of their sails and have agents throughout the Caribbean. They make good, high tech sails with modern computer designs and cutting edge equipment for very

---

1. *Because my name is Doyle, and Doyle Sails often advertise with me, a few people think I own the company, and I have even been congratulated for my fine sails! Unfortunately, the truth is I have no connection financial or familial.*

competitive prices. The man responsible is Andy Watts and he does a very fine job. The Doyle Sail Loft is on the east side of the island at Six Cross Roads, in the parish of St. Philip. Besides making a new sail for you they will repair any size sail, make awnings and related canvas work or supply 316 stainless tubing and fittings. Call them if you need a new sail or repairs and they will come to you to discuss it, or have a truck come by to pick up your old sail for repairs. Having a sail built while here will save the shipping costs and customs work in other islands and if you buy in the hurricane season they offer a special 10 percent discount on their already good prices.

For light sail repairs and canvas work you could also call Roger Edgehill (429-5800), who has Edge Hill Sails at Viking, Palm Beach in Hastings, Christ Church.

SHOPPING

Many fine modern supermarkets make provisioning in Barbados a pleasure. You can dinghy to the big Julie'n supermarket, just past the old swing bridge, on the left. For fresh produce, check out the local markets. The one closest to Carlisle Bay is adjacent to the Fairchild Street bus stand.

Souvenir and gift shoppers will find Barbados more than adequate for their needs. Barbados gets about half a million cruise ship passengers a year, in addition to a strong stay-over visitor population. The result is lots of shops selling everything from fine jewelry to local handicrafts. A good place to start is Broad Street with its large department stores and duty free shops. Cave Shepherd, on Broad Street is a Barbados institution. It opened in 1906 and was the Caribbean's first department store, as close as the Caribbean comes to having a Harrods. While it used to supply mainly practical items for the local population, it now includes lots of baubles attractive to visitors. Two restaurants within the store make good lunch spots. Harrison's, another Barbados institution, was founded in 1872 and they sell duty free items, including leather, jewelry and crystal. Pelican village on Princess highway offers local basketwork and other crafts and you can watch the artisans at work. If you are interested in fine art, check out Verandah Art Gallery, upstairs above Collins Pharmacy on Broad Street. They have a large selection of paintings, many by local artists.

RESTAURANTS

Barbados has hundreds of restaurants, from Kentucky Fried Chicken to top international chefs and gourmet French food. If Barbados is known for one special food, it is flying fish, usually deep fried in batter. You can even get them in a sandwich, known here as a cutter. Barbados also has its local brew, Banks Beer, which is very acceptable and reasonably priced.

The Boatyard Beach Club ($C), open every day from 0900, with its perfect beach setting, is a great daytime hangout. During the day they have a small entry charge that is fully redeemable at the bar and restaurant, which allows you use of

Opposite: the fishing harbor in Bridgetown

Barbados gingerbread

Cruising guide to Barbados

beach chairs, games, water sports, and more. You can choose between the yard bar and South Deck Grill Restaurant, with a big choice – from sandwiches to fine seafood. You can also get pizzas and pastas.

It is also the perfect place to drink a rum punch while you watch for the green flash at sunset and for fine dining after. They have an active entertainment schedule, including limbo and steel band, and dancing with IV De People, one of the big local bands. They also offer lots of happy hours. Drop by to find out what is happening, or check out their web site: theboatyard.com.

The Waterfront Café on the Careenage is one of Bridgetown's popular restaurants. It is informal, serving local food – anything from a cutter to a full meal. You can eat inside or out, overlooking the water. They have entertainment most nights, often jazz, but Tuesday night is Caribbean with a buffet and a steel band.

The Rusty Pelican ($C) is a pleasant second floor restaurant with seating on a verandah overlooking the local fishing fleet and charter boats. The variety of food should suit most tastes.

Mustor's Harbour Bar and Restaurant ($D) on McGregor Street (off Broad Street) serves traditional Bajan dishes such as flying fish and cucoo (made from breadfruit and corn meal). They are open from 1100-1600 and very reasonably priced.

For traditional Bajan dishes, check out Baxter's Road at night, where women barbecue dorado steaks by the sidewalk. Consider also visiting Oistins, a fishing village a few miles southeast of Bridgetown. They also have barbecues going at night for both locals and visitors, and it is easy to get there on a local bus.

WATER SPORTS

Barbados has excellent diving. The island is surrounded by a mass of fringing reefs, which generally slope gently and end in sand at about 80 feet. It also has banking reefs, which are a little way offshore and tend to be steeper and deeper. There are also numerous wrecks, both accidental and intentional. This, combined with clear water and a sand bottom, makes diving bright and pleasant.

Fish are fed in a number of places, which makes for good photographs and tons of fish and it delights the average tourist. A few nature divers may find it a bit aggravating to see the local piscine population turned into active beggars. In Alleynes Bay, there is even a place where you can swim and feed green turtles off the Royal Pavilion hotel.

You can dive on your own, but remember that damaging or collecting anything underwater is strictly against the law.

The easiest place to dive is on the wrecks in Carlisle Bay. The general area is outlined on our sketch chart. There are several wrecks fairly close together here starting at about 8 feet deep. The shallow one is the Berwyn. This was a 60-foot French tugboat scuttled by her crew. Amazingly for the shallow depth (8-20 feet), she is still more or less in one piece, and after 60 years of living on the bottom, well encrusted. The Ellion lies to her north and a little west a few hundred feet away in 35-55 feet. This is a 110-foot freighter confiscated and sunk in 1996 for drug trafficking. Pretty much due east of The Ellion in 20-40 feet is a 45-foot cement fishing boat deliberately turned into a diving wreck ten years ago. There are plenty of fish, some of which will approach for a hand out. Keep your eyes open for the well-disguised scorpion fish around the Berwyn. This dive is very popular and usually less crowded in the morning.

For other dives it would be best to go with one of the local dive shops, as they know all the best spots.

Roger's Scuba Shack is in the same complex as the boatyard restaurant, making it handy for those using their moorings. They are a Padi dive resort for a full range of dive tours, including wreck and naturalist dives and for snorkeling. They have a couple of boats and do small and large groups and will pick up people from their boats. They can provide full equipment or give you a special price if you have your own.

Just outside the Boatyard, is Hazell's Water World, a retailer of scuba and snorkeling gear and related items. They repair as well as rent equipment.

Midway down the beach is Underwater Barbados (VHF : 08), a Padi-certified resort run by Michel Young. They will fill your air tanks here as well as rent equipment or you can go on some of their many dive excursions. They will take you to some of the wrecks around Barbados, living reefs, or on night dives.

Further down (more convenient if you are anchored off the Yacht Club) is Barbados's oldest dive establishment; the Dive Shop, run by Haroon Degia, whose father "Paki" opened the store in 1966. From their location you can walk right into the water and do the wreck dive. Apart from regular dives, they run special bottle hunting dives in Carlisle Bay.

BETWEEN BRIDGETOWN AND SPEIGHTSTOWN

We show the coastline between Bridgetown and Speightstown in two charts. The first is from Bridgetown to Folkstone Park and the second is from Folkstone Park up to Speightstown. There are several anchoring possibilities along this coast, and as mentioned before, there is talk about opening up new yacht anchorages along this coast. These anchorages will be buoyed to keep you clear of the reefs. When this happens the port authority should be able to give you a map designating the permissible anchorages that you can then add to our charts. In the meantime it would be hard to get permission to anchor anywhere other than Carlisle Bay. You can try talking about it to members of the Barbados Yacht Club and they may be able to help.

We show anchors at the places you are most likely to get permission to anchor. One is in Paynes Bay south of Holetown and the Folkstone marine park, the other is in Speightstown south of the new fisheries jetty. Make sure you only anchor on sand or be prepared for massive fines! If we get more information about new anchoring areas being opened up we will post it on our website doyleguides.com.

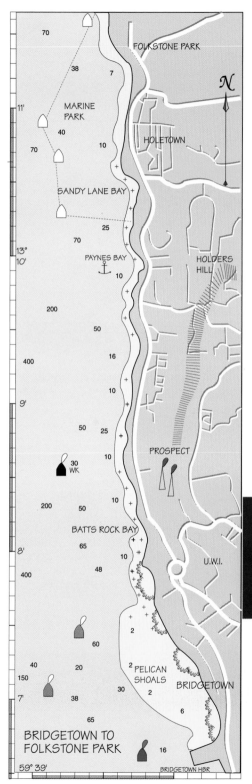

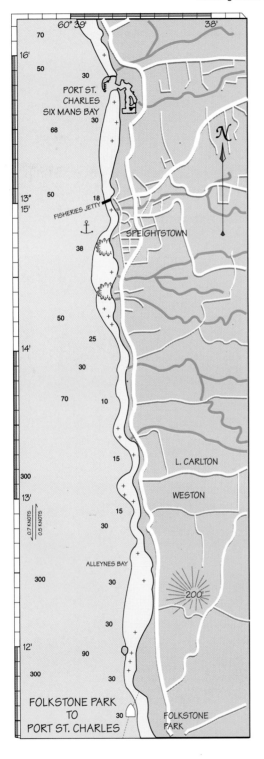

SPEIGHTSTOWN AND PORT ST. CHARLES

Speightstown, back in its heyday, was a major port and the commercial center of Barbados. Today, although it is the second largest town in Barbados, it is much smaller than Bridgetown. It was named after William Speight who owned the land in the early days of colonization and was a member of Barbados's first assembly. It is a pretty town, with a fishing fleet, fish market, and many colonial buildings.

Port St. Charles is in Six Mans Bay, about a mile north of Speightstown, and adjoins lovely beaches. It is an impressive new development built around a lagoon that includes some man made islands. The surrounding condominiums, many of which are for rent or sale, are super-luxurious and some have their own docks for yachts up to 8-foot draft. These inside berths at Port St. Charles are all for residents. However, a rock breakwater and small peninsula protects the port and contains a fuel dock, port of entry, and six visitor berths, particularly suitable for mega yachts. Transient yachts are welcome to stop by and take on fuel or clear in with customs. Keep in mind this is a very pristine place – more like driving your yacht into a swimming pool than into a marina, so treat it accordingly.

NAVIGATION

The entry channel to outer Port St. Charles is in about 14 ft of water and somewhat narrow. It is marked on the shore side by red flashing lights that mark the Tom Snooch Reef on the east side of the channel and a green beacon at the end of the breakwater. The channel has 14 feet of water at low tide.

Before entering, call the dock master, Derek Ince, on VHF: 16 or 77 for instructions. You will probably be directed to the fuel dock to tie up.

FACILITIES INCLUDE:
- 6 Berths from 60ft-200 ft. • Water
- Electricity –
  415V/3/50Hz/250AMPS
  208V/3/50Hz/200AMPS • Telephone • Cable TV
- Gasoline and Diesel • Garbage Incineration
- Customs, Immigration, Coastguard and Police Offices
- Restaurants • Sunset Isle Pool Bar
- Beauty Salon/Hairdressing • E-mail and Internet Facilities
- Gym • Beach • $13^1/2$ ft maximum draft.

PORT ST. CHARLES

ST. PETER BARBADOS

Contact: VHF channel 16 or 77 for reservations, Port St. Charles Dockmaster or customs.
email:dockmaster@portstcharles.com.bb
www.portstcharles.com
Tel: 246 419-1000 Fax: 246 422-4646

**Above
Port St. Charles
from the outer
docks**

Hassle's Yard

REGULATIONS

When you call for instructions to come into the port, tell the dock master you need to clear customs. If you fail to get him, you can try calling customs direct (VHF: 16/77). Once you have been instructed to berth, you should tie up and keep the Q flag flying till clearance is complete. Once tied up, stay on board till the officials arrive and clearance is complete. This is a full port of clearance and includes customs, immigration, health, coast guard, and police. Remember that you will need to get permission to move down to Carlisle Bay or to any other anchorage.

SERVICES

For transient yachts, the main service Port St. Charles provides is the 60-ft fuel dock by the heliport, supplying both diesel and unleaded gasoline. For those who want to stay longer, six visitor berths are available for yachts up to 200 feet (and most suitable for larger yachts). Water is piped to the docks, as are telephone lines and cable TV. Electricity is all 50-cycle and is available at 120, 208, 240 or 415 volts, single phase, or 208 and 415 volts, three phase. Holding tanks are mandatory on board and discharge of sewage, oil, or any other waste is strictly forbidden.

The complex will soon house a restaurant, pool bar, internet service, gym and other facilities.

Marine Management Services, run by Clint Brooks, takes

care of some of the yachts here, as well as elsewhere on the island. Clint has experience in absentee yacht care, general maintenance, rigging, and repair. He can oversee projects from major work to simple cosmetic jobs and make sure your boat is ready for you on your return.

PROVISIONING

Eddies and Jordans, two supermarkets in Speightstown, will take care of most of your needs. For more than that, it is about a five-mile drive to the massive Super Center in Holetown, which has everything and opens Monday-Thursday 0800-2000 and on Friday and Saturday till 2100.

Speightstown has several shops of interest to the visitor, including Mango's Art Gallery, showing the work of Michael Adams whose bright colors were inspired by his birthplace in Malaya.

RESTAURANTS

La Mer ($A) at Port St. Charles is a very

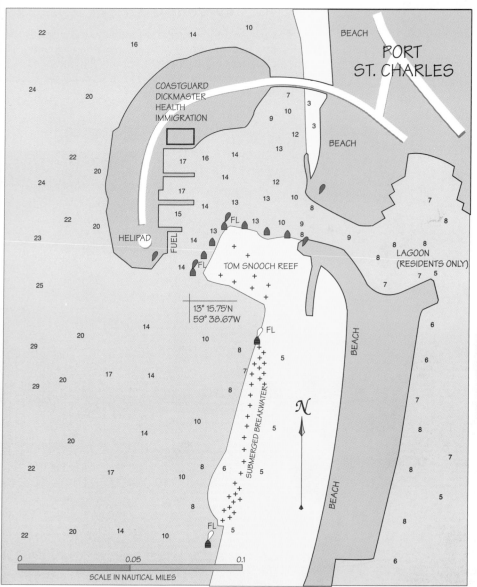

Cruising guide to Barbados

fancy restaurant overlooking the port under the direction of master chef Hans Schweitzer. This is a great place for a special night out and their menu includes such creations as grilled shrimp on sugar cane with tamarind rum glaze, and homemade extra old Mount Gay Rum and raisin ice cream on espresso sauce with caramelized banana.

On Sundays they throw a spectacular buffet lunch, with a huge variety of foods, including suckling pig, perfect roast beef, and shrimps. People come here from all over the island.

If you wander into Speightstown, there are several inexpensive local restaurants where you can get fish and also rum shops that sell ham cutters and Banks beer.

EXPLORING ASHORE

The new Arbib Nature and Heritage trail displays the natural and human history of Speightstown. There are two paths for different hiking levels. The more difficult one is 4.7 miles long; the easier one 3.4 miles long. Contact the Barbados Tourism Authority for details.

Inside
Port St. Charles

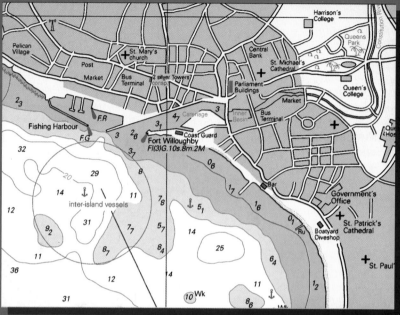

TRINIDAD DIRECTORY - SERVICES

EMERGENCY, OFFICIAL

Chaguaramas Security, 868-634-4227

Coast Guard Maritime Emergency, 868-634-4440

Community Hospital of Seventh Day Adventists, 868-622-1191/622-1192

Customs, 868-634-4341

Ferreira Optical, 868-623-3473, ferreira@wow.net

Fire/Ambulance, 990

General Hospital, 868-623-2951/623-2952

Glencoe Medical Clinic, 868-633-7744

Immigration, 868-634-4341/623-8147

Mount Hope Medical Sciences Complex, 868-645-4673/645-2640

Police, 999

St. Clair Medical Centre, 868-628-1451/628-1452

AIRLINE AGENTS

Lazzari & Sampson, (Coral Cove) 868-634-4052, F: 868-634-4045, lazzari@tstt.net.tt

Trans-Continental Travel, (Tropical Marine), 868-634-2949, F:634-2950, irena@tstt.tt

Travelsure (CrewsInn), 868-634-4000, VHF: 68, trvsure@ wow.net

CHANDLERY, FISHING GEAR, TECHNICAL SUPPLIES

Boaters Shop, (Power Boats), 868-634-4148

Budget Marine, 868-634-2006, F: 868-634-4382, sales@budmar.co.tt

Corsa Marine (Tardieu Marine), 868-634-1054, F: 868-634-1054, Cell: 868-680-7979

Echo Marine (Mariners Haven), 868-634-2027, F: 868-634-2026, info@echomarine.com

Eddo's Welding and Industrial Supplies, (San Fernando), 868-652-4924/5164, F: 868-653-3330

Eswil (Mariner's Haven) 868-634-2327, eswil@carib-link.net

Fluid Hose and Coupling, (Peake), 868-634-2076, F: 868-634-2076

General Store, (San Fernando), 868-652-7972

Hose & Equipment, (Point Lisas), 868-636-5668, F: 868-636-8628

Kiss Energy Systems, 868-634-2929, kissenergy @netscape.net

Low Tech (Trincity), 868-640-4918

LP Industrial and Marine, 868-633-3395/632-3441, F: 868-633-3858, lpmarine@tstt.net.tt

Marc One (Mariners Haven), 868-634-2259, marcone@wow.net

Marine Consultants Ltd. (POS), 868-625-2887/625-1309 F: 868-625-2270

Marine Safety Equipment, 868- 634-4410 F: 868-634-4410

Marine Warehouse (Tardieu), 868-634-4150, tiems@tstt.net.tt

Maska, (San Fernando), 868-653-3912, maska@tstt.net.tt

Peake Hardware (near TTYC) 622-8818,

Peake Chandlery (Peake), 868-634-4388 VHF:69

Point Lisas Steel Products, (Point Lisas), 868-636-7991/2

SGI (Coral Cove), 868-634-1034, F: 868-634-1034, skforbes @trinidad.net

Shiloh Enterprises (Tropical), 868-640-2363

Southern Wholesale stores, (Marabella), 868-658-7975/4506, msam@wow.net

SSL Indeserve Supply, (San Fernando), 868-657-5194, 652-8816, ssil@tstt.net.tt

Tackle Shop (Glencoe), 868-632-1782, F:632-1782 tackle@trinidad.net

Tan Yuk & Co. (Coral Cove), 868-632-0402, F: 868-632-6944, cety@cariblink.net

Vickers Distributors (Mariner's Haven), 868-634-1056

Tang How Bros., (Marabella), 868-658-1603

TOSL, (San Fernando), 868-657-7794/652-1686, F: 868-653-4187, naushad@tosl.com

United Bearings, (San Fernando), 868-638-2570/2571

West Indian Bearing Co, (San Fernando), 868-652-2424

William H. Scott, 868-634-2343, cs@wow.net

COMMUNICATIONS

Island Surf Café, (Mariners Haven), 868-634-2407, VHF: 68 islandsurfcafe @chaguarmas.com

Mariners Office, 868-634-4183

Ocean Internet Café, 868-634-2233/634-1205

Same but Different Communications, (Chag. convention center), 868-634-1360, F: 868 634-1361

GENERAL YACHT SERVICES (MARINAS, HAUL OUT, FUEL, LAUNDRY)

Bay View Beach Resort and Marina, 868-678-9002, VHF: 68

Chee's Laundry & Dry Cleaning, (Marabella), 868-658-6557/1660

Coral Cove Marina, 868-634-2040, F: 868-634-2248, coralcove@trinidad.net

CrewsInn, 868-634-4384/5, F:868-634-4542, e-mail crewsinn@tstt.net.tt

IMS Yacht Services, 625-2104/5 634-4328 F:634-4437 F:634-4329 VHF 68, ims@tstt.net.tt

Master's Laundromat (Tropical Marine), 868-634-1294/682-8514

Peake Yacht Services, 868-634-4420/4423/4427, F: 868-634-4387, VHF: 69, pys@cablenett.net

Pointe-a-Pierre Yacht Club call George Burne, 868-658-4200/658-2222

Power Boats Mutual Facilities Ltd. 868-634-4303 F: 868-634-4327, VHF: 72, pbmfl@powerboats.co.tt

Tardieu Marine, 868-634-2237, F: 868-634-4534

Trinidad and Tobago Yacht Club, 868-633-7420/637-4260, Fax: 868-633-6388, managers cell: 868-680-8611, ttyc@tstt.net.tt

Tropical Marine, 868-634-4502, F: 868-634-4453, hlanser@tstt.net.tt

Trinidad and Tobago Sailing Association, P.O. Box 3140, Carenage Post Office, Trinidad, 868-634-4519/4210, F: 868-634-4376, sesail@ttya.org

William Marine, 868-683-1818

MISCELLANEOUS

B &Tees (POS), 868-627-3648, b&tees@wow.net

Boaters' Enterprise Boca, Boaters Directory, (CrewsInn), 868-634-2055, info@boatersenterprises,com

Chaguaramas Development Authority (CDA) 868-634-4364/4349/625-1503, F: 868-625-2465

Sea of Styles (CrewsInn), 634-2142, VHF:68

TIDCO, 868-623-6022, UK: 0800-960-057, USA: 1-800-595-1868, Germany 49-06131-7337

YSATT, 868-634-4938, F:868-634-2160

Chaguaramas Military History & Aviation Museum, 868-634-4391

MISCELLANEOUS - PARKS

Asa Wright, 868--667-4655

National Park Department 868-634-4349/634-4227

Pointe-a-Pierre Wildfowl Trust, 868-637-5154/662-4040

Timberline 868-638-2263

WASA 868-622-2301/5 622-1965

SAILMAKERS AND CANVAS

Alpha Upholstery and Canvas, (Tardieu), 868-683-1713, alphacanvas@hotmail.com

Barrow Sails, (Power Boats) 634-4137, F: 868-634-2125, VHF: 68, barrow@tstt.net.tt

Calypso Marine Canvas, (Peake), 868-634-4012, VHF: 68, riadcmc@tstt.net.tt

Frankie's (Bones) Upholstery, (Point Lisas), 868-679-3295

Lensyl Products Ltd., 868-662-7534 F: 868-663-1454

Ocean Sails Ltd. (IMS) 868-634-4560 F: 868-634-4560

Soca Sails (CrewsInn), 868-634-4178, F: 868-634-1044, VHF: 68, info@socasails.com

The Upholstery Shop (Power Boats), 868-634-4134, VHF: 72

Webster's Canvas Work (Tardieu), 868-758-2956, VHF: 68

CANVAS- FABRIC STORES

Diamondtex (POS), 868-672-7760

Jimmy Aboud (POS), 868-625-2905

Mansoor & Son (POS), 868-623-2740

Radica Trading (POS), 868-627-2315,

Radica Trading (San Fernando), 868-652-0277/4186, radica@tstt.net.tt

Rahaman's Upholstery (San Fernando), 868-657-7400, F: 868-653-4861

Textile Corner (POS), 868-625-2904

TRANSPORT & TOURS

Avifauna Tours, 868-633-5614, Cell: 868-759-4084, F: 868-633-2580

Convenient Car Rentals (Tropical Marine), 868-634-4017, VHF: 68, crl@carib-link.net

EconoCar (CrewsInn), 868-634-2154

Geronimo's Bike Shop (POS), 868-622-BIKE

Hike Seekers, 868-632-9746 (Snake)

Ian Taxi, VHF:68

Mark's Rentals, 868-634-4003 VHF:68

Member's Only, 868-633-3486, cell: 868-683-5202, VHF: 68

Siewah's Taxi and Bus, 868-662-5071, Cell: 868-752-6021

Signal Car Rentals, 868-634-2277, VHF: 68, info@signalcars.com

Trump Tours (CrewsInn), 868-634-2189/624-0820, F: 868-624-3022, trumpluxury@hotmail.com Tranport- Courier

DHL, 868-625-9835

Federal Express, 868-623-4070

UPS 868-624-4895

TECHNICAL YACHT SERVICES

Ali's Machine Shop, 868-634-4420, VHF: 68

Ancil's Marine Painting and Services, 868-634-1071,

Antoine Woodworking, 868-634-1071, F: 868-634-1071, artantoine@hotmail.com

Awon's Marine Services, 868-638-4505 868-623-0859

Barrow Metal Works (Tardieu), 868-634-4137

Billy's Rigging, 868-634-4161/4423, Fax: 868-634-4161, VHF: 69, surveys@tstt.net.tt

Bowen Marine, 868-634-4543/634-4365 F: 868-634-4228

Budget Marine Rigging, 868-634-1110, F: 868-634-4382, rigging@budmar.co.tt

Calypso Marine Services, 868-634-4551/627-4550 VHF: 68

Caribbean Marine (Power Boats), 868-634-4561 F: 868-634-4561 VHF: 72

Clinton Brewster (Power Boats), 868-684-6746/632-4393

Ceejay Engineering, (Marabella), 868-628-7913/2149

Chaguaramas Metal Works (Tardieu Marine), 868-634-1164

Coastal Machine Shop (Tardieu Marine), 868-634-1280, F: 868-634-1280

Coatings Specialists, 868-634-2261, F: 868-634-2263, coatings @trinidad.net

Dockyard Electrics, 868-634-4933 F: 868-634-4933, VHF:68

Dynamite Marine, 868-634-4868/4663, F: 868 634-4269, dynamite@wow.net

Electropics (Tropical Marine), 868 634-2232, F: 868 634-2237 electropic@tstt.net.tt

Engines Engines (Tardieu), 868-6846260, VHF: 68

European Yacth Connection (EYC), 868-754-3352, F: 868-634-4327, VHF:72, europeanconnection @yahoo.com

Formula III, 868-634-4336 F: 868-634-4009, VHF 68

Fortress Woodworking (Power Boats), 868-634-4510 F: 868-634-4510, VHF: 72

General Diesel, (San Fernando), 868-657-6351

Gittens Engine Service (Tardieu Marine), 868-634-2233/632-3531

Goodwood Marine 868-634-2203, F: 868-634-2204, VHF: 68, goodwood@tstt.net.tt

Hugo de Plessis, F: 634-4376, VHF: 68

Ian Keizer, 868-634-4536

John Francois Woodworking (Peake), 868-634-2066, F: 868-634-2066, jfranwkg@tstt.net.tt , VHF: 68

KNJ Marine Services (Peake), 868-634-1021, F:868-634-4429 fmaingot@tstt.net.tt

Lennox Stewart (Tardieu), 868-634-1391

Lenny Sumadh, (San Fernando), 868-652-2930/3180/3055, F: 868-657-2237

Mark De Gannes (Power boats), 868-634-4025

Nadpat Corrosion Control, 868-634-1251, Cell:620-3110

Nau-T-Kol (CrewsInn), 868-634-2174, F: 868-634-2174, nautkol @cablenett.net

Navtech Electronics, 868-634-1231, navigationelectronics @hotmail.com

Peake Yacht Services, 868-634-4420/4423/4427, F: 868-634-4387, VHF: 69, pys@cablenett.net

Propeller & Marine Service (Peake), 868-634-4533 F: 868-633-6294

Rawle Walker, 868-640-5048 640-1982

Serge's Electrical Workshop, VHF:69

Ship's Carpenter, 868-634-2233, F: 868-634-2233, global@tstt.net.tt

Sign Lab (Tardieu), 868-634-2178, F: 868-634-2178

Soca Sailboats, 868-672-0092,

Stuart Electronics 868-634-1164, stutron@tstt.net.tt

Superior Machine Shop and Engineering (San Fernando), 868-653-1874/5, F: 868-657-2810

Trinidad Detroit Diesel (Coral Cove), 868-634-2177, tdad-detroit@carib-link.net

Trinidad Rigging, 868-634-2227, F: 868-634-2227, Home: 868-632-8473

Trojan Engineering (San Fernando), 868-652-5369/563-1904, F: 868-652-5369

Unity Metal Shop (IMS), 868-759-9118

Yacht Maintenance Services (Power Boats), 868-633-7846, 868-634-4303 868-634-4376

TRINIDAD DIRECTORY - RESTUARANTS, SHOPPING

HOTELS & RESTAURANTS

Bight Restaurant (Peake), 868-634-4420

Curry Bien, (Coral Cove), 868-755-8535

Galley Restaurant (IMS), 868-634-4438

Joe's Pizza, (Coral Cove), 868-634-2332

Lighthouse (CrewsInn), 868-634-4384

Mas Camp Pub (POS), 868-627-4042

Mt. Plasir Estate (Grand Riviere), 868-670-8381 F: 868-680-4553

Rafters, 868-628-9258

Roti Shop (Tardieu), 868-634-2061

Sails Restaurant (Power Boats), 868-634-4302/3

Skippers (TTYA), 868-633-1343

Soong's Great Wall, (San Fernando), 868-652-9255, great-wall@carib-link.net

Timmy's (TTSA), 868-634-4210

The Inn Place, (CrewsInn), 868-634-1096

The Pelican Inn Pub, 868-624-7486

Tiki Village, 868-622-6441

Timberline Resort, 868-638-2263

Timmy's Restaurant (TTSA), 868-634-2182

Verandah, 868-622-6287

Woodford Cafe, 868-622-2233

PROVISIONING

Dockside Foodmart (Power Boats), 868-634-4303

Hi-Lo Supermarkets, 868-632-1085, CrewsInn Branch: 868-634-4038

Linda's Bakery (Glencoe), 868-633-2650

OTHER SHOPPING

Creative Computers, (POS) 868-652-6860, marsha@creative-computers.com

TRINIDAD DIRECTORY - DIVING

Coastal Diving Services, (Tropical Marine), 868-634-2213, F: 868-634-4449, coastdive@wow.net

Dive Specialists Centre, 868-634-4319, F: 628-4524 VHF 68

Rick's Dive World (Tardieu), 868-634-3483, cell: 868-683-3684, rick@wow.net

TOBAGO DIRECTORY - SERVICES

EMERGENCY/OFFICIAL

Customs, 868-639-2415

Immigration, 868-639-2681

Ambulance, 868-639-2108

General Hospital, 868-639-2551

Coast Guard, 868-625-4939

Police, 868-639-1200

COMMUNICATIONS

Blue Waters Inn (Anse Bateau) 868-660-2583/4077, F: 868-660-5195 bwi@bluwatersinn.com

Cyber Café, (Crown Point), 868-639-0007/7461, F: 868-639-7546, sunfun@trinidad.net

Jupiter Tech, (Scarborough), e-mail and phone calls.

Matrix Technology, (Scarborough) 868-639-4220, matrixtechnology@tstt.net.tt, e-mail

Shenda's, e-mail (Charlotteville)

The Clothes Wash Café (Crown Point), 868-639-0007, e-mail, laundry, dry-cleaning, café

GENERAL YACHT SERVICES

The Clothes Wash Café (Crown Point), 868-639-0007, laundry, dry-cleaning

TECHNICAL YACHT SERVICES,

Francis Marine and Industrial Machine Shop, Crown Point, machining, engine repair, general yacht help.

MISCELLANEOUS

Club Pigeon Point, 868-639-0601, F: 868-639-0585

Look Out Stables, 868-639-9379, tobago@pobox.com, horse-riding, tours

Mt Irvine Water Sports, 868-639-9379

Mt. Irvine Bay Hotel, 868-639-8871/639-8872 F: 639-8800, Golf

Tobago Plantations, 868-639-800, marketing @Tobagoplantations.com, development, golf

Tourism Department, 868-639-2125

TRANSPORT

Blue Waters Inn, 868-660-2583/4077 F: 868-660-5195 bwi@bluwatersinn.com, Tours

David Rooks 868-639-4276 F: 868-639-4276, Tours

Pioneer Journeys 868-660-4327, 660-5175 F: 868-660-4328, Tours

TOBAGO DIRECTORY - RESTAURANTS, SHOPPING

ACCOMMODATION ONLY

Man-O-War Bay Cottages 868-660-4327 F: 868-660-4328

RESTAURANTS WITH ACCOMMODATIONS

Arnos Vale Hotel 868-639-2881 F: 868-639-4629

Blue Waters Inn 868-660-25834077 F: 868-660-5195 bwi@bluwatersinn.com

Coco Reef Resort 868-639-8571 F: 868-639-8574

Cocrico Inn (Plymouth) 868-639-2961

Grafton Beach Resort, 868-639-0191

Kariwak Village (Crown Point) 868-639-8442

King's Well Inn (Scarborough) 868-639-3883

Manta Lodge (Speyside) 868-660-5268 F: 868-660-5030

Mt. Irvine Bay Hotel 639-8871 639-8872 F: 868-639-8800

Rex Turtle Beach Resort 868-639-2851

Sea-side Garden Café, 868-639-0682

Zan's Village Inn (Buccoo), 868-639-9185

RESTAURANTS

Blue Crab Restaurant (Scarborough), 868-639-2737

Cascreole (Castara)

Eastman's Restaurant (Charlotteville,) 868-660-6150/5933

G's Restaurant (Charlotteville,) 868-660-5215

Gail's Local Food (Charlotteville,)

Golden Palace (Castara), 868-639-5673

Happy Lil Vibe (Buccoo), 868-639-9591, millers1@hotmail.com

TOBAGO DIRECTORY - RESTAURANTS, SHOPPING CONTINUED

Hendrix Hideaway, (Buccoo), 868-660-8633

Jane's Quality Foods (Charlotteville), 868-660-5733

Jemma's (Speyside), 868-660-4066

L&H Restaurant and Mini Market (Castara), 868-639-2973

La Tartaruga (Buccoo), 868-639-0940

Ocean View Bar, 639-0437

Pigeon Point Resort, 639-8141 F: 868-639-7232, VHF: 16/06

Richmond Great House, 868-660-4467,

Riverside Restaurant, (Parlatuvier), 639-5627 639-5628

Rouselle's 868-678-9003

Sharon & Phebe's Restaurant 660-5717

Shivan's Watermill, 868-639-0000, swmill@tstt.net.tt

Surfers (Mt. Irvine), 868-639-8407, F: 868-868-639-8226

The Old Donkey Cart House, (Scarborough), 868-639-3551

TJ's Bar & Restaurant, ,(Plymouth), 868-635-0731

Two Seasons Restaurant, 868-639-9461

Turtle Beach Hotel, 868-639-2851

PROVISIONING

Francis Supermarket (Crown Point), 868-639-8440

Jimmie's Mini Mart (Crown Point), 868-639-8292

Marie's Place, 868-639-0859

New Port Supermarket (Scarborough),

Penny Savers, (Highway from Crown Point and Scarborough)

Tobago Supermarket (Scarborough)

SHOPPING GENERAL

Culture House, 868-639-2646

New Reflections,

Sports and Games, 868-639-4435, sgltd@tstt.net.tt

The Cotton House, 868-639-2727

TOBAGO DIRECTORY - DIVING

Aqua Marine Dive Ltd., 868-660-4341 F: 868-639-4416 bwitobago@trinidad.net

Man Friday Diving, 868-660-4676, bjarne@manfriday.com

Manta Dive Centre, 868-639-9969/9209, cell: 868-678-3979, F: 868-639-0414 mantaray @tstt.net.tt,

Manta Lodge, 868-660-5268 F: 868-660-5030

Mount Irvine Watersports, 639-4008 T/F: 868- 639-9379

Prosucba, 868-639-7424, F: 868-639-7424, proscuba @tstt.net.tt,

Ron's Watersports, 868-622-0459 F: 868-673-0549

Tobago Dive Experience, 868-660-7034 F: 868-639-7845, info@ tobagodiveexperience.com

Wild Turtle Dive Safari, 868-639-7936, info @wildturtledive.com

BARBADOS DIRECTORY - SERVICES

EMERGENCY, OFFICIAL
Customs 246-430-2300
Immigration 246-426-1011
Health Offices 246-426-5080
Coast Guard 246-436-6185
Port Authority 246-430-4700
Police 211
Fire 311
Ambulance 511

CHANDLERY
Fishermans Corner, 246436-6049, F: 246-431-0799, VHF 06, Marine Store

Harris Paints, Ralph Johnson, T: 426-429-6500

GENERAL YACHT SERVICES (MARINAS, HAUL OUT, FUEL, LAUNDRY)
Barbados Sailing and Cruising Club, 246-426-4434

Barbados Yacht Club, J. Cecil Waterman, T: 246-427-7318, F: 246-435-7590, VHF: 16, byc@inaccs.com.bb

Port St. Charles, 246-419-1000, F: 246-422-4646, dockmaster @portstcharles.com.bb, fuel, port of clearance, limited berthing

The Boatyard, 246-436-2622, F: 246-228-7720, VHF: 16 boatyard @sunbeach.net, moorings, restaurant

MISCELLANEOUS
Almond Beach Village Golf Club, 246-422-4900, (9-holes)

Barbados Tourism Authority, 888-427-2623

Barbados Wildlife Reserve, 246-422-8826

Caribbean Riding Center, 246-420-1246, (horse riding)

Harrison's Cave, 246-438-6640, F: 246-438-6645

Mount Gay Rum Visitor Center, 246-427-8757

Rockley Golf Club, 246-435-7873, (9-holes)

The Barbados Museum, 246-427-0201, F: 246-429-5946

Sandy Lane Golf Club, 246-432-1145 (18-hole)

The Barbados National Trust, 246-436-9033

The Nature Commission, 246-425-1200

The Royal Westmoreland Golf Club, 246-422-4653 (18-holes)

Tony's Riding Stables, 246-422-1549, (horse riding)

Wilcox Riding Stables, 246-428-3610 (horse riding)

COMMUNICATIONS
Computer Internet Services, Larry Archer, T/F: 246-431-0756, cis1@sunbeach.net

Connect (Broad Street, 246-228-8648, info@connectbarbados.com

IInternet Access, Borad Street Mall, 246-431-0756

SAILMAKERS, CANVAS
Doyle Sails, 246-432-4600, F: 246-423-4499, doyle@caribnet.net

Roger Edgehill 429-5800, light canvas and sail work

TECHNICAL YACHT SERVICES
Andrew Burke, 246-228-1864, VHF 16 *Regent 1*, fiberglass repairs and construction

DI Manufacturing,(William Ince), 246-423-3866/425-4133, Fax: 246-423-0126, Mercury, John Deere, Yanmar, Mariner

Knowles Marine, 246-435-3068

Marine Management Services,, Clint Brooks, T: 246-234-4733/419-0432, F: 234-419-0432, mms @sunbeach.net (project management, rigging, general maintenance).

McEnearney's, 246-467-2400, F: 246-427-0764, cell: 246-427-0764, OMC Evinrude, Johnson outboards, Kubota and Ford inboards, Apex and Boston Whaler

Pelican Marine, (Shallow Draft Harbour) 246-430-6664, painting

Star Products, 246-426-3066, Yamaha dealers

Willie's Diving and Marine Services, 246-424-1808/230-4271, F: 246-425-1060,mikie@caribsurf.com, haul out and boat repair

TRANSPORT
Coconut Car Rentals Ltd., Neil Farmer, T: 246-437-0297, F: 246-228-9820, coconut@caribsurf.com

BARBADOS RESTAURANTS

RESTAURANTS

La Mer, 246-419-2000, hans@portstcharles.com.bb

Mustor's Harbour Bar and Restaurant, 726-5157

Rusty Pelican, 246-436-7778, rustypelicanbds@hotmail.com

The Boatyard, 246-436-2622, F: 246-228-7720

Victoria Hotel, 246-228-6488

Waterfront Café, 264-427-0093

BARBADOS DIVING

Roger's Scuba Shack, 246-436- 3483, scubashack@sunbeach,net

Hazell's Water World, John Hazell, T: 246-426-9423/4043/228-6734, F: 246-436-5726, hwwdivers @sunbeach.net, Divers supply shop

Underwater Barbados, 246-426-0655, F:246-426-0655, VHF 08, myoung@ underwaterbarbados.com

The Dive Shop, 246-427-9947, F: 246-426-0655

Advertisers Index

We Wrote The Books On Caribbean Cruising

We have literally written the books on Caribbean cruising, covering destinations ranging from the Virgin Islands south to Venezuela.

Our series of cruising guides provide colorful photography, up-to-date information on marinas, haul-out facilities, shops, restaurants and a wide variety of watersports activities. Accompanied by helpful sketch charts, these guides are indispensible aids for the cruising or chartering yachtsman.

We also distribute a wide variety of other titles ranging from cooking to travel, fishing and diving. Call for a FREE catalog or check out our website at www.cruisingguides.com.

CRUISING GUIDE PUBLICATIONS
The Caribbean Experts!
1130-B Pinehurst Road • Dunedin, FL 34698
Phone: (727) 733-5322 • (800) 330-9542
Fax: (727) 734-8179 • E-Mail: info@cruisingguides.com

General Index

CRUISING GUIDE PUBLICATIONS

ORDER FORM

☐ $22.50 CRUISING GUIDE TO THE VIRGIN ISLANDS
(10th Edition) by Simon and Nancy Scott. Expanded to include Spanish Virgin Islands.

☐ $24.95 VIRGIN ANCHORAGES (New color aerial photos and color graphics)

☐ $27.95 LEEWARD ANCHORAGES (Aerial anchorage photos from Anguilla through Dominica)

☐ $24.95 CRUISING GUIDE TO THE LEEWARD ISLANDS — *With GPS Coordinates* (7th Edition) by Chris Doyle.

☐ $22.50 SAILOR'S GUIDE TO THE WINDWARD ISLANDS
(10th Edition) by Chris Doyle, *With GPS Coordinates*

☐ $17.50 CRUISING GUIDE TO TRINIDAD AND TOBAGO plus BARBADOS (3rd Edition)
by Chris Doyle & Jeff Fisher, *With GPS Coordinates*

☐ $26.95 CRUISING GUIDE TO VENEZUELA & BONAIRE (2001 edition) by Chris Doyle and
Jeff Fisher. Provides anchorage information *GPS coordinates* and full color charts.

☐ $24.95 CRUISING GUIDE TO CUBA — *With GPS Coordinates* and Charts
(2nd Edition) by Simon Charles.

☐ $29.95 GENTLEMAN'S GUIDE TO PASSAGES SOUTH — 7th Edition *With GPS Coordinates*
— The "Thornless Path to Windward," by Bruce Van Sant.

☐ $15.95 CRUISING GUIDE TO THE SEA OF CORTEZ (From Mulege to La Paz)

☐ $19.95 CRUISING GUIDE TO THE FLORIDA KEYS by Capt. Frank Papy.

☐ $19.95 CRUISING GUIDE TO ABACO BAHAMAS by Steve Dodge. (8 1/2" x 11") Containing
charts from Walker's Cay south to Little Harbour. *Includes GPS coordinates.*

☐ $27.95 THE BAHAMAS – ABACO PORTS OF CALL AND ANCHORAGES by Tom Henschel.
(11x 8 ½") Stunning, color aerial photography of the anchorages of the Abaco Islands.

☐ $10.00 HOME IS WHERE THE BOAT IS by Emy Thomas. A glimpse into the
cruising way of life.

☐ $14.95 THE NATURE OF THE ISLANDS: PLANTS & ANIMALS OF THE
EASTERN CARIBBEAN by Virginia Barlow. Best nature book for cruisers.

☐ $12.95 CARIBBEAN by Margaret Zellers with breathtaking photos by Bob Krist; —
perfect tropical souvenir or gift. Also comes in a hardbound edition for $39.95.

COMPLETE DIVING GUIDE TO THE CARIBBEAN by Brian Savage and Colleen Ryan.
These definitive guides clearly describe dive sites and stores, with detailed dive plans aided
by spectacular color photos.

☐ $29.95 Volume I - The Windward Islands

☐ $29.95 Volume II - The Leeward Islands

☐ $29.95 Volume III - Puerto Rico & The Virgin Islands

☐ $19.95 STORE TO SHORE New from Captain Jan Robinson.– Proven menus from 50
international yacht chefs includes shopping lists, 400 delicious mouthwatering recipes -
cooking and entertaining for every occasion - informal to elegant.

☐ $16.95 SHIP TO SHORE by Jan Robinson (680 recipes and cooking tips from Caribbean
charter yacht chefs.) Jan Robinson's other cook books are described in full in our
catalog and on our web site.

| | $14.95 | RESTAURANT GUIDES AND RECIPE BOOKS TO THE LEEWARDS, PUERTO RICO, VIRGIN ISLANDS, CHESAPEAKE BAY, INTRACOASTAL WATERWAY AND FLORIDA GULF COAST, (separate books — $14.95 Each.) |
| ☐ | | |

☐ $14.95   RESTAURANT GUIDES AND RECIPE BOOKS TO THE LEEWARDS, PUERTO RICO, VIRGIN ISLANDS, CHESAPEAKE BAY, INTRACOASTAL WATERWAY AND FLORIDA GULF COAST, (separate books — $14.95 Each.)

☐ $35.00   SOUTHERN SHORES (2nd Edition, 9" x 12", 256 pp) by Roger Bansemer. Florida artist, Bansemer has captured on canvas the rich texture of the south from the shoreline to the native wildlife along Florida's coast, north to Savannah & Charleston with a stop in the Virgin Islands.

☐ $12.00   CALENDAR: THE BRITISH VIRGIN ISLANDS. Photography by Dougal Thornton (New year available in October of preceding year).

☐ $29.95   VIDEO (VHS), or (PAL Add $10): SAILING THE WINDWARD ISLANDS by Chris Doyle & Jeff Fisher.

☐ $29.95   VIDEO (VHS), or (PAL Add $10): CRUISING THE NORTHERN LEEWARDS by Chris Doyle.

CARIBBEAN YACHTING CHARTS.
Recently surveyed with the yachtsman in mind. *Includes GPS coordinates.*
small format, easy to handle and use.

☐ $69.00   CYC # 1 Virgin Islands - St.Thomas/Sombrero
☐ $69.00   CYC #2 Northern Leeward Islands - Anguilla/Antigua
☐ $69.00   CYC #3 Southern Leeward Islands - Guadeloupe/Martinique
☐ $69.00   CYC #4 Windward Islands - St. Lucia/Grenada

CALL FOR A COMPLETE CATALOG: Phone: 727-733-5322 or
VISIT OUR WEBSITE cruisingguides.com, or E-mail:info@cruisingguides.com

ORDER FORM

To order, check the appropriate boxes - fill out coupon and send check or money order to: *Cruising Guide Publications, P.O. Box 1017, Dunedin, FL 34697-1017. Florida residents add 7% sales tax. See schedule for shipping charges. All books are shipped within 10 days of receipt of order.*

SHIPPING & HANDLING

for US orders totaling	ADD	
under $15	$4.00	Larger orders will be charged according to weight
$15-25.99	$5.00	
$26-49.99	$7.00	
$50-74.99	$9.00	
$75-$99	$10.00	
Extra address add $3.25		

NON U.S. ORDERS: Orders will be shipped USPS at the losest available rate. Foriegn duties and taxes are the customers responsibility. If you need a firm shipping cost we will be pleased to fax a quote airmail versus surface mail shipping on your order. Fax: 727-734-8179

VISA **DISCOVER** **MasterCard**

$ _____ Total Merchandise

$ _____ Sales Tax (FL residents only)

$ _____ Shipping and Handling

$ _____ Total enclosed

Name _____

Address _____

City _____ State _____ Zip _____

Daytime telephone ( ) _____

Email: _____